THE PAPERS OF
Thomas Jefferson

CHARLES T. CULLEN,
EDITOR

SECOND SERIES

THE PAPERS OF THOMAS JEFFERSON

SECOND SERIES

✠

Jefferson's Literary Commonplace Book

DOUGLAS L. WILSON,

EDITOR

✠

PRINCETON UNIVERSITY PRESS

PRINCETON, NEW JERSEY

Copyright © 1989 by Princeton University Press
Published by Princeton University Press, 41 William Street,
Princeton, New Jersey 08540
In the United Kingdom: Princeton University Press,
Guildford, Surrey

Library of Congress Cataloging-in-Publication Data
Jefferson, Thomas, 1743-1826.
[Commonplace book]
Thomas Jefferson's Literary Commonplace Book
Douglas L. Wilson, editor.
p.   cm.—(The Papers of Thomas Jefferson. Second series)
Reprint.
Bibliography: p.
Includes index.
ISBN 0-691-04720-0 (alk. paper)
1. Jefferson, Thomas, 1743-1826—Literary art.
2. Jefferson, Thomas, 1743-1826—Books and reading.
3. Commonplace-books.   I. Wilson, Douglas L.
II. Title.   III. Title: Literary Commonplace Book.
IV. Series: Jefferson, Thomas, 1743-1826. Selections. 1983.
E332.9.C6J44 1989
973.4'6'0924—dc19
88-23381
CIP

This book has been composed in Linotron Monticello

Printed in the United States of America by
Princeton University Press
Princeton, New Jersey

CONTENTS

FOREWORD

One of the great pleasures of working as an editor of *The Papers of Thomas Jefferson* is the frequently repeated experience of discovery. Sometimes it comes from the research required to understand and explain the documents that must be edited, and sometimes it comes from the work one or more of the many Jefferson scholars produce. It was from this latter source that I had the pleasure of meeting Douglas Wilson and discussing his work on Thomas Jefferson.

Professor Wilson came to the Jefferson Office to examine and explore the copies of the manuscript of the Literary Commonplace Book on file there. His earlier interest and scholarship had focused on the influence of the classics on Jefferson, and this led him quite naturally into a pursuit of the significance of this relatively neglected manuscript from the least understood period of Jefferson's life, his young adulthood. Wilson's earlier work on Jefferson had been impressive, and as his interest in working on the Commonplace Book intensified, I invited him to prepare a new edition for publication in this series. Herein is presented the happy result of that invitation.

The Second Series of this edition of Jefferson's papers began publication in 1983 with the appearance of *Jefferson's Extracts from the Gospels*. Since then we have published a scholarly edition of his parliamentary writings, and currently in press is the long-awaited annotated edition of his memorandum books. Each of these projects had been commissioned by Julian P. Boyd, although he was not able to see them through publication prior to his death in 1980. The current edition of the literary commonplace book is the only manuscript in the Second Series that I authorized, and no other volumes are currently underway. The appearance of the present volume, therefore, marks a significant stage in the history of the Jefferson editorial enterprise, for now is the first time in almost three decades that work is concentrating solely on the correspondence series. While the actual editing of these topical volumes has been done in each instance by editors working alone, assisting them and publishing the manuscripts has required a great amount of the time of the Jefferson Office staff. Inasmuch as the previously completed Second Series volumes were in progress for much of the last twenty years of Mr. Boyd's tenure as Editor, and the present volume came to me by way of discovery, it is personally very satisfying to see all of this important work reach completion, and to make it available to the many scholars and interested readers who have waited so long for it. The Second Series now reaches a point where it may be considered as succeeding in the goals Mr. Boyd set for it when he launched the project, and at the same time additional future volumes may await some other opportunity of discovery by my successors.

In reading and using this volume, I should like to call attention to the important essay of introduction and the appendices. Professor Wilson shares in these contributions what he has learned about Jefferson's early and continuing education, and he explains his understanding of the sequence of the entries and the evolution of Jefferson's handwriting. No other scholar has done as much with this material, nor has the literary commonplacing ever been edited as well. Once

FOREWORD

again, I am pleased to present as an important addition to Jefferson scholarship a work of such quality.

Charles T. Cullen

Chicago, Illinois
January 11, 1988

PREFACE

The documentation for Thomas Jefferson's life and opinions is massive, most of it produced and preserved by Jefferson himself and in such quantity that, in spite of a multitude of editions and collections, it will be many years before it is published with reasonable completeness. But of this material, only a relatively few documents survive from the first 30 years of his life. As a result, there is a tendency for the students of Jefferson to take their bearings on a man who is already mature, already famous, whose attitudes and opinions are fully formed and whose guard against the prying public is already up. One of the few surviving documents from Jefferson's formative years, and one that offers prime evidence of his early literary and philosophical interests, is the manuscript presented here—his Literary Commonplace Book.

Jefferson's Literary Commonplace Book remained in the possession of his descendants nearly a hundred years before it was acquired by the Library of Congress, during which time it was unavailable to scholars and other students of Jefferson. In 1928, Gilbert Chinard performed a great service to Jefferson scholarship by publishing an edition of this notebook, the earliest that Jefferson is known to have kept. An unfortunate feature of Chinard's edition, however, was its limited editorial plan, which aimed at little more than an uncritical transcription of the text. As a consequence, this pioneering edition contained no analysis of the manuscript, virtually no supporting annotation, no means of assigning approximate dates for the entries, and an inaccurate rendering of the text.

A new edition of the Literary Commonplace Book on a more comprehensive editorial plan has been in prospect since the inception of *The Papers of Thomas Jefferson*, but the present editor's involvement came much later. It began with an inquiry concerning the dating of the entries, about which Chinard's edition and other authorities are largely silent. This inquiry developed into a study of the dating that was encouraged by Julian P. Boyd and Ruth W. Lester of the Jefferson Papers, and that eventually became, at the invitation of Charles T. Cullen, a full-fledged edition of the manuscript. In conformity with the aims and purposes of the Jefferson Papers, this edition represents an attempt to put the reader into possession of the document by presenting a reliable transcription of the text, together with appropriate annotation and critical analysis. The technical details regarding such things as the handwriting, the paper, the binding, and the composition of the manuscript, as well as statistical tables, have been placed in an appendix and may be consulted as needed. In the introduction, I have tried to present not so much what the diligent reader will find for himself by perusing the text, but rather what I have found and concluded in the course of an intensive study of the Literary Commonplace Book and related manuscripts.

An enterprise such as this is necessarily a collaborative effort, and I have attempted to acknowledge most of my many debts in the next section of the volume. But some debts are so basic to the completion of a project as to require special mention. My colleagues at Knox College have been helpful to me in more ways than they can properly be aware of, for merely to become part of such a faculty is to acquire scholarly assets and intellectual resources. Financial

PREFACE

resources for faculty research have always been available in my long tenure at Knox College, as well as other forms of institutional encouragement and support, and I am pleased to express my gratitude for continuing assistance from four successive Deans of the College: Hermann R. Muelder, Lewis S. Salter, Mary L. Eysenbach, and John Strassburger. In matters relating to American history and culture, I am deeply indebted to my teaching partner in courses in American Studies, Rodney O. Davis, whose historical knowledge and insights have been a constant source of illumination.

Stephen C. Fineberg of the Knox College Classics department made a considerable contribution by putting his knowledge of classical languages and literature at the disposal of the editor, who, like Shakespeare, has "small Latin and less Greek." Professor Fineberg spent a very substantial amount of time and effort in making trial transcriptions, examining the manuscript, verifying the Greek transcriptions, and advising me on various editorial problems. His worthy efforts in no way involve him in responsibility for whatever faults may be found in the handling of the classical material, for which I am alone responsible.

Charles T. Cullen commissioned this edition in the first year of his general editorship of the Jefferson Papers and was strongly supportive at every stage. My debt to him—for his expert advice and unfailing assistance—is deeply felt and gratefully acknowledged. My secretary, Rose Hane, is an important collaborator in all my scholarly and administrative activities, which I am pleased to be able publicly to confess.

It remains only to pay tribute to the most important collaborator of all, my wife, Sharon E. Wilson, without whom not.

Douglas L. Wilson

Galesburg, Illinois
January 2, 1988

ACKNOWLEDGMENTS

My obligations in this project are enormous and, of course, can never be properly acknowledged or repaid. Nonetheless, to list the people and institutions that have rendered assistance is a special pleasure. Much of the research that went into the project was done in libraries, where Jefferson would seem to have an endless number of friends and where I was able to take advantage of that friendship, and so the list begins with libraries.

The Library of Congress is the principal locus of Jefferson holdings. The Manuscript Division has charge of Jefferson's papers, and I am under particular obligation to its staff for attention and assistance over a long period. Paul G. Sifton played an important role in helping launch the project and rendered invaluable assistance. The head of the manuscript reading room, the late Fred Coker, was also understanding and helpful, as was his successor, Paul Chestnut. Others in the reading room who contributed much by their patience and cooperation were Gary Cohn, Charles Kelly, and John Hackett. The Rare Books and Special Collections Division, which has charge of Jefferson's library, was also extremely cooperative. Because of his familiarity with Jefferson's books and the extent of his knowledge in related areas, James Gilreath provided especially valuable assistance. His interest in the project and his willingness to provide a wide range of assistance are important elements in the completion of this edition. I am also obligated to Mr. Gilreath's very capable colleague, Peter Van Wingen. For an initial orientation and other favors, I am indebted to James R. Bowman, also of the Library of Congress.

The University of Virginia's Alderman Library is another prime location for Jefferson research, and I am grateful for assistance received there. In the Rare Book Department, acknowledgments are due Julius Barclay and Mildred Abraham; in the Manuscript Department, the same are due Edmund Berkeley, Jr., Gregory Johnson, and Janet Linde Kern. The Massachusetts Historical Society is yet another prime location for Jefferson material, and I am grateful for courtesy and consideration from its former Librarian, John D. Cushing, and for much helpful assistance from Peter Drummy. The Huntington Library is not only an important repository of Jefferson manuscripts, but is also one of the most pleasant and congenial settings imaginable in which to work. For financial assistance, I am indebted to its fellowship program, and for other assistance at the Huntington, to Martin Ridge and Virginia Renner. The Folger Shakespeare Library is another splendid place to work, and I am grateful for its hospitality and for the important assistance of the Manuscript Curator, Laetitia C. Yeandle, for useful advice and authoritative information on handwriting styles. Thanks are due also to Nati Krivatsy of the Reference department.

By naming the editor its first Lester J. Cappon Research Associate, the Newberry Library made possible the completion of this project, for which the editor is both extremely honored and grateful. Lawrence W. Towner, Richard Brown, Paul Gehl, Robert Karrow, Richard Johnson, Cynthia Peters, and John Tedeschi were all helpful, and the staff and program at the Newberry are generally to be commended for maintaining a truly exceptional environment in which to carry on scholarly work.

Other libraries and staff members that provided valuable assistance and

ACKNOWLEDGMENTS

earned my gratitude were the New York Public Library: David Stam; the Virginia State Historical Society: Sarah Sartain and Virginius C. Hall, Jr.; Earl Gregg Swem Library of the College of William and Mary: John Haskell and Margaret C. Cook; Colonial Williamsburg: Pearce Grove and John Ingram; and the Willard Library of Evansville: Joan Elliott. For making special arrangements for the examination of a Jefferson manuscript, I am grateful to Rosalie Sullivan of the James Monroe Law Office. Not the least of the libraries employed was the Knox College Library, where the service is always good. Special assistance was rendered by James K. Bracken and Jeffrey Douglas.

The Jefferson Office at Princeton University provided constant and invaluable support for this edition. Ruth W. Lester was present at the creation, so to speak, and with Julian P. Boyd lent encouragement in the very earliest stages of the study that preceded the editorial project. Mrs. Lester was not only vastly knowledgeable in matters regarding Jefferson and his manuscripts, but her willingness to respond knowledgeably and promptly to research needs made her an important asset in research, and I wish to acknowledge a special debt to her.

The American Philosophical Society provided a travel grant that made possible basic research in the early stages of the project. The American Council of Learned Societies earned my special gratitude by providing two grants to support travel for research, one in the earlier and one in the concluding phase. Grateful acknowledgment is made to the National Endowment for the Humanities for the award of a research fellowship which provided released time for extended research at the Library of Congress. Without these awards and those of the Huntington and Newberry Libraries already mentioned, this edition would still be in progress.

One of the pleasures of studying Jefferson is visiting Monticello, where the spirit of Jefferson is noticeably observed in the kindness and consideration afforded researchers. Both James A. Bear, Jr., and his successor as Director, Daniel P. Jordan, have been extremely considerate and cooperative. An important part of the work at the Thomas Jefferson Memorial Foundation is basic research on Jefferson, and two of its researchers have been especially generous: Lucia Stanton and William Beiswanger. Thanks are due also to Elizabeth Braswell, who has a special genius for finding ways to be helpful.

Thomas L. Gravell of Wilmington, Delaware assisted the editor immeasurably by examining the paper of which the manuscript is composed and providing related information. Willman Spawn of the American Philosophical Society made an invaluable contribution by identifying the binder and providing other relevant data. Thomas R. Coolidge of New York City kindly permitted me to examine a priceless family possession—Jefferson's Greek grammar. Two people associated with other founding fathers editorial projects were helpful in arranging for the examination of documents under their jurisdiction: Dorothy Bridgewater of the Benjamin Franklin Papers at Yale University, and Robert Taylor, formerly editor of the Adams Papers at the Massachusetts Historical Society.

Merrill D. Peterson of the University of Virginia took an early interest in this project and offered advice and support at several junctures, for which the editor is most grateful. The late Dumas Malone was friendly and generous in a way that was deeply appreciated. One of the editor's greatest regrets is that Mr. Malone did not live to see the completion of the project in which he took so

ACKNOWLEDGMENTS

keen an interest. Frank L. Dewey of Williamsburg, Virginia has been particularly helpful in sharing the results of his researches into Jefferson's career as a lawyer. Wilbur Samuel Howell of Princeton University was also very forthcoming regarding Jefferson's parliamentary notebooks.

For advice and assistance in dealing with the classical material in the Literary Commonplace Book, the editor is particularly indebted to two classicists: William Ziobro of the College of the Holy Cross, who shared his extensive knowledge of the classical curriculum in colonial period and offered helpful advice; and Meyer Reinhold of Boston University, answered many questions and made fruitful suggestions. Garry Wills of Northwestern University, who is a classicist as well as an authority on Jefferson, took a much-appreciated interest in the project generally and was helpful on classical subjects. The editor is also grateful to Timothy C. Wilson, whose special contribution it was to teach his father to transcribe Greek texts.

Eighteenth-century specialists were notably helpful, and grateful acknowledgment is here made to Maynard C. Mack of Yale University, for information on Pope; to R. G. Moyles of the University of Alberta and John T. Shawcross of the University of Tennessee for assistance with the Milton material; and to Howard C. Weinbrot and Eric Rothstein of the University of Wisconsin, Roger Lonsdale of Oxford University, Malcolm Goldstein of Queens College, City University of New York, and Douglas Canfield of the University of Arizona for assistance with other matters.

Though she may not be aware of it, Cynthia A. Wilson was a source of information on the law that was both material and relevant, and her father is grateful for this and much else. George Steckley, my colleague on the faculty of Knox College, provided useful advice on dealing with manuscripts and assistance on points of English history. For continuing interest and encouragement of long standing, I offer thanks to my colleague, Mikiso Hane, who is, among other things, a model of what a scholar should be. Two others, who are long-standing colleagues of another sort, deserve mention here because they have been constant sources of intellectual friendship and assistance: Terence C. Tanner and Sherman Paul.

Portions of the following copyrighted translations are used by permission: Richmond Lattimore, *The Illiad of Homer*, University of Chicago Press; Richmond Lattimore, *The Odyssey of Homer*, Harper and Row, Publishers; Samuel Solomon, *Complete Plays* (Jean Racine), Random House. For permission to reproduce Jefferson manuscript material, grateful acknowledgment is made to the Library of Congress, the Rosenbach Museum, the Huntington Library, New York Public Library, Yale University Library, University of Virginia Library, and the Rev. Dabney Carr III.

EDITORIAL APPARATUS

The text of the Literary Commonplace Book is presented as it appears in the manuscript. No changes have been made in spelling, capitalization, or punctuation, and nothing has been corrected or interpolated. Jefferson was a careful copyist, and while he frequently took liberties with the capitalization and punctuation of his copy-text, he rarely made copying mistakes. The few that occur have been retained and are indicated as such in the notes. The notes, rather than the reading text, have also been used to report the presence in the manuscript of interlineated insertions and crossed-out words, as well as manuscript and handwriting anomalies. Certain words, parts of words, and punctuation marks that appear originally to have been part of Jefferson's text have been cropped by the binder or otherwise lost. Where these could be identified from printed texts, they have been restored within square brackets. Headings, such as "Pope's Essay on Man," which sometimes recur on every leaf in the early material, are not repeated.

Transcription of handwritten material to printed form is not always the straightforward operation it appears to be. Though well over half of the Literary Commonplace Book was written during a time when Jefferson was still using the long *s*, this edition ignores it for the same reason Jefferson himself went to great lengths to rid his hand of it in the mid-1760s—because it causes the reader uncompensated difficulty and confusion. For the Greek entries, Jefferson also occasionally employed certain combined forms of Greek characters that occur in early printed editions but are no longer used. These have been transcribed in the standard Greek alphabet.

It is sometimes very difficult to determine whether Jefferson intended to write a capital or lower-case letter, just as it is occasionally unclear whether he intended to leave a space between words or run them together. This is especially true in transcribing the early material. And in the case of accents and diacritical marks, he appears to have been uncharacteristically careless or indifferent. In such cases, the text has been made to conform as closely as possible to what appears in the manuscript, and the matter is reported, where necessary, in the notes. Certain ambiguous diacritical marks in the Euripides section (§§85-154) constitute a special case, the treatment of which is discussed in the notes. It should be further noted that the capitalization of the entries is printed as found in the manuscript, including the treatment of the initial word in a sentence, and is thereby at variance with the established practice of the first series of the *Papers*.

Since all the entries in the Literary Commonplace Book have as their ultimate source a printed text, the editor has attempted to identify the precise edition or copy-text Jefferson used. While it has not been possible to specify the exact copy-text in all cases, Jefferson's entries have been compared with likely editions that were available to an eighteenth-century reader, as well as with well-edited modern editions. Annotation of textual variation is restricted to substantial differences, or matters that might otherwise affect meaning. Minor differences in punctuation or capitalization between Jefferson's entries and his copy-text are usually not reported. In noting textual variations, the published text used for comparison is identified by editor or publication data. However, in cases where the comparison of texts makes it appear likely that Jefferson himself is the source of the variation, either through error or emendation, the source of the correct reading is identified simply as the author. For example, Jefferson's first excerpt from Milton's *Paradise Lost* (§218) begins: "Round he threw his baleful Eyes." Though many editions of *Paradise Lost* were examined for comparison, none could be found that exhibited the word "threw" in this line. Thus, the note reporting this circumstance reads: "§218.1 *threw*] Milton: *throws*."

As is apparent in this example, for purposes of reference each entry has been assigned a number by the editor. This is printed to the left of the first line of the text in square brackets and is referred to in the notes and elsewhere with the section mark (§). The order of the numbers is the order in which the entries appear in the manuscript, but the reader should note that this is not the order in which the extracts were originally entered. The Literary Commonplace Book is an amalgamation of a number of manuscript components, which are described and analyzed in Appendix B. For a schematic approximation of the chronological order of the entries, the reader is referred to Table 1 in Appendix D. Only entries believed to have been entered by Jefferson have been included in the text. Entries in other hands and clippings from newspapers are printed in Appendix C.

SYMBOLS AND
SHORT TITLES OF
WORKS FREQUENTLY CITED

Cappon | Lester J. Cappon, ed., *The Adams-Jefferson Letters: The Complete Correspondence between Thomas Jefferson and Abigail and John Adams*, Chapel Hill, 1959, 2 vols.

Chinard | Gilbert Chinard, ed., *The Literary Bible of Thomas Jefferson*, Baltimore, 1928

DLC | Library of Congress

Family Letters | Edwin M. Betts and James A. Bear, Jr., eds., *Family Letters of Thomas Jefferson*, Columbia, Missouri, 1966

Ford | Paul Leicester Ford, ed., *The Writings of Thomas Jefferson*, "Federal Edition," New York, 1904-1905, 12 vols.

Garden Book | Edwin M. Betts, ed., *Thomas Jefferson's Garden Book, 1766-1824*, Philadelphia, 1944

Kimball | Marie Kimball, *Jefferson: The Road to Glory 1743-1776*, New York, 1943

L & B | Andrew A. Lipscomb and Albert E. Bergh, eds., *The Writings of Thomas Jefferson*, Washington, 1903-1905, 20 vols.

LCB | Literary Commonplace Book

Leavitt | *Catalogue of a Private Library . . . Also, the Remaining Portion of the Library of the late Thomas Jefferson, Comprising many Classical Works and several Autograph Letters, offered by his grandson, Francis Eppes, of Poplar Forest, Va.* [New York], 1873

Legal Commonplace Book | Gilbert Chinard, ed., *The Commonplace Book of Thomas Jefferson: A Repertory of his Ideas on Government*, Baltimore, 1926

Lives of the English Poets | Samuel Johnson, *Lives of the English Poets*, ed. George Birkbeck Hill, New York, 1967, 3 vols.

MHi | Massachusetts Historical Society

Malone | Dumas Malone, *Jefferson and his Time*, Boston, 1948-1981, 6 vols.

Notes on Virginia | William Peden, ed., *Notes on the State of Virginia*, Chapel Hill, 1955

Papers | Julian P. Boyd et al., eds., *The Papers of Thomas Jefferson*, Princeton, 1950-

Phil. Works	Henry Saint-John Bolinbroke, 1st Viscount, *The Philosophical Works of the Right Honorable Henry St. John, Lord Viscount Bolinbroke* . . . , London, 1754, 5 vols.
Poor	Nathaniel Poor, *Catalogue. President Jefferson's Library*, Washington, 1829
Randall	Henry Randall, *The Life of Thomas Jefferson*, New York, 1858, 3 vols.
Sowerby	E. Millicent Sowerby, comp., *Catalogue of the Library of Thomas Jefferson*, Washington, 1952-1959, 5 vols.
TJ	Thomas Jefferson
ViU	Alderman Library, University of Virginia

THE PAPERS OF
Thomas Jefferson

SECOND SERIES

INTRODUCTION

Life must be lived forward, Kierkegaard reminds us, even if it can only be understood backward. Thus, history and biography, in presenting earlier events as seen in the light of later ones, color our perceptions of what happened in the past and how things came about. Thomas Jefferson presents a classic case in point, for our awareness of his great accomplishments in later life—as a founding father of the American Republic, author of the Declaration of Independence, President of the United States, architect of Monticello and the University of Virginia—invariably affects the way we approach his earlier years. But the young man who kept the Literary Commonplace Book presented here, living his life forward from the age of about 15 to 30, was a very different Thomas Jefferson from the familiar figure of history.

Scarcely concerned with politics until he was in his twenties, he was very much concerned with and deeply affected by other things. He was an unusually avid and precocious student, and his most absorbing concern was his education, which included a mastery of foreign and classical languages, a broad acquaintance with the great books and writers, and a comprehensive view of "the expansion of science & of the system of things in which we are placed."[1] He was deeply affected by the death of his father, which occurred when he was only 14, and by the subsequent necessity of coming to terms with his mother. He liked to play chess and go to the theater, and he worked hard at becoming a competent violinist. During these years he followed horseracing, participated in fox hunts, and gambled for small stakes. As an adolescent, he was much interested in girls, and by the time he was twenty-five he had become entangled with a married woman. For virtually the whole of the time he was compiling his Literary Commonplace Book, he remained a bachelor, not marrying until he was nearly 29. Except for being elected by his neighbors to the colonial legislature near the end of this period, he achieved no wide public acclaim and was known as a person of great talent and potential only to his mentors and friends. What made him stand out from other members of his class, even more than his intelligence and ability, was a love of learning and a disciplined commitment to his intellectual endeavors. His letters to his college classmate, John Page, show that he was actively caught up in the social life of his circle, yet Page testified later that Jefferson could "tear himself away from his dearest friends, to fly to his studies."[2]

Jefferson was born in 1743 and, though his father, Peter Jefferson, was a self-made frontiersman without formal education, he seems to have encouraged his son's natural propensity for learning. According to a family tradition, the future president had read all the books in his father's small library by the time he was five, the age at which he started school. At the age of nine, he entered the boarding school of the Rev. William Douglas, where he learned the "rudiments" of Latin, Greek, and French. He continued there until the death of Peter Jefferson in August 1757. In accordance with the wish of his dying father, the young

---

[1] Autobiography, Ford, I, 6. The best accounts of Jefferson's early years are Malone, I, and Kimball, the latter providing the more detailed treatment of his youthful activities and particularly his literary interests.

[2] *Virginia Historical Register*, July 1850, p. 151, quoted in Malone, I, 58.

Thomas was to receive a classical education, and he was accordingly sent by his guardians in January 1758 to the school of the Rev. James Maury, where he remained for two years. In all likelihood, the Literary Commonplace Book was begun there. At about the time of his seventeenth birthday, in April 1760, he enrolled at the College of William and Mary, where he came under the tutelage of Dr. William Small. A learned young Scotsman who had been trained in the spirit of the Enlightenment, Small taught a full range of subjects, including belles-lettres, and took a personal interest in Jefferson's intellectual development. When Jefferson left the college after two years, it was to enter into an apprenticeship with Small's friend, George Wythe, who seems to have placed his learning, not only as a lawyer but also as a classicist, at the service of his nineteen-year-old apprentice. By the time he passed his bar examination three and a half years later in 1765, Jefferson had not only studied the law but had continued to pursue his interest in English poetry and Greek, had taken up history, and was teaching himself Italian.[3] And, characteristically, after passing the bar examination, he spent nearly a year and a half commonplacing dozens of law reporters and legal treatises before taking up his practice early in 1767.[4]

About the time he began the practice of law he also began seriously to plan for a place of his own across the river from Shadwell, the family residence, which he referred to as "my mothers house."[5] He was now 24. In the remaining half-dozen years in which he actively kept his Literary Commonplace Book, he would serve in the House of Burgesses, manage the family plantation and the affairs of his father's estate, attend to a legal practice that would average over 200 cases per year,[6] design and begin building the first Monticello, and pay court to a beautiful widow, Martha Wayles Skelton. By the time of his marriage on January 1, 1772, his literary commonplacing was coming to an end, and his political career was just beginning in earnest. The close conjunction of these developments is presumably no accident, for Jefferson's deep involvement in politics brought about dramatic and permanent changes both in his life and in what a biographer has called "the contours of his mind."[7] One of the conspicuous casualties thereof was his enthusiasm for literature generally and for English poetry in particular.

The Literary Commonplace Book is thus a product of Thomas Jefferson's formative years and as such belongs principally to a time when he was young, unmarried, not yet established in the world, and not yet caught up in politics. It was a time when, in spite of a full measure of cares and responsibilities, he was able to indulge what he believed were the pursuits most congenial to his nature, reading and study, or, as he might have termed them, the pleasures of

---

[3] On the date of TJ's bar examination, see Frank L. Dewey, *Thomas Jefferson, Lawyer* (Charlottesville, 1986), p. 117-21. On his reading during this period, see Douglas L. Wilson, "Jefferson's Library," in *Thomas Jefferson: A Reference Biography*, ed. Merrill D. Peterson (New York, 1986), p. 160-1.

[4] See Douglas L. Wilson, "Thomas Jefferson's Early Notebooks," *William and Mary Quarterly*, XLII (1985), 442-51.

[5] TJ to John Page, 21 Feb. 1770, *Papers*, 1: 34.

[6] The exact number of cases TJ handled in his law career is problematical. The investigator who has pursued this matter more thoroughly than anyone, Frank L. Dewey, has very kindly calculated for the Editor the number for this seven-year period at 1430 "with some allowance for error." Letter to the Editor, 26 July 1986.

[7] Merrill D. Peterson, *Thomas Jefferson and the New Nation* (New York, 1970), p. 37.

science. He would later complain that he should never have become involved in politics, for which he professed himself ill-suited, had not the times in which he lived demanded it. Upon his retirement, he returned with great relish to the books of his matchless library, which occupied the entire southern end of the expanded Monticello. Imaginative literature became something of a lapsed interest in his later years, but the moral and philosophical residue of his early reading, as inscribed in the Literary Commonplace Book, remained.

I

The Literary Commonplace Book is the earliest of a number of surviving notebooks kept by Thomas Jefferson.[8] It has come down to us as a bound manuscript of 123 leaves. He seems to have begun by folding sheets of foolscap paper three times, in octavo fashion, thereby creating fascicles of eight leaves, each measuring approximately four by six inches. Onto these leaves he copied extracts from his literary and philosophical reading from his mid-teens to the age of about thirty, after which he added very little. Most of the works represented are poetry, though by far the longest selection from a single source—the *Philosophical Works* of Henry St. John, Lord Bolingbroke—is in prose. The presence of at least two and possibly three sets of page numberings, plus a marginal note referring to a second volume, suggest that this compilation of quotations existed in a variety of physical arrangements and forms, and that the extracts were originally much more numerous than the 407 in the manuscript as it now exists.[9]

The evident rearrangement of the leaves (and consequently groups of entries) and the absence of many pages from the numbering sequences are clear indications that Jefferson selected some passages for inclusion, rejected others, and imposed a certain order on the manuscript that he sent to the binder in its final form in the 1780s. This order is not at once apparent, but it can eventually be discerned and may be described as constituting five basic categories: Works in Prose (§§1-84), Classical Poetry (§§85-202), English Poetry (§§203-85), English Dramatic Verse (§§286-341); and Poetic Miscellany (§§342-407). (For a complete listing of works by category, see Table 3.) The first category is essentially in prose; the rest are almost exclusively poetry. The last category differs from the other poetic categories in two ways: first, its entries are not segregated by era or type, so that ancient and modern, lyric and dramatic poetry, are intermingled; and second, the entries appear in an unbroken pagination series and seem to have been entered nearly chronologically from about 1768 to 1772-1773. It would appear from this that the extracts in the first four sections— which, with a few exceptions, were entered by 1766—must have been selected, arranged, and probably sewn together as a unit prior to 1768. Had these selections not constituted an already bound unit, the later entries, which constitute the fifth and final section, would surely have been treated like those in the first four sections and interspersed in the appropriate categories. The fifth section, herein called Poetic Miscellany, therefore appears to have been an extension of

[8] For an account of the other notebooks, see Wilson, "Jefferson's Early Notebooks."

[9] The Literary Commonplace Book is part of the *Thomas Jefferson Papers*, Manuscript Division, DLC. A descriptive analysis of the manuscript, detailing some of the original components, can be found in Appendix B.

the commonplace book created after an ordered selection of earlier material had been made between 1766 and 1768. The whole was bound in Philadelphia in the 1780s, before Jefferson went abroad in July 1784 to assume his ministerial duties in Paris.[10]

II

The evidence by which approximate dates may be assigned to the entries in Jefferson's Literary Commonplace Book is largely from the handwriting and is laid out in detail in Appendix A. It indicates that a substantial portion of the material—about 25 percent of the word count—was entered before December 1762, the date of the earliest extant letter in Jefferson's hand. This finding is corroborated by members of Jefferson's family, who report their understanding that the notebook was begun "before his hand was fully formed."[11] While it is safe to conclude that this early material comes from his student years, it is not possible to state with certainty how much of it might have been entered when Jefferson was enrolled at the Rev. James Maury's school between 1758 and 1760, or what portion, if any, might belong to the succeeding two years spent at the College of William and Mary. Since none of the various handwriting styles that Jefferson was experimenting with during this period very closely resembles the self-consciously italic hand that he was using at the end of 1762, it is possible that the bulk of these earliest entries belong to his school days in the 1750s rather than to his college years. Certainly the earliest entries—Horace, Virgil, and Ovid—are among the principal authors featured in the system of classical education that Jefferson received, and, though somewhat rearranged in the bound manuscript, they prove to belong to the pagination series that appears to be the earliest. It is perhaps not merely coincidental that, like most of the rest of the manuscript, these earliest entries are on paper that bears the same watermark as the account book kept by Jefferson's father in the 1750s.[12]

Peter Jefferson's dying wish that Thomas should have a classical education was a gesture that deeply endeared him to his son, who would often speak of this legacy in later life as the most valuable thing his father had left him. Jefferson remembered his teacher, the Rev. James Maury, in his autobiography as a "correct classical scholar,"[13] language that is calculated to set him apart from a previous teacher, the Rev. William Douglas, and also, apparently, to give Maury his due without professing affection. From what we know of him, Maury was unlikely to have been very congenial to his pupils. But while he disliked keeping a school—which he did only from financial necessity—he was serious

[10] Willman Spawn of the American Philosophical Society is the authority for dating the binding. For more information, see Appendix B.

[11] See the note inscribed in the manuscript itself by TJ's great-granddaughter, Martha Jefferson Trist Burke, in Appendix C. Her source may well have been her father, Nicholas P. Trist, who was Jefferson's personal secretary and who left a memorandum in which he called the Literary Commonplace Book "a 12° vol. of M.S. extracts made by Mr. Jefferson from various authors, many of which extracts were written before his hand became formed." *Nicholas P. Trist Papers*, Box 56, Manuscript Division, DLC.

[12] Peter Jefferson's Account Book is in the Huntington Library. For information on the paper, see Appendix C.

[13] Autobiography, Ford, I, 5. For a good account of Maury, see Malone, I, 40-6.

about education, knew his Latin and Greek, and was knowledgeable on a great many subjects. Even more to our purpose, he urged the kind of attention to one's reading that might suggest the keeping of a commonplace book, which was sometimes required by schoolmasters. "I would recommend it to you," he wrote his son, "to reflect, and remark on, and digest what you read; to enter into the spirit and design of your author; to observe every step he takes to accomplish his end; and to dwell on any remarkable beauties of diction, justness or sublimity of sentiment, or masterly strokes of true wit which may occur in the course of your reading."[14] These are features that the compiler of the Literary Commonplace Book frequently seems to have had in mind.

Jefferson probably began to keep his commonplace book about the time he enrolled in Maury's school, though possibly somewhat earlier. The entries that appear to be the earliest bear a striking similarity to certain examples of the model handwriting of Peter Jefferson, from whom the son is said to have learned penmanship. It is at least possible that a few of these earliest entries, which are the most elegantly inscribed, could actually have been penned by Peter Jefferson.[15] One of the baffling things about the manuscript is the variety of markedly different handwriting styles that are in evidence. A principal reason for thinking that Jefferson's father may have been responsible for the first few entries is that the hand of these entries is so much more elegant than most of the others, some of which seem too careless and unpolished to have been penned by the same person. Marie Kimball, who made a pioneering study of Jefferson's early handwriting, was led to conjecture that some of the entries may have been written by Thomas Jefferson's friends.[16] But the story told by this variety of hands is probably the familiar one of a young person trying out different handwriting styles as ventures in self-definition, explorations of how to present oneself to the world. In the differing styles of handwriting that he exhibits in the Literary Commonplace Book and in his other early notebooks and letters, Jefferson shows himself possessed of an extremely facile and versatile hand, capable of writing with conspicuous elegance and grace. (See the illustrations on pp. 191-204.) He experimented assiduously between the ages of 15 and 30 before settling into the plain, unpretentious version of the "round hand" that is seen in the familiar draft of the Declaration of Independence.

A careful study of the handwriting enables us to identify three principal periods during which extracts were entered: pre-1763 (i.e., prior to December 1762); 1762-1766; and 1768-1772/3. (A listing of authors and entries by period appears as Table 1 in Appendix D.) The first period comprehends his years of formal education. While some of the readings reflected in the entries were no doubt related to his schoolwork—particularly the Latin poets—it may be doubted that much of it represents reading that was assigned by his teachers as part of his curricular work. However, it is altogether likely that Jefferson, being an unusually eager student with a lively appetite for reading, sought the advice and probably borrowed the books of his teachers. The extracts belonging to this

[14] Quoted in Malone, I, 45.

[15] Randall, who is the authority for TJ's learning penmanship from his father, notes "a marked resemblance in the handwriting of father and son" (I, 15). The resemblance between Peter Jefferson's handwriting and that of the first six entries from Horace (§§167-72) is not striking in all instances but is quite discernible, for example, in the headings of his Account Book in the Huntington Library.

[16] Kimball, p. 115.

period are of two kinds: classical authors and English poets. The classical authors are all Latin poets except Cicero, an exception to be discussed later. The English selections feature Shakespeare, Milton, and Pope, but the poetry of the British dramatists and other dramatic verse is also strongly represented.

The next period chronologically, 1762-1766, coincides with Jefferson's years as a law student under the guidance of George Wythe. That Wythe was also known as one of the best classicists in the colony may help to explain why this period appears to foster most of the Greek entries. These consist of 70 entries from Euripides (more than from any other author), eight passages from Homer, and three from Herodotus. Lengthy excerpts from James Thomson's *The Seasons*, a short one from Livy, and certain of Pope's translations of Homer are the only English entries to be found in the distinctive italic hand that appears elsewhere only in Jefferson's earliest letters (1762-1764). The largest selection from a single author in the entire manuscript—54 excerpts and over 10,000 words from Bolingbroke—belongs to the end of this period, dating from 1765 or 1766.

The final period of significant activity in the Literary Commonplace Book, 1768 to 1772-1773, coincides with Jefferson's career as a lawyer. In later life, Jefferson told John Bernard that being trained in the law gave him a view of the dark side of life, so he turned to poetry for a view of the bright side.[17] This may relate principally to the fact that his intensive course of reading for the law, which is reflected in his other commonplace books kept during the years 1766-1768, interrupted his literary pursuits, to which he returned in the period under review. Or it may refer to the balancing of his legal practice with readings in poetry, of which these extracts may be taken as a sample.[18] What is clear is that the miscellaneous character and unclassifed, chronological order of this section of the Commonplace Book afford us an interesting look at the range of the young lawyer's reading in poetry, classical and contemporary: Mark Akenside, Horace, Anacreon, Thomson, David Mallet, Edward Moore, Young, George Buchanan, Seneca, Catullus, Pope, Horace, Nicholas Rowe, Ossian, Terence, Racine, John Langhorne, Homer, Ossian, and Thomas Moss.

The entries added after 1773 are very few (see Tables 1 and 2 in Appendix D). While Jefferson continued to read and take an interest in poetry, there is no doubt that his early enthusiasm for it began to fade, a development that went hand in hand with his deep immersion in politics. He still retained his relish for Ossian in 1782, when it proved a common bond with the Marquis de Chastellux. He even carried their friendly dispute over the basis of English prosody so far as to compose a substantial essay on the subject in 1786. But in it he theorized that the youthful pleasure one takes in poetry recedes with age until "we are left at last with only Homer and Virgil, perhaps with Homer alone."[19] By the time he became president in 1801, he confessed that his taste for poetry had almost entirely deserted him.[20]

[17] John Bernard, *Retrospections of America, 1797-1811*, ed. Mrs. Bayle Bernard (New York, 1887), p. 238.
[18] The relationship of TJ's legal and literary commonplace books is discussed in Wilson, "Jefferson's Early Notebooks," p. 433-52.
[19] "Thoughts on English Prosody," L & B, XVIII, 448. This text (415-51) has never been carefully edited and is somewhat garbled in this, the only published version.
[20] TJ to John D. Burke, 21 June 1801, Ford, IX, 267.

III

Near the end of his long life, Thomas Jefferson wrote out precise instructions for the design and inscription of his tombstone, prefacing these with some verses from Anacreon. It was the last of a number of such memorial inscriptions he authored, and like those that he had fashioned for his favorite sister, Jane, his best friend, Dabney Carr, and his young wife, Martha, it owed an obvious debt to his early readings in poetry. The chief repository for the lines of verse gleaned from these readings, containing the lines from Anacreon and many other poems he was to refer to in the course of his writings, was his Literary Commonplace Book.[21] Though he virtually ceased adding to it in the 1770s, there is abundant evidence to show that Jefferson continued to consult his Literary Commonplace Book—to refer to it and quote from it—throughout the rest of his life. The first direct quotation of which we have a record is a passage in his 1771 pocket memorandum book in which he sketches some ideas for creating a burying ground at Monticello. Perhaps in imitation of what he had read in Robert Dodsley's description of William Shenstone's ornamented farm, The Leasowes, about the placement of inscribed urns and brass plates at certain sites, he proposed as suitable inscriptions for the burying ground passages from Horace and Nicholas Rowe that he had recently entered in his Commonplace Book. Designing the burying ground as a resting place for his family, he added to these ruminations the Latin epitaph for his sister, Jane, who had died in 1765. But only two years later he was forced by the sudden loss of his brother-in-law and closest friend, Dabney Carr, to prepare a burying ground in earnest. On a leaf from an early notebook, he drafted a long epitaph for Carr's tombstone, on which he considered affixing inscriptions from David Mallet and Pope, both recorded somewhat earlier in the Literary Commonplace Book.[22]

The most concentrated and extensive use Jefferson made of his collection of literary extracts was in Paris in 1786 when he came to write the essay intended for the Marquis de Chastellux, "Thoughts on English Prosody." Although he consulted other books and cited passages not included in the Literary Commonplace Book, a large number of the verses he used to illustrate English prosody were drawn directly from its pages, sometimes in the exact order in which they occur in the bound manuscript. That he should carry this Commonplace Book with him to Paris at all is noteworthy and would seem to indicate his attachment to it; on the other hand, he may have had expressly in mind the project to prepare a demonstration of his prosodical arguments for the Marquis. In any case,

---

[21] The manuscript containing instructions for his tomb is in the Manuscript Division, DLC, and often reprinted. His epitaph for his wife from the *Iliad*, in Greek and in Pope's translation, can be seen in Randall, I, 383. For those for his sister Jane and Dabney Carr, see below. The verses from Anacreon (actually the *Anacreontea*) can be seen in the present edition at §347.3-4.

[22] Robert Dodsley, "A Description of The Leasowes," in *The Works in Verse and Prose of William Shenstone, Esq.* (London, 1764), II, 356. TJ's epitaph for his sister Jane, an imitation of Shenstone's for Maria Dolman reproduced by Dodsley, appears in the pocket Memorandum Book for 1771 and is printed in the *Garden Book*, p. 26. His proposed epitaph for Dabney Carr, with its excerpts from Mallet, Pope, and Ossian, is in the Manuscript Department, ViU, and is partially reproduced in Sarah N. Randolph, *The Domestic Life of Thomas Jefferson* (Charlottesville, 1978 [1871]), p. 47 (see p. 172 below).

Jefferson's reliance on the Literary Commonplace Book in working out his contentions in the essay on prosody is fully evident.[23]

There is relatively little discussion of poetry in Jefferson's voluminous correspondence, but there are occasional quotations, usually no more than a line or two. Some of these prove to be from his Literary Commonplace Book, such as a reference to Horace or an allusion to "the dark and narrow house of Ossian" in a letter to Adams.[24] Perhaps more telling are two versions of the same passage from Young's *Night-Thoughts* that Jefferson included in letters written five years apart to Abigail and John Adams. In both he draws on a passage of 13 lines (§254), but each version is sufficiently different in its inclusion of certain phrases and suppression of others as to suggest that he must have had the assistance not only of his memory but of his Commonplace Book. "Is this life?" he wrote to John,

> With lab'ring step
> To tread our former footsteps? pace the round
> Eternal?—to beat and beat
> The beaten track? to see what we have seen
> To taste the tasted? o'er our palates to decant
> Another vintage?[25]

Copied out when Jefferson was about 25, this passage, much condensed in Jefferson's versions, came to characterize for the man in his seventies the ennui of his declining years.

A final example of the uses Jefferson made of his Literary Commonplace Book also underscores its abiding utility and philosophical relevance from youth to old age. In 1816, he sent to Amos J. Cook, a Maine schoolmaster who had requested a sample of his handwriting and a message for his students, two passages of the same stoical import he had copied into the Literary Commonplace Book as a school boy more than fifty years before—one in the prose of Cicero (§79), the other in the verse of Horace:

> Who then is free? [asks Horace] The wise man, who is lord over himself, whom neither poverty nor death nor bonds affright, who bravely defies his passions, and scorns ambition, who in himself is a whole, smoothed and rounded, so that nothing from outside can rest on the polished surface, and against whom Fortune in her onset is ever maimed. (§177)

Jefferson thus shared with Mr. Cook's students something he had recorded when he was in their situation and to which, at the age of 73, he could still recur.[26]

IV

The real significance of the Literary Commonplace Book lies in what it has to reveal about Thomas Jefferson. When he began to keep it, he was a school-

[23] For example, a dozen lines from Milton's *Paradise Lost* that occur in the LCB are cited individually as examples in the early pages of "Thoughts on English Prosody."

[24] TJ to John Adams, 25 May 1785, *Papers*, 8: 162. See §387.

[25] Both letters are printed in Cappon: TJ to Abigail Adams, 11 Jan. 1817, p. 504; TJ to John Adams, 1 June 1822, p. 577. The letter to Mrs. Adams even employs a phrase ("leaden iteration") that was taken from a neighboring entry (§256).

[26] TJ to Amos Cook, 21 Jan. 1816, L & B, XIV, 403-6.

boy—naive, orthodox, and adolescent. By the time he ceased to keep it, he was a man of 30—cultivated, independent of mind, and marked for leadership. The Literary Commonplace Book may not reflect every change along the way, but it marks some of the stages. For example, Gilbert Chinard has called attention to the fact that many of the selections "reflect the natural dispositions of a man who distrusts the masses and takes pride in his birth and in his ancestry," representing a stage "before he had formulated his democratic creed."[27] There are also elements of an unmistakable misogyny in the earlier entries that are conspicuously absent in the later. And the entries from Bolingbroke, made when Jefferson was 22 or 23, record the unfolding of a momentous event in his intellectual development, the awakening of a skeptical and rationalistic deism in matters of religion. In addition to illuminating certain stages in his education and development, the manuscript provides glimpses of what would prove the unchanging bedrock of Jefferson's intellectual character, such as his uncompromising materialism and his ubiquitous concern with utility.

As a guide to his literary interests, the Literary Commonplace Book tells more about Jefferson's interest in poetry than prose. The long sections from Bolingbroke and Cicero are in prose and are indeed important, but they are not nearly so indicative of his literary as his personal and religious concerns. Of the 407 entries, 339 are poetry, and of 41 authors represented, 35 are poets. Insofar as it can be considered a literary sampler, the Literary Commonplace Book is representative only of Jefferson's interest in poetry.

Except for a single passage from Sterne's *Tristram Shandy*, nothing from prose fiction is present. In a sense, this is itself representative, for Jefferson seems never to have been an avid reader of fiction, as he was of poetry, and in later years he read almost no fiction at all. In fact, he came to regard the growing popularity of novels with disdain. But as a young man he read Sterne, Swift, and other writers with pleasure, and in a letter accompanying a list of recommended books he offered a staunch defense of fiction against the standard puritanical objections.[28] Part of this defense was repeated in 1800 in a letter to the American novelist Charles Brockden Brown, in which he allowed that "some of the most agreeable moments of my life have been spent in reading works of the imagination."[29] Ever a believer in the efficacy of moral examples, he read and commended to others the moral tales of Jean François Marmontel and the great eighteenth-century favorite, François de Fénélon's *Télémaque*. He may not have read Cervantes until he began to learn Spanish in the 1780s, but *Don Quixote* seems to have been a favorite and is sometimes said to be the only novel he ever re-read.[30]

Besides telling virtually nothing about his taste in fiction, the Literary Commonplace Book fails to inform us of some other literary interests that Jefferson had. Notebook citations, marginalia, and his essay on prosody attest to his fa-

[27] Chinard, p. 10.

[28] TJ to Robert Skipwith, 3 Aug. 1771, *Papers*, 1: 76-7.

[29] TJ to Charles Brockden Brown, 15 Jan. 1800 (DLC), quoted in William Peden, "Thomas Jefferson and Charles Brockden Brown," *Maryland Quarterly*, 1 (1944), 2, 68.

[30] Copies of *Don Quixote* were in both of TJ's Monticello libraries (Sowerby 4347 and Poor 746-7). William H. Peden, the author of the most detailed study of Jefferson's library, writes: "Don Quixote, one his favorites and considered by most critics the only book of prose fiction he ever read twice, was the only novel listed in Jefferson's catalogue for the University of Virginia." *Thomas Jefferson: Book-Collector* (Ph.D. diss., Univ. of Va., 1942), p. 66.

miliarity with William Collins, Thomas Percy's *Reliques of English Poetry*, and William Shenstone, no evidence of which appears in the Commonplace Book.[31] Jefferson was greatly attracted to Shenstone's light, pastoral lyrics and experiments in verse forms, quite independently of his more famous interest in The Leasowes and Shenstone's ideas on landscape gardening. This and other evidence aside, it seems an obvious mistake to conclude that the absence of certain writers or works from the Literary Commonplace Book proves their lack of attraction for the young Jefferson. The reader must bear in mind that the book is highly selective and that its importance to its compiler was not simply literary. "He that reads many books must compare one opinion or one style with another," wrote Samuel Johnson, "and when he compares, must necessarily distinguish, reject, and prefer."[32] But it will not follow that whatever is preferred will be written down in a commonplace book and whatever is not included has been rejected.

But the Literary Commonplace Book does indeed reveal a great deal about Jefferson's literary interests. It affords, for one thing, a look at his early literary education. The early excerpts in Latin are predictably from the most prominent authors in the classical curriculum in which he was trained—Horace, Virgil, and Ovid. In English, the earliest excerpts are from the leading poets—Pope, Milton, and Shakespeare. That James Thomson and Edward Young are classed with them as major poets shows Jefferson's perceptions about the stature of these relatively contemporary poets. Such preferences bespeak his affinity not only for their principal subjects—the rural landscape and death, respectively—but for their "romantic" and "sentimental" treatment of these subjects as well. The Literary Commonplace Book also tells a good deal about Jefferson's more mature poetic tastes and preferences, insofar as these are represented in the final section begun in 1768. There one sees that in addition to "major" poets, such as Pope, Thomson, and Young, he was keeping up his earlier interest in the drama of Nicholas Rowe and the verse of David Mallet. At the same time, he continued to indulge his decided taste for Latin verse, not only with Roman poets like Horace and Catullus, but in the verse drama of the Renaissance humanist George Buchanan, whose "pure latinity" earned him a revival in the eighteenth century.

Reference has been made to Jefferson's early interest as a student in plays and dramatic verse, but this interest is evident in all three of the principal periods during which the Literary Commonplace Book was being kept. Excerpts from plays, sometimes taken from a collection of memorable speeches but most often extracted from the works themselves, account for over a third of all entries, not counting a great many that contain speeches from epics and dramatic poems. Nearly half of the excerpts from plays are from Euripides (§§85-154), a circumstance that may provide a clue to the nature of Jefferson's attraction for dramatic literature. What apparently captured his attention and busied his pen was Euripides' penchant for apostrophe and moralizing speeches. The declamatory

[31] Lines from Collins' "Ode Written in the Beginning of the Year 1746" appear in the 1774 pocket Memorandum Book and in "Thoughts on English Prosody." Excerpts from several poems by Shenstone appear in both the 1771 pocket Memorandum Book and "Thoughts on English Prosody." Percy's *Reliques* is cited several times by TJ in the margins of a copy of Capell's edition of Shakespeare (1767) now in the possession of the Thomas Jefferson Memorial Foundation and on deposit in ViU.

[32] "Pope," *Lives of the English Poets*, III, 94.

nature of the drama readily lends itself to this mode, and the English dramatists favored by Jefferson in the Commonplace Book—Shakespeare, Otway, Rowe, and Young—fully availed themselves of their opportunities. There are, of course, many instances in the extracts from dramatic speeches where Jefferson seems drawn by the affecting nature of the language and imagery, but the substance of the speeches is very often philosophical or moralistic.

Had the Literary Commonplace Book been lost, the extraordinary place in Jefferson's literary pantheon occupied by Ossian, the supposedly ancient Celtic bard whose epics were actually the work of James Macpherson, would still be evident. In a remarkable letter dated 25 Feb. 1773, Jefferson requested the assistance of a relative of Macpherson's in obtaining a copy of Ossian's poems in their original language and such grammars and dictionaries as to make possible the mastery of the language. "I am not ashamed to own," he wrote, "that I think this rude bard of the North the greatest Poet that has ever existed."[33] Moreover, the Marquis de Chastellux has left a memorable account of sitting up late around the punch bowl at Monticello nearly ten years later and taking turns with his host reciting favorite passages from Ossian.[34]

Because of its footnoted parallels to classical sources, the Ossian section in the Commonplace Book strongly suggests that part of Jefferson's attraction to Ossian must have been the supposed similarity of his epic devices to those of the ancients. This comparing of texts turns out to be a significant aspect of the Literary Commonplace Book and indicates something quite revealing about Jefferson's literary interests. As in his historical and legal researches, Jefferson's attention in reading poetry was frequently drawn to precedents and counterparts. An obvious example is his commonplacing from Homer's originals and Alexander Pope's translations, which proves for the most part to be focused on corresponding passages. This is true also of his excerpts from Shakespeare's *Julius Caesar* and the Duke of Buckingham's rewritten version. The classical parallels to Ossian referred to above are partly drawn from Macpherson's own footnotes highlighting the "similarities" to famous epics, but Jefferson found and recorded some of these comparisons on his own. His letter to the Maine schoolmaster proves that the philosophical parallels between the passage from Cicero's *Tusculan Disputations* and the one from Horace, both entered when Jefferson was in his teens, had been more than mere coincidence. And even part of his interest in the misogynistic material may have been the striking similarity of disparate texts. The latest entries of this sort are from Euripides (§§132, 146), and their similarity to a passage in Milton (§241) that Jefferson had commonplaced earlier is obvious, a similarity that may have been called to his attention by the notes in Thomas Newton's edition of *Paradise Lost*. Thus, a noteworthy feature of Jefferson's commonplacing seems to have been "intertexuality," to use a current phrase, an expression of his interest in allusive relationships and the ways in which literary works anticipate and reflect one another. While Jefferson's literary tastes and preferences are, for their time, thoroughly conventional and unexceptional, the individual selections are decidedly his own and present a distinctive array of choices. He rarely contents himself

[33] TJ to Charles Macpherson, 25 Feb. 1773, *Papers*, 1: 96.

[34] Marquis de Chastellux, *Travels in North America in the Years 1780, 1781 and 1782*, ed. Howard C. Rice, Jr., 2 vols. (Chapel Hill, 1963), p. 392; quoted in the note on Macpherson in the Register of Authors.

with copying out the most celebrated passages from a work, and he often ignores what is most characteristic. As many commentators have noted, Jefferson's literary interests were never purely aesthetic, but were always closely tied to the moral and philosophical content of the works. Thus, in commonplacing Samuel Butler's *Hudibras*, a particular favorite of Virginians because of its rollicking satire at the expense of the Puritans, Jefferson records only non-humorous passages about honor, a frequent Commonplace Book theme. Or in reading the revelrous drinking songs of Anacreon, he extracts brief, philosophical sidelights on envy and the brevity of life. This concern with the moral and philosophical content is, of course, not surprising in so earnest a young man living in the eighteenth century. He probably subscribed wholeheartedly to the definition given by Dr. Johnson in his iife of Milton: "Poetry is the art of uniting pleasure with truth by calling imagination to the help of reason."[35] The study of poetry he regarded not only as a pleasurable but as a useful undertaking, affording instructive examples in both morality and composition. Even when he lost his zest for poetry in later life, he retained his belief in the educational value of reading the best poets.[36]

V

By training and temperament, Thomas Jefferson seems always to have been a reserved person, indisposed to speak of his personal concerns outside the circle of his family and closest friends. Finding himself a man of consequence in the world, he went to extraordinary lengths to preserve a full record of his public life, but he took equal pains to protect his privacy, and in so doing erected a barrier of silence and secrecy regarding his personal feelings and affairs. This barrier was and still is formidable. The problem has regularly been alluded to by historians and Jefferson biographers since the time of Henry Adams. One of the ablest of these, Merrill D. Peterson, has described the difficulties presented by "the wall of silence Jefferson threw around his emotional life," and in the preface to his own biography has confessed with mortification that, in this respect, Jefferson remains for him "an impenetrable man."[37]

The very existence of such a barrier has been used by others as evidence that Jefferson must have had something embarrassing or shameful to hide—a hatred of his mother or, more sensationally, an illicit sexual liaison with a slave. This is highly speculative, to say the least, for it hardly follows that because he wanted to keep his personal life out of public view, he must have been ashamed of it. Nonetheless, there is little doubt that Jefferson did dispose of letters relating to his mother and his wife, and there were other materials that he put into the hands of members of his family that, because of their personal associations, he probably did not expect to be made public. Though his descendants to this day are known to possess materials that have never been published, a surprising amount of this material has found its way into permanent repositories, where its safety and preservation have been deemed more important considerations than

[35] *Lives of the English Poets*, I, 170.

[36] For example, see his letter to Nathaniel Burwell, 14 Mar. 1818, L & B, XV, 166.

[37] Peterson describes the difficulties of the "wall of silence" in his introduction to *Thomas Jefferson: A Profile*, ed. Merrill D. Peterson (New York, 1967), p. x-xi. The prefatory remark is from *Thomas Jefferson and the New Nation*, p. viii.

the original wish to restrict its circulation to members of the family. One of the most interesting and significant things about the Literary Commonplace Book is that it belongs to this category of intimate personal effects.

At Jefferson's death, the manuscript passed to his daughter, Martha Randolph, who, according to her granddaughter, "always kept this book of her father's among her treasures."[38] On the first leaf Martha inscribed a Latin motto that her father had encountered in his youth and presumably had currency in the family—"Heu! quanto minus est cum reliqui[s] versari quam tuie memminisse." This motto had personal associations with his favorite sister, Jane, and appears in another family document with a translation which may derive from Jefferson himself: "To live with them is far less sweet / Than to remember thee!"[39] Its importance for Martha Randolph is underscored by a remark she made about the memory of her father nearly two years after his death: "One image has possession of my brain, in company or alone, sleeping or waking, it is always there."[40] From Martha, the Literary Commonplace Book passed to her daughter and son-in-law, Virginia and Nicholas P. Trist, and from them to their daughter, Martha Jefferson Trist Burke, who had been born at Monticello. Late in life Mrs. Burke placed many family items with such established Jefferson repositories as the University of Virginia, but the Literary Commonplace Book was one of the things she never relinquished. It was finally purchased from her heirs in 1918 by the Library of Congress.[41]

Having thus remained a family possession for nearly a century after his death, Jefferson's Literary Commonplace Book had apparently never been examined by scholars or biographers, nor does it seem to have been noticed as an important Jefferson source, until it was edited for publication by Gilbert Chinard in 1928 as *The Literary Bible of Thomas Jefferson*. Sensing its potential as a new source of insight into an intensely private man, Chinard went so far as to declare in his introduction that the Literary Commonplace Book affords "an opportunity to penetrate to the real personality of the man" and that it might be titled "Jefferson Self-revealed."[42] But Chinard seems to have meant something less dramatic than his language implies, for both in his introduction and in the biography that he published a year later he pursued this notion no further than to observe that the Commonplace Book contained "maxims and principles" that Jefferson followed through life. Chinard's edition quickly became a standard source for students of Jefferson, and though it has regularly been consulted as a gauge of Jefferson's literary and philosophical interests, little use has been made of it as a means of penetrating his personality.

That his Literary Commonplace Book was more to Jefferson than a literary sampler and was in some respects a deeply personal notebook with direct con-

---

[38] From a testimonial written on a blank leaf near the beginning of the LCB. For the full text, see Appendix C.

[39] For a discussion of the motto and the family documents relating to it, see Appendix C.

[40] Martha Jefferson Randolph to Thomas Jefferson Randolph, 2 Mar. 1827 (Edgehill-Randolph Papers, ViU), quoted in Elizabeth Langhorne, *Monticello: A Family Story* (Chapel Hill, 1987), p. 268.

[41] Mrs. Burke died in 1915. The editor is indebted to Paul G. Sifton of the Library of Congress for researching the provenance of the LCB in the internal files of the Manuscript Division and sharing the results of his investigation.

[42] Chinard, p. 3.

nections to the emotional events and preoccupations of his formative years becomes more evident when the dating of the entries is clarified. What one makes of any historical document is, of course, largely dependent on its date, and this is particularly true of the entries in a notebook such as Jefferson's. Copying out a passage into a commonplace book might suggest one thing if done as a schoolboy exercise but something very different if done in maturity. The present edition provides a rationale for dating most of the entries within a few years of their having been written, and enables the reader to determine, as Chinard's edition did not, the approximate order in which the extracts were entered and the biographical context to which they may belong. Thus it is now possible to correct or amend previous conjectures that were based on erroneous assumptions about date and, by the same token, to see in certain extracts personal associations that were hitherto obscured from view. His courtship of Rebecca Burwell may serve as an example. A common speculation is that the strain of misogyny in the Literary Commonplace Book reflects his disappointment at having lost Rebecca to another suitor. But as most of the misogynistic passages were entered several years before this courtship ended suddenly in March 1764, such speculation proves wide of the mark.[43] By the same token, knowing that the lengthy passages from Thomson on "the charming agonies of love" (§§283-5) were entered during the period of that courtship and at about the time that Jefferson was describing the same "symptoms" in his letters to John Page presents these passages in something more than a literary light and shows why they should have seemed to a perceptive biographer less moralistic and "much more poetical in character that those Jefferson usually selected."[44]

This pair of examples scarcely suggests the depth or significance that other personal associations discernible in the Literary Commonplace Book may be seen to have. Jefferson's infatuation with Rebecca Burwell was certainly an important experience of his youth, but it was carried on mostly from afar and in his imagination, and it seems not to have touched his deepest feelings and to have left no permanent scar. But Jefferson does seem to have been profoundly affected by other things that one may glimpse in these pages. Perhaps the most persistent motif in the Literary Commonplace Book is death. It appears early and late, in poetry and in prose, in English, Latin, and Greek. A passage from Horace in the earliest section of the manuscript invokes the specter of death, which appears at the door of rich and poor alike (§171), and the final entry, written as a kind of valedictory in Jefferson's old age, concludes, "no man may live for ever: each man's fate is foreordained" (§407). Jefferson's early interest in Young's gloomy and often lugubrious *Night-Thoughts* is to some extent, of course, simply the attraction of the age, which relished the melancholy brooding that would later seem sententious and self-indulgent. But Young's poem, whatever else it does, evokes the inner experience of deep personal loss resulting from the deaths of those closest and most dear. For a young man of tender sensibilities who had lost a father and a favorite sister, the inclusion of Young's meditations must be regarded as something more than poetic posturing.

There is material in Jefferson's Literary Commonplace Book that relates directly or indirectly to the death of his wife, to the death of his dearest friend

[43] See TJ to William Fleming, 20 Mar. 1764, *Papers*, 1: 16.
[44] Kimball, p. 114. Of his letters to Page about Rebecca Burwell, 1762-1764, see especially TJ to John Page, 20 Jan. 1763, *Papers*, 1: 7.

Dabney Carr, and, as noted, to the composition of his own epitaph.[45] But the most revealing passages on death must surely be those from Cicero's *Tusculan Disputations*, which it can now be demonstrated were entered not long after the death of Jefferson's own father. Through Cicero, who was himself writing in bereavement over the loss of his daughter, the boy confronts the fact that "all have to die" (§60) and faces the question: "What satisfaction can there be in living, when day and night we have to reflect that at this or that moment we must die?" (§61) Coming to terms with this necessity is the burden both of the *Tusculan Disputations* and of Jefferson's commonplacing, as he traces Cicero's thoughts on such topics as immortality and the afterlife, on belief in God, on suicide, and on the assistance to be sought from reason, the "mistress and queen of the world." The boy receiving the benefits of a classical education arranged for by his dying father notes Cicero's remark that death "does not frighten the wise man from considering the interests of the State and of his family for all time; and it follows that he regards posterity, of which he is bound to have no consciousness, as being really his concern" (§68). Death is inevitable, but "the man who is afraid of the inevitable cannot live with a soul at peace" (§72). Once one is alerted to the circumstances, the entire section of 21 philosophical extracts resonates with personal significance. It culminates in a passage, later to be used by Jefferson as a touchstone of his philosophy, on the overriding need for control of the passions:

> Therefore the man, whoever he is, whose soul is tranquilized by restraint and consistency and who is at peace with himself, so that he neither pines away in distress, nor is broken down by fear, nor consumed with a thirst of longing in pursuit of some ambition, nor maudlin in the exuberance of meaningless eagerness—he is the wise man of whom we are in quest, he is the happy man who can think no human occurrence insupportable to the point of dispiriting him, or unduly delightful to the point of rousing him to ecstasy.(§79)[46]

This encounter with Cicero and the consolations of stoic philosophy in the shadow of his father's death may well have been pivotal in the development of the young man's personality. It is distinctly present in the philosophical stance Jefferson subsequently devised for himself and tried out a few years later on his friend John Page:

> The most fortunate of us all in our journey through life frequently meet with calamities and misfortunes which may greatly afflict us: and to fortify our minds against the attacks of these calamities and misfortunes should be one of the principal studies and endeavors of our lives. The only method of doing this is to assume a perfect resignation to the divine will, to consider that whatever does happen, must happen, and that by our uneasiness we cannot prevent the blow before it does fall, but we may add to its force after it has fallen. These considerations and other such as these may enable us in some measure to surmount the difficulties thrown in our way, to bear up with a tolerable degree of patience under this burthen of life, and to proceed

[45] For the death of his wife, see §81 and notes. For Dabney Carr, see §354, §376 and notes.

[46] This is the passage sent along with the one from Horace to Amos J. Cook, the Maine schoolmaster, in 1816. See above.

with a pious and unshaken resignation till we arrive at our journey's end, where we may deliver up our trust into the hands of him who gave it, and receive such reward as to him shall seem proportioned to our merit. Such dear Page, will be the language of the man who considers his situation in this life, and such should be the language of every man who would wish to render that situation as easy as the nature of it will admit. Few things will disturb him at all; nothing will disturb him much.[47]

The "calamities and misfortunes" that Jefferson knew at first hand were centered in the death of his father, and the passages commonplaced from the *Tusculan Disputations* lent expression, if not direction, to the intellectual means he adopted to cope with them.

As he grew older, Jefferson added, as appendages to the Cicero section, other seemingly interrelated extracts having to do with inevitability and death (§§80-4). The first is from Livy on facing unpleasant truths, and another is from Cicero's *De Fato*. One is a passage from Laurence Sterne's *Tristram Shandy* that was to have personal associations with Jefferson's wife, Martha, and her early death. Another proves to be a reworking of a famous epitaph that Jefferson may have adapted to apply to himself. The last is a brief passage from Virgil's *Aeneid*, apparently entered late in life, that sums up the lesson taught by Cicero as Jefferson had learned and applied it: "whither the Fates, in their ebb and flow, draw us, let us follow; whatever befall, all fortune is to be o'ercome by bearing." The theme of bearing whatever the fates or fortune may bestow, which is mentioned in the letter to Page, is one that occurs frequently in the Literary Commonplace Book and is closely allied to the stoic attitude toward death and misfortune. Typical are two passages from Homer entered both in Greek and in Pope's translation at about the same time that the letter to Page was written:

> To labour is the lot of man below;
> And when Jove gave us life, he gave us woe. (§200)

> ——Let reason mitigate our care:
> To mourn, avails not: man is born to bear. (§202)

If these braided strands constitute an indicative theme of personal significance, there is, at the same time, an important thematic strain in the Literary Commonplace Book that runs opposite to this, a counter-theme of defiance and rebellion. One may see this exemplified in the sharp outcry of Cassius against Julius Caesar or in Satan's famous speech from Book 1 of *Paradise Lost*:

> ——What tho the Field be lost?
> All is not lost; the unconquerable Will,
> And Study of Revenge, immortal Hate
> And Courage never to submit or yield:
> And what is else not to be overcome? (§219)

Among these passages which feature defiance are a number of dramatic

---

[47] TJ to John Page, 15 July 1763, *Papers* 1: 10-11. For a different approach to this letter and its relationship to the LCB, see Adrienne Koch, *The Philosophy of Thomas Jefferson* (New York, 1943), p. 1 ff. She proceeds on the notion that "Jefferson's interest in the ancients was [not] primarily to cull personal comfort or guidance for his immediate problems," but she took this position with no clear idea of when the Cicero entries were made.

speeches that are characterized by emphatic outbursts. This example from
Thomas Otway is tinged with a misogyny that is more blatant elsewhere:

> ———Wed her!
> No! were she all Desire could wish, as fair
> As would the vainest of her Sex be thought,
> With Wealth beyond what Woman's Pride could waste,
> She should not cheat me of my Freedom. Marry!
> When I am old & weary of the World,
> I may grow desparate,
> And take a Wife to mortify withal. (§301)

Given the earnest stoicism of so many other passages, Jefferson's attraction for
strongly-worded, defiant speeches is quite noticeable and suggests a personal
application for this telling excerpt from Nicholas Rowe's *Tamerlane*:

> The firey Seeds of Wrath are in my Temper,
> And may be blown up to so fierce a Blaze
> As Wisdom cannot rule. (§314)

The ability to date these entries brings to light an important circumstance,
namely, that the passages voicing defiance and rebellion all belong to the early
part of the book and that no passage of this sort was entered after 1762. Inter-
estingly, too, most are inscribed in the same energetic and flamboyant hand, the
most exuberant in the manuscript, which Jefferson used only briefly in his student days and which stands in striking contrast to the subdued and self-consciously plain hand of his maturity.[48] The fiery seeds of wrath were indeed in
the young man's temper, but, as his letter to Page indicates, he was learning to
control them. This firm grip on even his deepest emotions would characterize
his personality for the rest of his life.

But if these passages of defiance and rebellion are indeed indicative of Jefferson's carefully concealed emotional makeup, why did he retain them in his
Commonplace Book? Outspoken defiance and rebellion, as well as a frank misogyny, were presumably things he had either outgrown or gained control of
by the time he made his final selection and seemingly should no longer have
been attractive, either as models or mementoes. Since the Literary Commonplace Book is the earliest of his notebooks and was not intended for public scrutiny, it seems possible that he retained them as a reminder of what he had mastered, as a measure of the distance he had come and the degree of control he had
achieved.

The personal dimensions of the Literary Commonplace Book are manifold,
and no attempt is made to name or discuss them exhaustively here. While it
would be too much to claim that such a document—or any single document—
contains the key to the complex and elusive personality of Thomas Jefferson,
the Literary Commonplace Book nonetheless contains potentially rich and provocative clues. It is an early record that speaks from both the Head and the
Heart and helps us to better understand the dialogue between those comple-
mentary but contending forces. It reveals the early directions and tendencies of
Jefferson's inner life as no other document is able to do—its fantasies, its pos-

---

[48] In Table 1 of Appendix D, which lists the entries by period and handwriting style,
this is called the "Shakespeare" hand.

turing, its varying attempts to find, in the situations and utterances of imaginative characters, suitable images for the self. Adam and Satan, Caesar and Cassius, Coriolanus and Falstaff are but a few from the varied host that present themselves. Looking back on Jefferson's early life from our accustomed perspective, *Samson Agonistes* would seem an unlikely work in which the future president might glimpse himself or his own apparently fortunate and promising situation in life. But the Commonplace Book, which records his life being lived forward, shows us that at the age of about 16 or 17 he took a long, careful look at Milton's Samson (§§324-41). It is evident from the uncharacteristically large number of extracts from a single work that the sufferings of Samson—the futility of strength without wisdom, the sense of being friendless and alone, of being deeply troubled and in despair, of suffering at the hands of a woman—these somehow spoke to the young student and were still meaningful in some wise to the grown man who, many years later, decided to preserve them. His other early notebooks, which deal more or less straightforwardly with legal, historical, and political pursuits, are invaluable for the light they shed on his development, but the special challenge of the Literary Commonplace Book, for those who would better understand Thomas Jefferson, is to do justice to the personal as well as the aesthetic and intellectual character of what he recorded and preserved.

THE
LITERARY COMMONPLACE
BOOK

[1] μουνοι παντων ανθρωπων Κολχοι και Αιγυπτιοι και
Αιθιοπες περιταμνονται απ' αρχης τα αιδοια. Φοιν-
ικες δε και Συροι ὁι εν τη Παλαιϛινη και αυτοι ὁμ-
ολογεουϛι παρ' Αιγυπτιων μεμαθηκεναι. compare with
Gen c.17.v.10.

Herodot. l.2. c.104.

[2] πρωτοι δε και τονδε τον λογον Αιγυπτιοι ειϛι ὁι ει-
ποντες, ὡς ανθρωπου ψυχη αθανατος εϛτι· του ϛωμα-
τος δε καταφθινοντος, ες αλλο ζωον αιει γινομενον
εϛδυεται· επεαν δε περιελθη παντα τα χερϛαια και
τα θαλαϛϛια και τα πετεινα, αυτις ες ανθρωπου ϛωμα
γινομενον εϛδυνειν· την περιηλυϛιν δε αυτη γινε-
ϛθαι εν τριϛχιλιοιϛι ετεϛι.

Herod. l.2. c.123.

[3] Ὁι δε Γεται αθανατιζουϛι τονδε τοντροπον· ουτε
αποθνηϛκειν ἑωυτους νομιζουϛι, ιεναι τε τον απολ-
λυμενον παρα Ζαμολξιν δαιμονα.——ὡς δε εγω πυν-
θανομαι τον Ζαμολξιν τουτον εοντα ανθρωπον, δου-
λεῦϛαι Πυθαγορη και——καταϛκευαϛαϛθαι ανδρεωνα,
ες τον πανδοκευοντα των αϛτων τους πρωτους, και
ευωχεοντα, αναδιδαϛκειν ὡς ουτε αυτος, ουτε ὁι
ϛυμποται αυτου, ουτε ὁι εκ τουτων αιει γινομενοι
αποθανεονται, αλλ' ἡξουϛι ες χωρον τουτον ἱνα αει
περιεοντες ἑξουϛι τα παντα αγαθα.

Herodot. l.4. c.94, 95.

§§1-3 These entries from Herodotus' history of the Persian wars were probably entered in the mid-1760s. Translations are from the Loeb Classical Library edition: A. D. Godley, trans., *Herodotus*, 4 vols. (London, 1921).

§1 Translation: . . . the Colchians, the Egyptians, and the Ethiopians are the
only nations that have from the first practised circumcision. The Phoenicians
and the Syrians of Palestine acknowledge of themselves that they learnt the
custom from the Egyptians.

Herodotus, 2.104. Herodotus' testimony about circumcision bears directly
on Bolingbroke's charge in succeeding entries, entered at about the same time
(*c.* 1765), that certain Jewish customs supposedly ordained by God in the Old
Testament were actually borrowed from others. Bolingbroke's forceful challenge to the historicity of the Bible, as the LCB reveals, was of great interest to
the young TJ, but his attention to this passage may also have been piqued by
reading *Tristram Shandy*, echoes of which appear elsewhere in TJ's writing.
(See Sterne in the Register of Authors.) In the novel, Tristram's accidental
circumcision causes his philosophical father to wonder "whether the *Jews* had
it from the *Egyptians*, or the *Egyptians* from the *Jews*." See *Tristram Shandy*,
Book 5, Chapter 27.

§1.4 *Gen c.17.v.10*] Genesis 17: 10: "This is my covenant, which you shall

[4] It is said that the sacred authors writ agreeably to all the vulgar notions of the ages and countries in which they lived, out of regard to their ignorance and to the gross conceptions of the people: as if these authors had not writ for all ages and all countries, or as if truth and error were to be followed, like fashions, where they prevailed.

> Bolingbroke's philosoph. works.
> Essay 1. sect. 5.

[5] It may be said that an extraordinary action of god on the human mind, which the word inspiration is now used to denote, is not more inconceivable, than the ordinary action of mind on body, and of body on mind: and I confess that it is not. but yet the cases are so widely different, that no argument can be drawn from one in favor of the other. it is impossible to doubt of an action which is an object of intuitive knowledge, and whereof

---

keep, between me and you and thy seed after thee; Every man child among you shall be circumcised." King James version.

§2 Translation: Moreover, the Egyptians were the first to teach that the human soul is immortal, and at the death of the body it enters into some other living thing then coming to birth; and after passing through all creatures of land, sea, and air (which cycle it completes in three thousand years), it enters once more into a human body at birth.

Herodotus, 2.123.

§3 Translation: As to [the claim of the Getae] to be immortal, this is how they show it: they believe that they do not die, but that he who perishes goes to the god Salmoxis——For myself, I have been told by the Greeks that this Salmoxis was a man who was once a slave of Pythagoras——he made himself a hall, where he entertained and feasted the chief among his countrymen, and taught them that neither he nor his guests nor any of their descendants should ever die but that they should go to a place where they would live for ever and have all good things.

This extract is pieced together by TJ from Herodotus, 4.93-5.

§3.4-5 δουλεῦςαι Πυθαγόρῃ καὶ] Inserted with a caret between the lines. καὶ seems to have been added by TJ as a connective.

§§4-34, 36-58 All extracts from Bolingbroke were taken from *Phil. Works*. Volume and page numbers indicate locations for the passages commonplaced.

TJ uses a long dash (——) to indicate material that he has omitted within an entry, and these are printed as part of the text. The few instances in which he makes significant silent omissions are noted.

Nine of these entries are truncated, representing either the beginning or ending (and in one case both) of an entry TJ, by eliminating one or more leaves, chose not to include in toto. In these entries, a bracketed ellipsis ([...]) indicates an indeterminate amount of material TJ omitted.

§4 *Phil. Works*, I, 135.

§5 Same, 154-5.

we are conscious every moment; and it is impertinent to deny the existence of any phaenomenon merely because we cannot account for it; but then this phaenomenon must be apparent, and the proof that it exists, or has existed, must be such as no reasonable man can refuse to admit; otherwise we shall be exposed to make frequently the ridiculous figure that philosophers have sometimes made, when it has been discovered after they had reasoned long about a thing, that there was no such thing.

Id. Ib.

[6] We must not assume for truth, what can be proved neither à priori, nor à posteriori. a mystery cannot be proved à priori; it would be no mystery if it could: and inspiration is become a mystery, since all we know of it is, that it is an inexplicable action of the divine on the human mind[.] it would be silly, therefore, to assume it to be true, because god can act mysteriously, that is, in ways unknown to us, on his creature man: for just so Asgyll did prove, or might have proved, that men do not die but are translated, because god can translate them. there is then no possibility of proving inspiration à priori; and the proofs that are brought à posteriori for Christian inspiration, are not more decisive to Christians, than those, which the Stoicians brought in favor of vaticination and divination, were to them; nor than those which the Mahometans and the worshippers of Foe bring of the same kind, are to them.

Id. Ib.

[7] No hypothesis ought to be maintained if a single phaenomenon stands in direct opposition to it.

Id. sect. 8.

§6 Same, 155. In Bolingbroke's text, this passage follows immediately after that given in §5. TJ at first skipped the first sentence and wrote "a mystery cannot be proved à priori," but then struck this out and began his entry with the previous sentence.

§6.9 Asgyll] John Asgill (1659-1738), English author of *An argument proving that according to the covenant of eternal life reveal'd in the Scriptures, man may be translated from hence into that eternal life without passing thro death* . . .

§7 *Phil. Works*, I, 195. This entry, which has been frequently cited by commentators, is derived from the following passage: "They who plead for hy-

[8] If nothing which is an object of real knowledge could be opposed to the immateriality and immortality of this substance, the insuperable difficulty of accounting for the action of mind on body, and of body on mind, that are reciprocally and in their turns both active and passive, would stop our philosophical enquiries.

Id. Ib.

[9] Solidity and extension are the primary qualities, and in our ideas the essence of matter, of which we can frame no conception exclusively of them. what then are the primary ideas of spirit or immaterial substance?

Id. Ib.

[10] it will cost a reasonable mind much less to assume that a substance known by some of it's properties may have others that are unknown, and may be capable, in various systems, of operations quite inconceivable by us, according to the designs of infinite wisdom; than to assume that there is a substance, concerning which men do not pretend to know what it is, but merely what it is not.

Id. Ib.

[11] As long as matter is senseless and inert, it is not a thinking substance, nor ought to be called so. but when, in any system of it, the essential properties, extension, solidity &c. are maintained, that system is material still, tho' it become a sensitive plant, a reasoning elephant, or a refining metaphysician. it would be nonsense to assert, what no man does assert, that the idea of incogitativity can be the idea of thinking: but it

---

potheses urge, not very unreasonably, that they may be of some use in the investigation of truth, whilst they are employed; and that they may serve to the same purpose, even when they are discovered to be false and are laid aside: as men who have missed their way give some instruction to others who find it. Besides which, they do not so much as pretend that any hypothesis ought to be maintained, if a single phaenomenon stands in direct opposition to it. I do not agree to this plea in the whole, but to the latter part of it entirely."

§8 Same, 206-7.
§9 Same, 209.
§10 Same, 210.
§11 Same, 219-20.

is nonsense, and something worse than nonsense, to assert what you assert, that god cannot give the faculty of thinking, a faculty in the principle of it entirely unknown to you, to systems of matter whose essential properties are solidity, extension &c. not incogitativity. this term of negation can be no more the essence of matter, than that other, immateriality, can be the essence of spirit. our ideas of solidity and extension do not include the idea of thought, neither do they include that of motion; but they exclude neither:

Id. Ib.

[12] Body or matter is compounded and wrought into various systems before it becomes sensible to us. we behold some that are indeed inert, senseless, stupid, and in appearance merely passive, but we behold others that have vegetative life juices and spirits that circulate and ferment in them, by which they are nourished, and by which they grow. they have not the power of beginning motion; but motion, which is renewed in them after it has entirely ceased, and both by causes as material as themselves, continues in them, and they live, and move, and propagate their species; till their frame is dissolved by age or sickness, or some external violence. we behold others again that have animal life, and that go from rest to motion, and from motion to rest, independently of any outward cause that determines such effects by a physical necessity in this case, as we observe to be done in the former. we discover, by the help of microscopes, an immense variety of these animal systems. where they begin, god alone their creator and ours can tell:——As these animal systems come to be more and more sensible to us, and as our means and opportunities of observing them increase, we discover in them, and according to their different species, or even among individuals of the same species, in some more in others fewer, of the same appearances that denote a power of thinking in us, from the lowest conceivable degrees of it, up to such as are not far, if at all, remote from those in which some men enjoy it. I say some men, because I think it indis-

§12 Same, 227-9.

putable that the distance between the intellectual faculties of different men, is often greater, than that between
the same faculties in some men and some other animals.
If now we are to form a general conclusion from all
these concurrent phaenomena, without any further reasoning about them than such as they justify, what must
it be? it must be plainly this, that there is in the whole
animal kind one intellectual spring, common to every
species, but vastly distinguished in it's effects; that tho'
it appears to be the same spring in all, yet it seems to
be differently tempered, and to have more elasticity and
force in some and less in others; and that, besides this,
the apparent difference in the constitutions and organiza-
tions [of] animals seems to account for the different de-
terminations of it's motion, and the surprising variety of
its effects.

Id. sect. 9.

[13] The power of thinking, that very power whereof we are
conscious is as necessary to the perception of the slight-
est sensation as it is to geometrical reasoning. there is
no conceivable difference in the faculty or power: the
sole difference arises from the degree in which it is or
can be exerted.

Id. Ib.

[14] It is absurd to affirm that a god sovereignly good, and
at the same time almighty and alwise, suffers an inferior
dependent being to deface his work in any sort, and to
make his other creatures both criminal and miserable.

Id. Essay. 2. sect. 7

[15] To say of a monarch in the true sense of the word, who
is invested with absolute power, that he suffers one of
his subjects to abuse the rest without controll, and to
draw them into crimes and revolts for which he pun-
ishes them afterwards, is the most injurious accusation
that can be brought.

Id. Ib.

§13 Same, 235.
§14 Same, II: 30.
§15 Same, 31.

[16] I combat the pride and presumption of metaphysicians in a most flagrant instance, in the assumption by which man is made the final cause of the whole creation; for if the planets of our solar system are worlds inhabited like ours, and if the fixed stars are other suns about which other planets revolve, the celestial phaenomena were no more made for us than we were for them. That noble scene of the universe, which modern philosophy has opened, gives ample room for all the planetary inhabitants, whom it leads, and even constrains us to suppose, where the spirits of the other system reside was [a] question easily answered, when superstition and hypothesis made up the sum of religion and philosophy. but it is not so easy to be answered now. are the good and pure spirits in heaven? but where is heaven? Is it beyond all the solar systems of the universe? or is it, like the intermundia of Epicurus, in expanses between them? are the evil and impure spirits in hell? but where is hell? is it in the center of any one planet for every system? or is it in the center of every planet? do others wander in air? or reside latent in every element?

Id. Postscript Essay. 2.

[17] A polytheist who beleives one self-existent being, the fountain of all existence, by whose immediate or communicated energy all things were made, and are governed, and who looks on all those other beings whom he calls gods, that is, beings superior to man, not only as inferior to the supreme, but as beings all of whom proceed from him in several subordinate ranks, and are appointed by him to the various uses and services for which he designed them in the whole extent of the divine economy; such a polytheist, I say, will approach nearly to true theism, by holding in this manner nothing that is absolutely inconsistent with it: whilst the monotheist, who beleives that there is but one god, and ascribes to this god, whom he should conceive as an all-perfect being, the very worst of human imperfections, is

---

§16 Same, 154-5. This passages is a condensation of the original.
§16.17 *Epicurus*] Epicurus (342-270 B.C.), Greek philosopher.
§17 *Phil. Works*, II, 161-2.

most certainly ignorant of the true god, & as opposite to true theism as the atheist: nay he is more injuriously so.
Id. Essay. 3. sect. 1.

[18] They who compare the ideas and notions concerning the supreme being that reason collects from the phaenomena of nature, physical and moral, which we know to be the work of god, with those that the books of the old testament, which we suppose to be his word, give us, will be apt to lay these spectacles aside, and to conclude that the god of Abraham, Isaac, and Jacob, cannot be that glorious supreme all-perfect being whom reason shewed them, and whom they discerned with their naked eyes.
Id. sect. 2.

[19] A polytheist, who worshipping many gods, that is, inferior divinities, acknowledged still one supreme being, the monarch of gods and men; was scandalised when he saw this being, of whom he had the sublimist conceptions that the mind of man can frame, degraded into the rank of a local, tutelary divinity, the god of Abraham, of Isaac, and of Jacob, the god of one family, and one nation, of a family who had strolled into Egypt for bread, of a nation who had been long slaves in that country.
Id. Ib.

[20] If we take the words of some divines that the beleif and worship of one god could be communicated no other way to mankind than by revelation, and that this sacred deposite was trusted to a people chosen to preserve it till the coming of the messiah; this assumption will appear as little conformable to the reason of things, as several others are which the same men advance to be parts of the divine economy and for which they appeal to the reason of mankind. reason will pronounce, that no people was less fit than the Israelites to be chosen for this great trust on every account. they broke the trust continually; and the miracles, that were wrought to pre-

§18 Same, 221.
§19 Same, 230-1.
§20 Same, 232-4. TJ has added a few words to provide the context.

serve it notwithstanding their apostasies, would have preserved it at least as well all over the world. besides, the revelations made to them were 'shut up in a little corner of the world, amongst a people by that very law, which they received with it, excluded from a commerce and communication with the rest of mankind,' as mr Locke observes very truly. a people so little known, and contemned, and thought vilely of by those nations that did know them, were therefore very 'unfit, and unable to propagate the doctrine of one god in the world.'

But wherefore then was this deposite made to them[?] it was of no use to other nations before the coming of Christ, nor served to prepare them for the reception of his gospel; and after his coming, it was in this great respect of little use, if of any, to the Jews themselves. they beleived universally one god, but they were not universally disposed to beleive in his son. monotheism might indispose them to the gospel, as well as their attachment to the law of Moses. the expectation of the Messiah did not clash with monotheism. but they might imagine, that the beleif of god the son, and god the holy ghost, did so very manifestly; the trinity not having been early reconciled to the unity of god. other nations seemed to be better prepared by philosophy, by that of Plato particularly, and by the polytheistical notions of divine natures, some in the godhead, and some out of it, for the reception of the gospel, or of the theology which the teachers of the gospel taught. accordingly we find, that when Christ came, and threw down the wall of partition, if he did throw it down, and not St Paul, the miracles wrought to propagate Christianity had greater effect out of Judaea than in it. on the whole matter, it is impossible to conceive, on grounds of human reason, to what purpose a divine economy, relative to the coming of Christ, should have confined the knowledge of the true god to the Jews, and have left the rest of mankind without god in the world.

Id. Ib.

§20.19 *mr Locke*] John Locke (1632-1704), English philosopher, greatly admired by Bolingbroke, and regarded by TJ, with Bacon and Newton, as one of the three greatest men who ever lived.

[21] To recapitulate, therefore, and to conclude: I think it plain, that the knowledge and worship of the one true god must have been the religion of mankind for a long time, if the mosaical history be authentic, and was not therefore confined from the beginning to the family of Sem, nor to the Israelites who pretended to be of it. I think it plain, that the assumed confinement of this orthodox faith and worship could answer no imaginable design of a divine economy, preparatory to the coming of Christ; since the Jews who had it, were not better prepared than the Gentiles, who are said not to have had it, to receive and embrace the gospel; and since this doctrine was propagated much more by heathen philosophers than by Jewish doctors. I think it plain, that, if we suppose the unity of god to have been discovered by reason, and to have been propagated by human authority merely, the beleif of it must have gone through all the vicissitudes, and have been exposed to all the corruptions, that appear to have attended it.

Id. Ib.

[22] When we consider the great and glorious purposes of this revelation, the manner in which, and the person, even the son of god himself, by whom it was made; and all the stupendous miracles in the heavens, and on earth, that were wrought to confirm it; we are ready to conclude that such a revelation must have left reason nothing to do, must have forced conviction, and have taken away even the possibility of doubt. this consequence seems so necessary, that if such events were stated hypothetically the hypothesis would be rejected as defective and inconsistent, unless they were supposed to have had their full effect: and yet in fact, an universal submission of all those, who were witnesses of the signs and wonders that accompanied the publication of the gospel, did not follow. the learned men among the Jews, the scribes, the pharisees, the rulers of the people, were persecutors of christianity, not converts to it: and the vulgar, as well as they were so far from beleiving Jesus to be the messiah their nation expected, or any divine person sent by god, that when Pilate inclined to save him, instead of Barrabbas a notorious criminal, the whole crowd cried out, 'let his

§21 *Phil. Works*, ii, 237-8.
§22 Same, 259-61.

blood be upon us and our children;' and insisted, with a sort of mutinous zeal, on his execution.

What are we to say now?——the infidel will insist, that all these miracles were equivocal at best, such as credulous superstitious persons, and none else, beleived, such as were frequently and universally imposed by the first fathers of the christian church, and as are so still by their successors, wherever ignorance or superstition abound.

Essay. 4. sect. 1.

[23]   if we suppose ourselves transported back to that time, and inquiring into the truth of this revelation on the very spot where it was made, we shall find that, far from being determined by authority in favor of it, our reason would have had much to do in comparing the various and contradictory testimonies, and in ballancing the degrees of probability that resulted from them.

Id. sect. 2.

[24]   We have the concurrent testimony of the sacred writers: and it has been asked, whether we have not as much knowledge of them as we have of several profane writers whose histories pass for authentic?——we read the histories of Arrian, and even of Q. Curtius, tho' we do not know who the latter was, and the commentaries of Caesar, as authentic histories. such they are too for all our purposes; and if passages which we deem genuine should be spurious, if others should be corrupted, or interpolated, and if the authors should have purposely, or through deception, disguised the truth, or advanced untruth, no great hurt would be done. But is this the case of the scriptures? in them, besides all the other circumstances necessary to constitute historical probability, it is not enough that the tenor of facts and doctrine[s] be true; the least error is of consequence.

Id. Ib.

§23 Same, 262.
§24 Same, 270-1.
§24.1 *testimony*] TJ first wrote, then struck out, *proof*, a word that appears in the line above.
§24.4 *Arrian*] Flavius Arrianus (2nd century A.D.), Greek historian and philosopher.
§24.5 *Q. Curtius*] Quintus Curtius Rufus (1st century A.D.), biographer of Alexander the Great.

[33]

[25]   When we meet with any record cited in history, we accept the historical proof, and content ourselves with it, of how many copies soever it may be the copy. but this proof would not be admitted in judicature, as mr Locke observes, nor any thing less than an attested copy of the record. the application is obvious: and if it be reasonable to take such a precaution in matters that concern private property, and wherein the sum of ten pounds may not be at stake, how much more reasonable is it to neglect no precaution, that can be taken to assure ourselves that we receive nothing for the word of god, which is not sufficently attested to be so?

Id. Ib.

[26]   The missionary of supernatural religion appeals to the testimony of men he never knew, and of whom the infidel he labors to convert never heard, for the truth of those extraordinary events which prove the revelation he preaches: and it is said that this objection was made at first to Austin the monk by Ethelred the saxon king. but the missionary of natural religion can appeal at all times, and every where, to present and immediate evidence, to the testimony of sense and intellect, for the truth of those miracles which he brings in proof: the constitution of the mundane system being in a very proper sense an aggregate of miracles.

Id. sect. 3.

[27] No man can beleive he knoweth not what nor why. and therefore he, who truly beleiveth, must apprehend the proposition, and must discern it's connection with some principle of truth, which, as more notorious to him, he before doth admit. now let me ask again, can any man be said to apprehend a proposition which contains a mystery, that is something unintelligible; or any thing more than the sound of

§25 *Phil. Works*, II, 272-3.
§26 Same, 279-80.
§26.5 *Austin the monk*] St. Augustine of Canterbury (d. *c.* 605), Benedictine monk who converted King Ethelbert (called Ethelred by Bolingbroke) to Christianity.
§26.12 *Id. sect. 3.*] TJ originally wrote *Id. Ib.*
§27 *Phil. Works*, II, 281-2. The first part of this entry ("No man can beleive . . . doth admit.") is quoted by Bolingbroke from the English theologian, Isaac Barrow (1630-1677).

words? will not the argument against beleiving become still stronger, if a proposition is repugnant to any principles of truth, which we have before admitted on evident demonstration?

Id. Ib.

[28] It is not true that Christ revealed an entire body of ethics, proved to be the law of nature from principles of reason, and reaching all the duties of life. if mankind wanted such [a] code, to which recourse might be had on every occasion, as to an unerring rule in every part of the moral duties, such a code is still wanting; for the gospel is not such a code[.] moral obligations are occasionally recommended and commanded in it, but no where proved from principles of reason, and by clear deductions, unless allusions, parables, and comparisons, and promises, and threats, are to pass for such. were all the precepts of this kind, that are scattered about in the whole new-testament, collected, like the short sentences of antient sages in the memorials we have of them, and put together in the very words of the sacred writers, they would compose a very short, as well as unconnected system of ethics. a system thus collected from the writings of antient heathen moralists of Tully, of Seneca, of Epictetus, and others, would be more full, more entire, more coherent, and more clearly deduced from unquestionable principles of knowledge.

Id. sect. 7.

[29]   Christianity consists
    1. of the duties of Natural religion
    2. duties added thereto 1. by the gospel and 2. by the church
    3. articles of faith.

Id. Ib.

§28 *Phil. Works*, ii, 305-6.
§28.17 *Tully*] Marcus Tullius Cicero (106-43 B.C.), Roman philosopher and statesman.
§28.17 *Seneca*] Lucius Annaeus Seneca, (*c.* 3 B.C.-A.D. 65), Spanish-born philosopher and dramatist.
§28.17 *Epictetus*] Epictetus (b. *c.* A.D. 60), Greek philosopher.
§29 This entry was not actually copied from the text but was rather abstracted by TJ from Bolingbroke's general discussion in Section 7 of *Essay IV*.

[30] If we do not acknowledge the system of beleif and practise, which Jesus, the finisher as well as the author of our faith, left behind him, in the extent in which he revealed and left it, complete and perfect, we must be reduced to the grossest absurdity, and to little less than blasphemy. we assume that the son of god, who was sent by the father to make a new covenant with mankind, and to establish a new kingdom on the ruins of paganism, executed his commission imperfectly; we assume, that he died to redeem mankind from sin, and from death the wages of sin, but that he left them at the same time without sufficient information concerning that faith in him, and that obedience to his law, which could alone make this redemption effectual to all the gracious purposes of it. in short, we assume that they, who were converted to Christianity by Christ himself, and who died before the supposed imperfection of his revelation had been supplied by the apostles, by Paul particularly, lived and died without a sufficient knowledge of the terms of salvation; than which nothing can be said more abominable.——religion, revealed by god himself immediately, must have been complete and perfect, from the first promulgation in the mind of every convert to it, according to all our ideas of order: and if we consider it as a covenant of grace, the covenant must have been made at once, according to all these ideas, and all those of justice. no new articles of beleif, no new duties, could be made necessary to salvation afterwards, without changing the covenant: and at that rate how many new covenants might there not be? how often, I say it with horror, might not god change his mind?——since these additions are made by the same authority, and since they make a change in the covenant, for a covenant is changed by additional conditions, tho' the original remain still in force, the objection is confirmed.
Id. sect. 8.

[31] The council of Laodicea admitted four gospels and rejected all the rest. but it is very possible that this council might

§30 *Phil. Works*, ii, 329-31. TJ has condensed this passage by silently deleting three portions of the original.
§30.7 *new kingdom*] Bolingbroke wrote of Christ being sent to establish a *spiritual* kingdom on the ruins of paganism; TJ has substituted the word *new*.
§31 *Phil. Works*, iii, 37.

proceed as councils have generally done, under the influence of an ecclesiastical faction, and decree accordingly; or else on some such reasons as Irenaeus called a demonstration (lib. 3.) 'There are four parts of the world. there are four cardinal winds. there have been four covenants, under Adam, Noah, Moses, and Christ. there can be but four gospels therefore.'
Id. sect. 19.

[32] The truth is, that as every man, in the most early days of Christianity, judged of his own inspiration, and of the gifts of the spirit he received, so every church judged of the inspiration of authors, and of the divine authority of books. the first led to the last, and these authors were deemed inspired, and those books were canonised, in which every particular church found the greatest conformity with her own sentiments. it is astonishing to consider how far this extravagance was carried. to consider, for instance, that Clement of Alexandria (*pa. 348. line 49.*) should look on an Apocalypse of Peter as genuine, and it should be rejected afterwards. that St Paul should insert in his epistles several passages of the apocalypse of Elias, as Origen assures that he did, and it should be refused admittance into the canon. but it is still more astonishing to observe how much respect Origen himself had for the visions of Hermas, and the oracles of the Sibyl, as well as others of the fathers. Irenaeus having cited the former, uses this expression (lib. 4) 'scriptura pronuntiavit': and honest Justin, in his admonition to the greeks, exhorts them in a most solemn manner to beleive the antient and

§32 Same, 37-8.
§32.9 *Clement of Alexandria*] Clement of Alexandria (b. *c.* 150), Greek anti-Nicene father of the church. TJ's footnote to Clement of Alexandria, placed at the bottom of the page in the manuscript and rendered parenthetically in the present text, is not found in Bolingbroke and would therefore appear to be a product of TJ's own reading. In fact, the reference conforms to a sixteenth-century edition of Clement's writings from TJ's library, still extant in the Library of Congress (Sowerby 1582).
§32.13 *Elias*] Greek form of Elijah.
§32.13 *Origen*] Origen (*c.* 185-*c.* 254), early Christian scholar and theologian.
§32.16 *Hermas*] Reputed author of *The Shepherd* (*c.* 150), an apocalyptic work highly regarded by early Christians.
§32.17 *Irenaeus*] St. Irenaeus (*c.* 125-*c.* 202), Greek theologian and father of the church.
§32.19 *Justin*] Justin Martyr (b. *c.* 100), early Christian apologist.

venerable Sybyl, who was extraordinarily inspired 'by almighty god.'

Id. Ib.

[33] I conclude from the little that has been said on a most voluminous subject, that as tradition furnishes very precarious anecdotes to those who write at great distances of time, so it may become difficult, nay impossible, to ascertain the authority even of books that were written, perhaps, at the time they suppose themselves to have been written, if the attempt to fix their authenticity, and to reduce them into a canon, is made at a great distance of time. they may be neither received nor rejected on grounds absolutely sure. they may be rejected at one time, and received at another: a remarkable example of which we find in the adventures of the apocalypse.——the council of Laodicea left it out of the canon in the year 360: and altho' Asiatic bishops might pass, in this case, for judges more competent than those of the west, the council of Carthage put it into the canon in the year 397.

Id. Ib.

[34] [...] are contained, and by which they are all promulgated.——the children of the first couple were certainly brothers and sisters: and by these conjunctions, declared afterwards incestuous, the human species was first propagated.——it is evident on the whole, that marriages, within certain degrees of consanguinity and affinity, are forbid by political institutions, and for political reasons; but are left indifferent by the law of nature, which determines nothing expressly about them.——'increase and multiply' is the law of nature. the manner in which this precept shall be executed with greatest advantage to society, is the law of man[.]

Id. Fragm. 19.

[35] The natural reason, why marriage in certain degrees is prohibited by the civil laws and condemned by the moral sentiment[s] of all nations, is derived from men's care to pre-

§33 *Phil. Works*, III, 38-9.
§34 Same, IV, 129-32. TJ has written "—wanting—" at the top of the page to indicate the omission of the leaf which contains the beginning of this entry.
§35 In 1764, a year or two before this entry was made, TJ purchased a set of the first full-length edition of David Hume's *History of England* (1754-

serve purity of manners; while they reflect, that if a commerce of love were authorised between the nearest relations, the frequent opportunities of intimate conversation, especially during early youth, would introduce an universal dissoluteness and corruption. but as the customs of countries vary considerably, and open [a]n intercourse more or less restrained, between different families or between the several members of the same family, so we find that the moral precept, varying with it's cause, is susceptible, without any inconvenience, of very different latitude in the several ages and nations of the world. the extreme delicacy of the Greeks, permitted no converse between persons of the two sexes, except where they lived under the same roof; and even the apartments of a stepmother, and her daughters, were almost as much shut up against visits from the husband's sons, as against those from any strangers or more remote relations: hence in that nation it was lawful for a man to marry, not only his neice, but his half-sister by the father: a liberty unknown to the Romans and other nations, where a more open intercourse was authorized between the sexes.——even judging of this question by the scripture, the arguments for the king's (Henry. 8.) cause appear but lame and imperfect. marriage in the degree of affinity which had place between Henry and Catherine, is indeed prohibited in Leviticus; but it is natural to interpret that prohibition as a part of the Jewish ceremonial or municipal law: and tho' it is there said, in the conclusion, that the gentile nations, by violating these degrees of consanginity, had incurred the divine displeasure, the extension of this maxim to every precise case before specified, is supposing the scriptures to be composed with a minute accuracy and precision, to which,

1762) in six volumes (*Virginia Gazette Daybooks*). This excerpt was taken from the third volume: David Hume, *The History of England Under the House of Tudor* (London, 1759), p. 167. The point made by Hume about the natural and civil law is an elaboration of the same point made by Bolingbroke in the preceding entry. TJ's interest in this question may have been prompted by reading Laurence Sterne's *Tristram Shandy*, where a similar distinction (Book 4, Chapter 29) is raised between natural and levitical law. For information on TJ and Hume, see the Register of Authors.

§35.8 *dissoluteness and corruption*] TJ apparently made a copying mistake at this point, for these words, which correctly follow Hume, are overwritten in the manuscript.

§35.24-46 *even judging . . . have enjoined it.*] This portion of the entry is drawn from a footnote.

we know with certainty, the sacred penmen did not think proper to confine themselves. the descent of mankind from one common father, obliged them in the first generation to marry in the nearest degrees of consanguinity: instances of a like nature occur among the patriarchs: and the marriage of a brother's widow was in certain cases, not only permitted, but even enjoined as a positive precept by the Mosaical law. it is in vain to say that this precept was an exception to the rule; and an exception confined merely to the Jewish nation. the inference is still just. that such a marriage can contain no natural or moral turpitude; otherwise god, who is the author of all purity, would never, in any case, have enjoined it.

Hume's hist. Henry. 8. chap. 4.

[36]   I say that the law of nature is the law of god. of this I have the same demonstrative knowledge, that I have of the existence of god, the all-perfect being. I say that the all-perfect being cannot contradict himself; that he would contradict himself if the laws contained in the thirteenth chapter of Deuteronomy, to mention no others here, were his laws, since they contradict those of nature; and therefore that they are not his laws. [of] all this I have as certain, as intuitive, knowledge, as I have that two and two are equal to four, or that the whole is bigger than a part.

Bolingbroke. Fragm. 21.

[37] To shew, then, the more evidently how absurd, as well as impious, it is to ascribe these mosaical laws to god, let it be considered that neither the people of Israel, nor their legislator perhaps, knew anything of [a]nother life, wherein the crimes committed in this life are to be punished;——if Moses knew that crimes were to be punished in [a]nother life he deceived the people in the covenant they made by his intervention with god. if he did not know it, I say it with horror, the consequence, according to the hypothesis I oppose, must be that god deceived both him and them. in either case, a covenant or bargain was made, wherein the conditions of obedience and disobedience were not fully, nor

§36 *Phil. Works*, IV, 148.
§37 Same, 153-4. TJ has written "—wanting—" at the bottom of the page to indicate that the conclusion of this entry has been omitted, though the portion present contains all but the last few words of the conclusion to *Fragment 21.*

the consequence fairly, stated. the Israelites had better things to hope, and worse to fear, than those that were expressed in it: and their whole history seems to shew how much need they had of these additional motives, to restrain [. . .]

[38] [. . .] as universal charity or benevolence was the broad foundation of their moral system.——when we consider the means of reforming mankind, which the heathen philosophers, and the christian divines, have had in their turns, and compare the progress made in this great work by both, it will appear that the former had not sufficient means, nor the latter a success proportionable to the means they had. in short, if Clarke's way of reasoning be good, some extraordinary and supernatural assistance to reform the world, is still wanting.
Id. Fragm. 25.

[39] Since the precepts and motives, offered by the best philosophers, have been never able to reform mankind effectually, without the assistance of some higher principle, and some divine authority, nor even when both of these have been assumed, may we not be led to think that such a reformation is impracticable? may w[e] not conclude from the experience of all ages, that no means can bring it about, and those which have been emploied less than any? there is a perpetual conflict in the breast of every man, who endeavors to restrain his appetites, to govern his passions, and to make reason the law of his life. just such a conflict there is between virtue and vice, in the great commonwealth of mankind[.]
Id. Fragm. 26.

[40] Suppose a theist objecting to some modest reasoner a posteriori, who is firmly persuaded of the authenticity of the scriptures, that they contain many things repugnant to the justice and goodness of god, and unworthy of his majesty, his wisdom, and power. the beleiver might reply——that assurance founded on probability is the utmost which can be had in all cases of this kind; and, therefore, that he thinks

§38 *Phil. Works*, IV, 183.
§38.8 *Clarke*] Samuel Clarke (1675-1729), English divine.
§39 *Phil. Works*, IV, 193.
§40 Same, 257-9.

himself obliged to receive these books for the word of god, tho' he cannot reconcile every thing that they contain to his ideas of the attributes of an infinite, all-perfect being——the theist would answer——must I respect probability more than you respect certainty, and a probability which is either not established, or is established by halves? it is not established, if the book contains anything which implies an absolute contradiction with any conceivable perfection even of the human nature. it is established by halves, whatever external proofs you may bring, unless you can shew that the things contained in it, which seem repugnant to all our ideas of a perfect nature, are really consistent with them.

Id. fragm. 36.

[41] Is it agreeable to reason to beleive a proposition true, merely because it does not manifestly imply contradiction? is every thing that is possible, probable?

Id. Ib.

[42] If the redemption be the main fundamental article of the christian faith, sure I am, that the account of the fall of man is the foundation of this fundamental article. and this account is, in all it's circumstances, absolutely irreconcileable to every idea we can frame of wisdom, justice, and goodness, to say nothing of the dignity of the supreme being, who is introduced so familiarly, and emploied so indecently, in taking the cool air, in making coats of skins, to serve instead of aprons of fig-leaves which Adam and Eve had sewed together; and not only in cursing the serpent, and them, but their whole posterity, and the world itself for their sakes.

Id. Ib.

[43] Did mankind stand in more need of a revelation four thousand years after their race began than at any other period?

Id. Fragm. 37.

[44] God sent his only begotten son, who had not offended him, to be sacrificed by men, who had offended him, that he

§41 Same, 261.
§42 Same, 263.
§43 Same, 265. TJ makes this into a question.
§44 Same, 268-71. This is from *Fragment 37*. TJ has written "—wanting—" at the bottom of the page to indicate that the conclusion of this entry has been omitted.

might expiate their sins, and satisfy his own anger. surely our ideas of moral attributes will lead us to think that god would have been satisfied, more agreeably to his mercy and goodness, without any expiation, upon the repentance of the offenders, and more agreeably to his justice with any other expiation rather than this.——a heathen divine would have challenged a christian to produce an example, in the pagan system, of a god sacrificing his son to appease himself, any more than of a god who was himself his own father and his own son.——can the innocence of the lamb of god, and the sufferings and ignominious death of Christ, be reconciled together?——let us suppose a great prince governing a wicked and rebellious people. he has it in his power to punish, he thinks fit to pardon them. but he orders his only and beloved son to be put to death to expiate their sins, and to satisfy his royal vengeance. would this proceeding appear to the eye of reason, and in the un- [. . .]

[45] [. . .] on it, and requires no broader foundation.——what now has artificial theology pretended to add to that knowledge of the deity, which natural theology communicates? it pretends to connect, by very problematical reasonings a priori moral attributes, such as we conceive them, and such as they are relatively to us, with the physical attributes of god; tho there be no sufficient foundation for this proceeding in the phaenomena of nature: nay, tho the phaenomena are in several cases repugnant. god is just, an[d] good, and righteous, and holy, as well as powerful and wise.——such were their notions.

Id. Ib.

[46]   Man is the principal inhabitant of this planet, a being superior to all the rest. but will it follow from hence, that the system, wherein this planet rolls, or even this plane[t] alone, was made for the sake of man? will it follow, that infinite wisdom had no other end in making man, than that of making an happy creature? surely not. the suppositions are arbitrary, and the consequences absurd. there is no pretence

§45 Same, IV, 303-4. This is from *Fragment 41*.
§46 Same, 316-17, 320, 318-19. This entry is one of the few instances of TJ's rearranging the order of Bolingbroke's material. The passage "modern discoveries . . . above our conceptions." (ll. 13-33) is inserted between passages that precede it by a few pages in Bolingbroke's text.

to say that we have any more right to complain of the evils which affect our state than our fellow creatures of the evils which affect theirs, or which are common to both.——because god has given us intellectual powers superior to theirs——is he cruel and unjust because he has not given us invulnerable and impeccable natures?——modern discoveries in astronomy have presented the works of god to us in a more noble scene. we cannot doubt that numberless worlds and systems of worlds compose this amazing whole, the universe and as little, I think, that the planets, which roll about our sun, or those which roll about a multitude of others are inhabited by living creatures fit to be the inhabitants of them. when we have this view before our eyes, can we be stupid or impertinent and vain enough to imagine, that we stand alone, or foremost among rational created beings; we, who must be conscious——of the imperfection of our reason? shall we not be persuaded rather, that as there is a gradation of sense and intelligence here from animal beings imperceptible to us, for their minuteness, without the help of microscopes, and even with them, up to man, in whom, tho this be their highest stage, sense and intelligence stop short and remain very imperfect; so there is a gradation from man, through various forms of sense, intelligence, an[d] reason, up to beings who cannot be known by us because of their distance from us, and whose rank in the intellectual system is even above our conceptions.——Let me ask now the greatest flatterers of human nature, what proportion there is between the excellencies of it, and the goodness of god, that should determine his infinite wisdom to judge it essential to his goodness, when he resolved to make man, to make a planet the more for this ideal creature? the habitation is fit for him, and he is fitted to live in it. he coul[d] not exist in any other. but will it follow, that the planet was made for him, not he for the planet? the ass would be scorched in Venus or Mercury, and be frozen in Jupiter or Saturn. will it follow that this temperat[e] planet was made for him, to bray and to eat thistles in it[?]

Id. Frag. 42.

[47]   To chuse the best end, and to proportion the means to it, is the very definition of wisdom. two things are then evident.

§47 *Phil. Works*, iv, 323, 327. These passages are from *Fragment 43*. TJ has

one, that, since infinite wisdom determined to call into existence every being that does exist, and to constitute that
universal system, which we call the system of nature, it was
right and fit that infinite power should be exercised for this
purpose. the other, that, since infinite wisdom not only established the end, but directed the means, the system of the
universe must be necessarily the best of all possible systems:
which it could not be, nor even a consistent scheme, unless
the whole was the final cause of every part, and no one nor
more parts the final causes of the whole.——why does the
rain pour down into the sea, whilst the sandy desarts of Ly-
bia are parched with drought? why do wintry storms happen in the summer, and irregular seasons destroy our har-
vests? such questions as these have been often asked, and all
of them relatively to man. they have been answered in many
instances by new discoveries, after the deaths of those who
asked them: and posterity has been convinced, tho they did
not live to be so, that when they triumphed in them, they
[. . .]

[48] [. . .] several rites of external devotion: and to keep up a
belief that they are few, and that the providence of god, as it
is excercised in this world, is therefore on the whole unjust,
serves to keep up the belief of another world, wherein all,
that is amiss here, shall be set right. the ministry of a clergy
is thought necessary on both these accounts by all.
Id. frag. 55

[49] Nothing can be less reconcileable to the notion of an all-perfect being, than the imagination that he undoes by his power
in particular cases what his wisdom, to whom nothing is
future, once thought sufficient to be established for all cases.
Id. Ib.

[50] who are to be reputed good Christians? go to Rome, they
are papists. go to Geneva, they are Calvinists. go to the

---

written "—wanting—" at the bottom of the page to indicate that the conclusion
of this entry has been omitted, though it seems likely, judging from the source,
that the entry was within a few words of being completed.
  §48 *Phil. Works*, v, 34.
  §49 Same, 35.
  §50 Same, 49-50. The "you" refers to Alexander Pope, to whom these essays are addressed, and to his fellow Roman Catholics.

north of Germany, they are Lutherans. come to London, they are none of these[.] orthodoxy is a mode. it is one thing at one time and in one place. it is something else at another time, and in another place, or even in the same place: for in this religious country of ours, without seeking proofs in any other, men have been burned under one reign, for the very same doctrines they were obliged to profess in another. you damn all those who differ from you. we doubt much about your salvation. in what manner, now, can the justice of god be manifested by particular providences? must the order of them change as the notions of orthodoxy change, and must they be governed by events, instead of governing them? if they are favorable to those of your communion, they will be deemed unjust by every good protestant, and god will be taxed with encouraging idolatry and superstition. if they are favorable to those of any of our communions, they will be deemed unjust by every good papist, and god will be taxed with nursing up heresy and schism. god can do nothing more, than to furnish arms against himself, by the dispensations of particular providences in the christian world; and every one of these will pass in the minds of some men for a proof of injustice, if it passes in the minds of others for a proof of justice.

Id. frag. 57.

[51] if providences were directed according to the different desires, and even wants of men, equally well entitled to the divine favor, the whole order of nature, physical and moral, [. . .] providences are exercised so rarely, so secretly, or some ho[w] or other so ineffectually, that his government continues l[i]able to the same charge of injustice, and cannot be reconciled to his attributes, without the help of another hypothesis.

Id. frag. 62.

§51 Same, 85, 91-2. This excerpt consists of two partial sentences, the first apparently the beginning of an entry and the second, an ending. Whether they originally belonged to the same entry or to separate entries is unknown, though both sentences appear in the same essay, *Fragment 62*. Because the first partial sentence comes at the end of one leaf and the second, at the beginning of the next, these fragments may not have been included for their substance, but rather because they each happened to be on the same page as extracts that TJ did wish to preserve.

[52]   That a due proportion of reward and punishment, that reparation and terror, are objects essential to the constitution of human justice, will not be denied. that whi[ch] falls short of these is partial: that which goes beyond [them] cruel. men are liable to err on both sides: god on neither[.] men may have, therefore, amends to make; god never c[an] and when we say amends have been made, we imp[ly] that injustice has been committed. now, as absurd a[s it] appears to say this when we speak of the proceedings [of] god towards good men in the other life, we must say [it] for we have nothing else to say, if we assume that he h[as] dealed unjustly by them in this life; since it is beyo[nd] omnipotence to cause that, which has been done, not to have been done. the happy state of good men in hea[ven] according to this bold hypothesis, is not so much the reward of the virtue they practised on earth, as an act of god's justice against himself, as it were; an act, in short, by which he makes them reparation, and an ample one it is, for the injustice he did them here. the miserable state of wicked men in hell is an exercise of justice delayed, but exercised so severely at last, that it would [e]xceed vastly all the necessary degrees of terror, if any of these creatures remained after it in an undetermined condition wherein terror might have it's effect.——— justice requires that punishments, and we must say the same of rewards, the two sanctions of all laws, be measured [o]ut in various degrees and manners, according to the various [c]ircumstances of particular cases, and in a due proportion to them.———I ask the men who maintain that justice is the same in god as it is in our ideas of it, and who presume, on these ideas, to censure the divine providence when they see such as they esteem good involved sometimes in publick calamities with such as they esteem wicked, whether this be a jot more repugnant to their ideas of justice and of the moral fitness of things, whereon they insist so much, than it is to reward the greatest and the least degr[ee] of virtue, and to punish the greatest and the least degr[ee] of vice, alike? the particular rules of justice consist in the distinction and proportion that have been mentioned and unless they are preserved, the general rules must be of course perverted. I ask what these persons would say if they beheld a man, who had

§52 Same, 127-30.

done some trifling good to society, recompensed like one who had saved his country or if they, who were convicted of petty larceny, should be delivered over to the hangman, at one of our sessions, wit[h] those who had been found guilty of assassination and robbery[.]

Id. fragm. 68.

[53] If the immortality of the soul could be proved by physical arguments, the eternity of rewards and punishments would be no necessary corollary deducible from it. but this immortalit[y] is a consequence necessarily deducible from this eternity[.] this immortality therefore, seems to rest on a moral proof, and an inverted order of reasoning, since if the justice of god requires that there should be a state of eternal rewards and punishments, the soul of man is immortal certainly.

Id. frag. 69.

[54] Compare the greatest human virtue you can imagine, [e]xposed to all the calamities of life during a term of fifty or threescore years, and recompensed with happiness which exceeds vastly in every instance of it, as much as in it's duration, the sum total of all these calamities, that is, with happiness infinite and eternal. compare the greatest human wickedness you can imagine, accompanied with an uninterrupted unmingled affluence of every thing which can go to the constitution of human felicity during the same number of years, and after that punished in a state of excessive and never-ending torments. what proportion, in the name of god, will you find between the virtue and the recompense, between the wickedness and the punishment? one of these persons has amends made to him beyond all conceivable degrees of a just reparation. the other has punishment inflicted on him beyond all conceivable degrees of a necessary terro[r] again. suppose two men of equal virtue, but of very opposite fortunes in this life; the one extremely happy, the other as unhappy during the whole course of it. are these men recompensed alike in the next? if they are, there arises such a disproportion of happiness in favor of one of these

§53 Same, 135-6.
§54 Same, 140-1.

virtuous men, as must appear inconsistent with justice, and can be imputed to nothin[g] but partiality, which theism will never impute to the supreme being, whatever artificial theology may do, and does in many instances. are these two men not recompensed alike? has one of them a greater, and the oth[er] a less, share of happiness in that heaven to which they both go? if this be said and allowed, the same dispro-portion, nay, a disproportion infinitely greater, will remain. the difference must be made by the degree[,] it cannot be made by the duration, of this happiness, which both of them are to enjoy eternally. now any [d]egree of happiness the more, tho' never so small, enjoyed [e]ternally, will exceed infinitely not only all the happiness of earth, but all that of heaven which can be enjoyed in any determined number of years. if you [s]uppose two persons of equal guilt, one of whom has been [a]s happy as a wicked man can be, and the other of whom has suffered as much misery in this life as a wicked man can be thought to deserve; the same reasoning will hold good: the disproportion of punishments [i]n one case will be like the disproportion of rewards in the other; and that justice, which is said to be the same [i]n god as in our ideas, will be acquitted in neither.

Id. frag. 69.

[55]   To reform offenders is neither the sole, nor the principal end of punishments. those of an inferior kind may have this intention. those that are capital must have some other: and it would be too ridiculous to make the hangman, who exe-cutes a criminal, pass for the reformer of his manners. the criminal is executed for the sake of others, and that he, who did much hurt in this life, may not only be deprived of the power of doing any more, but may do some good too by the terror of his death.——but what effect of this kind can fur-ther punishments have when the system of human govern-ment is at an end; and the state of probation over; when there is no further room for reformation of the wicked, nor reparation to the injured by those who injured them; in fine, when the eternal lots of all mankind are cast, and terror is of no further use?

Id. frag. 70.

§55 Same, 144-5.

[56]   natural religion represents an allperfect being to our ado-
ration and to our love; and the precept 'thou shal[t] love the
lord thy god with all thy heart' will be effectua[l] in this
system.——can any man now presume to say that the god
of Moses, or the god of Paul, is this amiable being? the god
of the first is partial, unjust, and cruel; delights in blood,
commands assassinations, massacres[,] and even extermi-
nations of people. the god of the secon[d,] elects some of his
creatures to salvation, and predestinates others to damna-
tion, even in the womb of their mothers.

Id. frag. 81.

[57]   Tho we cannot strictly speaking, have a certain knowledge of any fact whereof we have not been ourselves witnesses, yet are there several such facts whereof we cannot
doubt. high probability must stand often in lieu of certainty;
or we must be, every moment, at a loss how to form [o]ur
opinions and to regulate our conduct. such is our
[c]ondition; and we cannot think it unreasonably imposed,
since we are able by a right use of our reason, to ascend
through various degrees from absolute improbability, which
is little distant from evident falshood to that degree of probability which is little distant from evident truth.——an historical fact which contains nothing that contradicts general
experience, and our own observation, has already the appearance of probability; and if it be supported by the testimony of proper witnesses, it acquires all the appearances of
truth; that is, it becomes really probable in the highest degree. a fact, on the other hand, which is repugnant to experience, shock[s] us from the first; and if we receive it afterwards for a tru[e] fact, we receive it on outward authority,
not on inward conviction. now to do so is extremely absurd;
since the same experience, that contradicts this particular
fact, affirms this general fact, that men lie very often, and
tha[t] their authority alone is a very frail foundation of as-
sen[t.]——a fact may be indifferent. we may discover in our
experience, none of the same sort; and yet none tha[t] imply
contradiction, with it. such a fact, therefore, is merely new;

§56 Same, 216-17.
§57 Same, 230-1, 233, 268, 269-70, 273, 276, 301.
§57.76 *m'r de Pouilly*] Louis-Jean Lévesque de Pouilly (1691-1750),
French savant and friend of Bolingbroke.

and experience will be far from teaching us to reject any fact on this account alone. when such facts, therefore, new to us, according to the extent of ou[r] knowledge, but not so to other men, are attested by credible witnesses, he must act very unreasonably, who refuses to give that degree of assent to them, which is proportionable to the credibility of the witnesses. again, the fact may be conformable to experience by a [c]ertain analogy physical or moral, if not by particular examples; and may be admitted therefore, on proper testimony: more easily still, than one of those which I called indifferent. one rests wholly on testimony, but experience gives to the other an indirect, if not a direct confirmation.——a story circumstantially related, ought not to be received on the faith of tradition; since the least reflection on human nature is sufficient to shew how unsafely a system of facts and circumstances can be trusted for it's preservation to memory alone, and for it's conveiance to oral report alone; how liable it must be to all those alterations, which the weakness of the human mind must cause necessarily, and which the corruption of the human heart will be sure to suggest.——history has this advantage over tradition. the authors of authentic history may be known; but those of tradition whether authentic or unauthentic, are not known. the probability of facts must diminish by length of time, and can be estimated, at no time, higher than the value of that original authority from which it is derived. this advantage then authentic history has, which no traditio[n] can have. the degree of assent which we give to history may be settled in proportion to the number, character[,] and circumstances of the original witnesses; the degree of assent to tradition cannot be so settled.——we are deceived, grossly, very often about the number of witnesses, two ways. sometimes by applying testimonies that have no relation to the thing testified, and sometimes by taking different repetitions of the same testimony, for different testimonies.——history to be authentic must give us not only the means of knowing the number but of knowing the character of the witnesses who vouch for it.——when the motives and designs of authors ar[e] not the same, when they had no common principle, and when they cannot be suspected to have had any concert togethe[r,] nothing but a notoriety of facts can make their relation coincide.——common sense requires that every thing proposed to the understanding should be accompanied with such proofs as the nature of it can furnish. he who requires more, is guilty of absurdity. he who requires less, of rashness. as the nature of the proposition decides what proofs are exigible and what not, so the kind of proof determines the class into which the proposition is to be ranged.

Id. Letter to m'r de Pouilly.

[58]   Tillotson says 'I ask no more, than that the same credit may be to Moses, as we give to every other historian. now this cannot be reasonably refused, since he is quoted by the most antient heathen historians, and since the antiquity of his writings has never been contested by any of them, as Josephus maintains.' this is my text. I shall make some few remarks upon it, and this general remark in the first place. it has been said truly enough that the court of Rome has established many maxims and claims of right, by affirming them constantly and boldly against evident existent proofs of the contrary. the jewish and the christian church have proceeded by the same rule of policy: and the authority of the pentateuch, to say nothing here of the other book[s] of the old testament, has been established entirely an[d] solely on affirmation, the affirmation of the Jews; or, a[t] best, on seeming, and equivocal proofs, such as Josephus brings; against such evident marks of falshood as can be objected to no other writings, except to professed romances, nor even allways to them.——To constitute the authenticity of any history, these are some of the conditions necessary. 1. it must be writ by a cotemporary author, or by one who had cotemporary materials in his hands. 2. it must have been published among men who are able to judge of the capacity of th[e] author, and of the authenticity of the memorials on

§58 *Phil. Works*, v, 332-3, 337-8, 336, 338, 343, 344, 345, 346, 347, 359-60, 361-2, 364-5, 367, 370. The passages that comprise this long entry are all from *A Letter Occasioned by one of Archbishop Tillotson's Sermons*. The numbering of the propositions is TJ's. The parenthetical passage, "(for had Moses . . . was created)," is interpolated from an earlier portion of the work. TJ has written "—wanting" at the bottom of the page to indicate that the conclusion of this entry has been omitted.

§58.1 *Tillotson*] John Tillotson (1630-1694), English divine and Archbishop of Canterbury.

§58.6 *Josephus*] Flavius Josephus (*c*. 37-*c*. 95) Jewish historian.

whic[h] he writ. 3. nothing repugnant to the universal experience of mankind must be contained in it. 4. the principal
facts at least, which it contains, must be confirmed by collateral testimony, that is, by the testimony of thos[e] who had
no common interest of country, of religion, or of profession,
to disguise or falsify the truth.

1. that Moses was not a cotemporary author is allowed;
and that he could have no co-temporary authority for the
greatest part of what he advanced concerning the creation,
is proved. (for had Moses taken his materials from the
mouth of Adam himself, they would not have been sufficient
vouchers of what passed on the five first days, wherein the
whole material world was created.) 2. were the writings of
Moses published among people able to judge of them and of
their author? a book, to be deemed authentic, must have
been received, as such, in the age which followed immediately the publication of it, and in all the ages which followed
this. has it been sufficiently proved that the mosaical history
was so received? I beleive not. 3. things repugnant to the
experience of mankind are to be found in many histories
which pass however for authentic; in that of Livy for instance, but then these incredible anecdotes stand by themselves as it were, and the history may go on without them.
but this is not the case of the pentateuch, nor of the other
books of the old testament. incredible anecdotes are not
mentioned seldom and occasionally in them[:] the whole
history is founded on such, it consists of little else, and if it
were not an history of them, it would b[e] an history of nothing.——— two or three incredible anecdotes, in a decade of
Livy, are easily passed over: I reject them, and I return, with
my author, into t[he] known course of human affairs, where
I find many things extraordinary, but none incredible. I cannot do this in reading the history of the old testament. it is
founded in incredibility. almost every event contained in it
is incredible in it's causes or consequences: and I must accept or reject the whole, as I said just now. I can do no otherwise, if I act like an indifferent judge, and if I give no more
credit to Moses than to any other historian.———4. an history
is deemed to be true, when other cotemporary, or nearly cotemporary histories relate the same fact and in the same
manner. but if the authors of these books had a common
interest of country, of religion, or of profession, to disguise

or falsify the truth, all these testimonies would be in effect
but one; as all those of the old testament, which confirm the
mosaical history are in truth but one, the testimony of Moses
himself. whenever any circumstance is found in profane history or tradition that has any seeming relation to sacred history, it is produced as a collateral testimony; and sometimes
even the similitude of sounds is emploied for the same purpose, with a great apparatus of learning. but nothing can be
more impertinent than this learning.——that the Israelites
had a leader and legislator called Moses, is proved by the
consent of foreigners whom I call collateral witnesses. be it
so. but surely it will not follow that this man conversed with
the supreme being face to face; which these collateral witnesses do not affirm. the Israelites were an egyptian colony,
and conquered Palestine. be it so. it will not follow that the
red sea opened a passage to them, and drowned the Egyptians who pursued them. it will not follow, that the possession of the land of Canaan was promised to their father
Abraham four hundred years before, as a consequence of the
vocation of this patriarch, and of an alliance which god
mad[e] with him and his family.——the most excellen[t]
constitutions of human government and systems of human
law become often useless, and even hurtful either in a natural course of things, or by extraordinary conjunctures,
which the wisdom of legislators could not foresee. one of the
most conceivable perfections of a law is, that it be made with
such a foresight of all possible accidents, and with such pro-
visions for the due execution of it in all cases, that the law
may be effectual to govern and direct these accidents instead
of lying at the mercy of them.——another of the most conceivable perfections of a law consists in the clearness and
precision of it's terms.——tho' this is ideal, not, real perfection among men, it will be found, no doubt, and ought to be
expected, when god is the legislator.——on the first head,
we cannot read the bible without being convinced that no
law ever operated so weak and so uncertain an effect as the
law of Moses did. far from prevailing against accidents and
conjunctures, the least was sufficient to interrupt the course,
and to defeat the designs of it: to make that people not only
neglect the law, but cease to acknowledge the legislator. —
—if this be ascribed to the hardness of heart and obstinacy

of the people, in order to [s]ave the honor of the law, this
honor will be little saved and it's divinity ill maintained. this
excuse might be admitted in the case of any human law; but
we speak here of a law supposed to be dictated by divine
wisdom, which ought, and which would have been able, if
it had been such, to keep in a state of submission to it, and
of national prosperity, even a people rebellious and obstinate
enough to break throu[gh] any other.——on the second
head: the language in which this law was given is, the
learned say, of a[ny] languages the most loose and equivocal;
and the st[yle] and manner of writing of the sacred authors,
whoev[er] they were, or whenever they lived, increase the
uncertainty and obscurity even of any other language[.] how
should it be otherwise, when the same passage[s] may be
taken in historical, mystical, literal, and allegorical, senses;
and when those who writ them knew so little what they
writ, that they foretold som[e] future, when they imagined
they were relating [some] past event——there may be some
defects in human laws, some falsities or mistakes in human
histories, and yet both of them may deserve all the respect
and all the credit, on the whole, that the writi[ng] of fallible
men can deserve. but any one defect, an[y] one falsity, or
mistake, is sufficient to shew the frau[d] and imposture of
writings that pretend to contain the infallible word of god.
now there are gross defects, [a]nd palpable falshoods, in almost every page of the [s]criptures, and the whole tenor of
them is such as no man who acknowleges a supreme all-
perfect being [c]an beleive to be his word. this I must
prove.——Moses, they say, was divinely inspired; and yet
Moses was as ignorant of the system of the universe, as [a]ny
of the people of his age.——to evade the objection we are
told that he conformed himself to the ignorance of the people. he did not write to instruct the Israelites [i]n natural
philosophy, but to imprint strongly on their minds a beleif
of one god, the creator of all things. was [i]t necessary to that
purpose that he should explain to them the Copernican system? no most certainly[.] but it was not necessary to this
purpose, neither, that he should give them an absurd account, since he [t]hought fit to give them one, of the creation
of our physical, and we may say, of our moral system. it was
not necessary, for instance, he should tell them, that [. . .]

[59] "Honos alit artes: omnesque incenduntur ad studia gloriâ: jacentque ea semper, quæ apud quosque improbantur."
Cic: Tusc: Quæst: Lib: 1.

[60] "Moriendum est enim omnibus: esset tamen miseriæ finis in morte."
Id:

[61] "Quæ enim potest in vita esse jucunditas, cu[m] dies, & noctes cogitandum sit, jam jamque esse moriendum?"
Id:

[62] Nam si cor, aut sanguis, aut cerebrum est animus, certe, quoniam est corpus, interibit cum reliquo Corpore: si anima est, fortasse dissipa[bi]tur, si ignis extinguetur.
Id:

[63] Ut porro firmissimum hoc afferri videtur, cur Deos esse credamus, quod nulla gens tam fera, nemo omnium tam sit im-

§§59-79 These extracts from Cicero's *Tusculan Disputations* were entered before 1763, quite possibly as early as the late 1750s, when TJ was a student in the school of the Rev. James Maury. Translations are from the Loeb Classical Library edition: J. E. King, trans., *Cicero: Tusculan Disputations* (Cambridge, Mass., 1971). For further information, see Cicero in the Register of Authors.

§59 Translation: Public esteem is the nurse of the arts, and all men are fired to application by fame, whilst those pursuits which meet with general disapproval, always lie neglected.
Cicero, *Tusculan Disputations*, 1.2.

§59.1 The *n* in *omnesque* has been written above the line.

§60 Translation: for all have to die—still there would have been an end of wretchedness in death. . . .
Tusculan Disputations, 1.5.

§61 Translation: What satisfaction can there be in living, when day and night we have to reflect that at this or that moment we must die?
Same, 1.7.

§62 Translation: For if the soul is the heart or blood or brain, then assuredly, since it is material, it will perish with the rest of the body; if it is breath it will perhaps be dispersed in space; if fire it will be quenched;
Same, 1.11.

§63 Translation: Furthermore, as this seems to be advanced as the surest basis for our belief in the existence of gods, that there is no race so uncivilized, no one in the world, we are told, so barbarous that his mind has no inkling of a belief in gods—true it is that many men have wrong notions about the gods, for this is usually the result of a corrupt nature; nevertheless all men think that a divine power and divine nature exist, and that is not the result of human conference or convention, it is not belief established by regulation or by statute,

manis, cujus mentem non imbuerit Deorum opinio. Multi
d[e] Diis prava sentiunt: id enim vitioso more effici solent:
omnes tamen esse vim, & naturam divinam arbitrantur. Nec
vero id collocatio hominum, aut consensus efficit: non insti-
tutis opinio est confirmata, non legibus. Omni autem in re
consensio omnium gentium, lex naturæ putanda est."
                    Id:

[64] "Tantumque valuit error,—ut corpora cremata cum scirent,
tamen ea fieri apud inferos fingerent, quæ sine corporibus
nec fieri possent, nec intelligi."
                    Id:

[65] "Has autem imagines loqui volunt: quod fieri nec sine lin-
gua, nec sine palato, nec sine faucium, laterum, pulmonum
vi, & figurâ potest."
                    Id:

[66] "Vetat enim dominans ille in nobis injussu hinc nos suo de-
migrare. Cum vero causam justam Deus ipse dederit, ut
tunc Socrati, nunc Catoni, sæpe multis: næ ille medius fidius
vir sapiens, lætus ex his tenebris in lucem illam excesser[it,]

---

but in every inquiry the unanimity of the races of the world must be regarded
as a law of nature.
   Same, 1.13.
   §64 Translation: And such was the extent of deception . . . that though they
knew that the bodies of the dead were consumed with fire, yet they imagined
that events took place in the lower world which cannot take place and are not
intelligible without bodies;
   Same, 1.16.
   §64.1 Following the word "error," the text calls for "*qui mihi quidem jam
sublatus* videtur," which King translates "now to my thinking dissipated." TJ
originally entered the portion shown in italics and then struck it out.
   §65 Translation: Yet none the less they wish the phantoms to speak and this
cannot take place without tongue and palate, or without a formed throat and
chest and lungs in active working.
   Tusculan Disputations, 1.16.
   §66 Translation: For the God who is master within us forbids our departure
without his permission; but when God Himself has given a valid reason as He
did in the past to Socrates, and in our day to Cato, and often to many others,
then of a surety your true wise man will joyfully pass forthwith from the darkness here into the light beyond. All the same he will not break the bonds of his
prison-house—the laws forbid it—but as if in obedience to a magistrate or some
lawful authority, he will pass out at the summons and release of God.
   Same, 1.30.
   §66.1 *nobis injussu*] Loeb: *nobis deus iniussu*.

nec tamen illa vincula carceris ruperit: leges enim vetant: sed
tanquam a magistratu, aut ab aliqua potestate legitima, sic a
Deo evocatus, atque emissus exierit."

Id:

[67] "Quid aliud agimus, cum a voluptate, id est a corpore, cum
a re familiari, quæ est min[is]tra & famula corporis, cum a
Rep: cum a negotio omni sevocamus animum? Quid, in-
quam, tum agimus, nisi animum ad se-ipsum advocamus,
secum esse cogimus, maximeque a corpore abducimus? se-
cernere autem a corpore animum, nequicquam aliud est,
quam emori discere. Quare hoc commentemur, mihi crede:
disjungamusque nos a corporibus, id est consuescamus
mori. Hoc et dum erimu[s] in Terris, erit illi cælesti vitæ
simile."

Id:

[68] "Itaque non deterret sapientem mors, quæ propter incertos
casus quotidie imminet, propter brevitatem vitæ nunquam
non longe potest abesse, quo minus in omne tempus Reip[:]
suisque consulat, & posteritatem ipsam, cujus sensum habi-
turus non sit, ad se putet pertinere."

Id:

§67 Translation: What else do we do when we sequester the soul from pleasure, for that means from the body; from private property, the handmaid and
servant of the body; from public interests; from any kind of business: what, I
say, do we then do except summon the soul to its own presence, force it to
companionship with itself and withdraw it completely from the body? But is
severance of the soul from the body anything else than learning how to die?
Let us, therefore, believe me, make this preparation and dissociation of ourselves from our bodies, that is, let us habituate ourselves to die. This will, for
the time of our sojourn on earth, resemble heavenly life. . . .
Tusculan Disputations, 1.31.
§67.3 *Rep:*] Abbreviation: *Republica.*
§67.6 *nequicquam*] Loeb: *ecquid.*
§68 Translation: Consequently death, which because of the changes and
chances of life is daily close at hand, and because of the shortness of life can
never be far away, does not frighten the wise man from considering the interests of the State and of his family for all time; and it follows that he regards
posterity, of which he is bound to have no consciousness, as being really his
concern.
Tusculan Disputations, 1.38.
§68.3 *non longe potest abesse*] Loeb: *potest longe abesse.*
§68.3 *Reip*] Abbreviation: *Rei publiciae.*

[69] "Etsi enim nil in se habeat gloria, cur expetatur: tamen vir-
tutem tanquam umbra sequitur."

Id:

[70] "Nam hæc quidem vita, mors est: quam lamentari possem,
si liberet."

Id:

[71] "Nam si supremus ille dies non extinctionem, sed commu-
tationem affert loci, quid optabilius? sin autem perimit, ac
delet omnino, quid melius, quam in mediis vitæ laboribus
obdormiscere, & ita conniventem somno consopiri sempi-
terno?

Id:

[72] "Nam qui id, quod vitari non potest, metuit is vivere animo
quieto non potest: sed qui, non modo quia necesse est mori,
verum etiam quia nîl habet mors quod sit horrendum, mor-
tem non timet, magnum is sibi præsidium ad beatam vitam
comparat."

Id. Lib: 2.

[73] "Est in animis omnium fere natura molle quiddam demis-
sum, humile, enervatum quodam modo, & languidum. Si
nihil esset alius, nihil esset homine deformius. Sed præsto

§69 Translation: There is, it may be, nothing in glory that we should desire
it, but none the less it follows virtue like a shadow.
Tusculan Disputations, 1.45
§70 Translation: For this life is indeed death, and I could sorrow over it if so
I would.
Same, 1.31.
§71 Translation: For if the final day brings, not annihilation, but a change
of place, what more can be wished for? But if on the other hand that day brings
total destruction and obliteration, what can be better than to fall asleep in the
midst of the toils of life and so, closing one's eyes, be lulled in everlasting slumber?
Same, 1.49.
§72 Translation: . . . for the man who is afraid of the inevitable cannot live
with a soul at peace; but the man who is without fear of death, not simply
because it is unavoidable but also because it has no terrors for him, secures a
valuable aid towards rendering life happy.
Same, 2.1.
§73 Translation: As a rule, all men's minds contain naturally an element of
weakness, despondency, servility, a kind of nervelessness and flaccidity. Had
human nature nothing else, no creature would be more hideous than man; but
reason, the mistress and queen of the world, stands close at hand and striving

est domina omnium, & regina ratio, quæ conni[xa] per se, & progressa longius, fit perfecta virtus. Hæc ut imperet illi parti animi, quæ obedire debet, id videndum est viro.

Id:

[74] "Non enim silice nati sumus: sed est, naturale in animis tenerum quiddam, atque molle, quod ægritudine, qua[si] tempestate, quatiatur."

Id: Lib: 3.

[75] "Sunt enim ingeniis nostris, semina innata virtutum: quæ si adolescere liceret, ipsa nos ad beatam vitam natura perduceret. Nunc autem, simul atque editi in lucem, & suscepti sumus, in omni continuo pravitate, & in summa opinionum perversitate versamur, ut pene cum lacte nutricis errorem suxisse videamur. Cum vero parentibus redditi, id est magistris traditi sumus, tum ita variis imbuimur erroribus, ut vanitati veritas, & opinioni confirmatæ natura ipsa cedat."

Id:

[76] "Est causa omnis in opinione, nec vero ægritudinis solum, sed etiam reliquarum omnium perturbationum.["]

Ib:

---

by her own strength and pressing ónward she becomes completed virtue. It is man's duty to enable reason to have rule over that part of the soul which ought to obey.

Same, 2.21.

§73.3 *nihil*] TJ first wrote *nil*, then inserted the *hi* with a caret.

§73.3 *alius*] Loeb: *aliud*.

§73.3 *homine*] This word had been written above the line and its place indicated by a caret.

§74 Translation: Or we are not sprung from rock, but our souls have a strain of tenderness and sensitiveness of a kind to be shaken by distress as by a storm. *Tusculan Disputations*, 3.6.

§75 Translation: The seeds of virtue are inborn in our dispositions and, if they were allowed to ripen, nature's own hand would lead us on to happiness of life; as things are, however, as soon as we come into the light of day and have been acknowledged, we at once find ourselves in a world of iniquity amid a medley of wrong beliefs, so that it seems as if we drank in deception with our nurse's milk; but when we leave the nursery to be with parents and later on have been handed over to the care of masters, then we become infected with deceptions so varied that truth gives place to unreality and the voice of nature itself to fixed prepossessions.

Same, 3.1.

§76 Translation: It is wholly in an idea that we find the cause not merely indeed of distress but of all other disturbances as well. . . .

Same, 3.11.

[77] "His autem perturbationibus, quas in vita hominum stultitia quasi quasdam immittit furias, atque incitat omnibus viribus: atque opibus repugnandum est, si volumus hoc, quod datum est vitæ, tranquille, placideque traducere."
Ib:

[78] "Nihil est enim, quod tam obtundat, elevetque ægritudinem, quam perpetua in omni vita cogitatio, nihil esse quod accidere non possit: quam meditatio conditionis humanæ, quam vitæ lex, commentatioque parendi: quæ non hoc affert, ut semper mæreamus, sed ut nunquam."
Ib:

[79] "Ergo is, quisquis est, qui moderatione, & constantia quietus animo est, sibique ipse placatus, ut neque tabescat molestiis, neque frangatur timore, nec sitienter quid appetens ardeat desiderio, nec alacritate futili gestiens deliquescat: is est sapiens, quem quærimus: is est beatus, cui nihil humanarum rerum aut intolerabile ad demittendum animum, aut nimis lætabile ad efferendum videri potest.
Ib: Lib: 4.

[80] "His ego gratiora dictu alia esse scio: sed me vera pro gratis loqui, etsi meum ingenium non moneret, necessita[s] cogit.

---

§77 Translation: We must, however, with all our might and main resist these disturbances which folly looses and launches like a kind of evil spirit upon the life of mankind, if we wish to pass our allotted span in peace and quiet.
Same.

§78 Translation: For there is nothing so well fitted to deaden and alleviate distress as the continual life-long reflection that there is no event which may not happen; nothing so serviceable as the consideration of our state as human beings, as the study of the law of our being and the practice of obedience to it; and the effect of this is not to make us always sad but to prevent us from being so at all.
Same, 3.16.

§79 Translation: Therefore the man, whoever he is, whose soul is tranquilized by restraint and consistency and who is at peace with himself, so that he neither pines away in distress, nor is broken down by fear, nor consumed with a thirst of longing in pursuit of some ambition, nor maudlin in the exuberance of meaningless eagerness—he is the wise man of whom we are in quest, he is the happy man who can think no human occurrence insupportable to the point of dispiriting him, or unduly delightful to the point of rousing him to ecstasy.
Same, 4.17.

§80 Translation: I know that there are other things more pleasant to hear; but even if my character did not prompt me to say what is true in preference to what is agreeable, necessity compels me. I could wish to give you pleasure,

Vellem equidem vobis placere, Quirites; sed mult[o] malo
vos salvos esse, qualicumque erga me animo futur[i] estis.
Orat: T. Quinctii Capitolini ad populum Ro[m.]
Liv: Lib: 3. cap: 68.

[81] Time wastes too fast! every letter I trace tells me with what
rapidity life follows my pen. the days & hours of it are flying
over our heads like clouds of a windy day never to return
more! everything presses on: and every time I kiss thy hand
to bid adieu, every absence which follows it, are preludes to
that eternal separation which we are shortly to make!
Sterne.

[82]   Diodorus id solum fieri posse, dicit, quod aut sit verum,
aut futurum sit verum: et, quidquid futurum sit, id dicit fieri
necesse esse; et, quidquid non sit futurum, id negat fieri
posse. Cicero de fato. c. 7.

Quirites, but I had far sooner you should be saved, no matter what your feeling
towards me is going to be.

Livy, *Ab Urbe Condita*, 3.68. This quotation, the only one from Livy in LCB,
is from an oration in which Titus Quinctius, as consul, accuses the Roman
citizens (Quirites) of neglecting their duty, while the enemies of Rome vandal-
ize their lands and heap ignominy upon them. The translation is from the Loeb
Classical Library edition: B. O. Foster, ed. and trans., *Livy*, 13 vols. (London,
1922), II, 233. For more on TJ and Livy, see the Register of Authors.

§81 This is commonplaced from Laurence Sterne's novel, *The Life and
Opinions of Tristram Shandy, Gentleman* (1760-1767), Book 9, Chapter 8.
Sterne's passage reads:

> I will not argue the matter: Time wastes too fast: every letter I trace
> tells me with what rapidity Life follows my pen; the days and hours of it,
> more precious, my dear Jenny! than the rubies about thy neck, are flying
> over our heads like light clouds of a windy day, never to return more——
> everything presses on——whilst thou art twisting that lock,——see! it
> grows grey; and every time I kiss thy hand to bid adieu, and every absence
> which follows it, are preludes to that eternal separation which we are
> shortly to make.——
> ——Heaven have mercy upon us both!

Melvyn New and Joan New, eds., *The Florida Edition of the Works of Laurence
Sterne* (Gainesville, Fla., 1978), II, 754.

For a discussion of the special significance this passage apparently had for
TJ and his wife, Martha, as well as for other information relating to TJ and
Sterne, see the Register of Authors.

§82 Translation: Diodorus says that only what either is true or will be true
is a possibility, and whatever will be, he says, must necessarily happen, and
whatever will not be, according to him cannot possibly happen.

Cicero, *De Fato*, Chapter 7. The *De Fato*, which belongs to the larger philosophical project into which Cicero entered after the death of his daughter, is
a dialogue between Cicero and Hirtius on the freedom of the will. TJ also

[83] Dubius, non impius vixi;
Incertus morior, non perturbatus:
Humanum est nescire et errare:
Ens entium miserere mei!
                    D. of Buckingham's epitaph.

[84] —quo fata trahunt, retrahuntque, sequamur.
Quicquid erit, superanda omnis fortuna ferendo est.

---

wrote this passage in the Legal Commonplace Book (§865 in Chinard's edition), in a large-paper legal notebook dated 1772 (MHi), and in a copy of Helvétius, *La Vrai sens du Système de la Nature*, now in the Manuscript Department, ViU. These circumstances, as well as the handwriting, suggest that this entry belongs to the period of the 1770s. The translation is from the Loeb Classical Library edition: H. Rackham, ed. and trans., *Cicero De Oratore . . . Together with De Fato, Paradoxa Stoicorum, De Partitione Oratoria*, (Cambridge, Mass., 1942), III, 207. For more on TJ and Cicero, see the Register of Authors.

§82.1 TJ has substituted *Diodorus* for *Ille enim*.

§83 Translation:

Doubtful, not undutiful I lived;
Uncertain I die, not perturbed;
It is human to be unknowing and to err;
Being of beings, have mercy on me!

This is a condensed and somewhat altered version, presumably fashioned by TJ himself, of a well-known and controversial epitaph by John Sheffield, Duke of Buckingham (1648-1721). In his will, which was published with his works, Buckingham specified that these lines be put on any monument erected to his memory:

Dubius, sed non improbus vixi,
Incertus morior, sed inturbatus;
Humanum est nescire & errare:
Christum adveneror, Deo confido
Omnipotenti, benevolentissimo:
Ens entium, miserere mei.

[Doubtful, but not improper I lived,
Uncertain I die, but unperturbed;
It is human to be unknowing and to err:
Honoring Christ, I confide in
Almighty and most benevolent God:
Being of beings have mercy on me.]

This entry is difficult to date from the handwriting, but it is certainly much later than most LCB entries. TJ's alterations and the aptness of the result give rise to a strong presumption that, in framing the epitaph, he had his own life and career in mind. For a discussion of TJ's changes and other information on Buckingham, see the Register of Authors.

§84 Translation: Whither the Fates, in their ebb and flow, draw us, let us follow; whatever befall, all fortune is to be o'ercome by bearing.

Virgil, *Aeneid* 5. 709-10. Judging by the handwriting, TJ entered this passage without attribution late in life. It is the last of what appears to be a series

Euripides.

[85] Αχάριςτον ὑμων σπερμ᾽, ὅςοι δημηγόρους
ζηλουτε τιμὰς, μηδὲ γινώςκοιςθέ μοι,
οἱ τους φιλους βλαπτοντες, ου φροντιζετε
ην τοῖσι πολλοῖς πρὸς χάριν λέγητέ τι.
Hecuba. v: 254.

[86] Ου του κρατοῦντας χρὴ κρατεῖν ἃ μη χρεών.
ουδ᾽ εὐτυχουντας, εὖ δοκεῖν πράξειν αεί.
Id: v: 282.

[87] ——Λόγος γὰρ εκ τ᾽ αδοξούντων ιών,
κᾳκ των δοκούντων αυτὸς, ου ταυτὸν ςθένει.
Id: v: 294.

---

of thematically interrelated entries on belief, death, and fate that begins with the extracts from Herodotus. Translation: Loeb Classical Library edition: H. Rushton Fairclough, trans., *Virgil*, 2 vols. (New York, 1932). For other entries from Virgil, see §§163-6. For information on TJ and Virgil, see the Register of Authors.

§§85-154 These entries from Euripides seem to have been copied from the edition of Joshua Barnes, first published in two large quarto volumes in 1694. The tragedies commonplaced here by TJ are all from the first volume and appear in the order in which they occur in Barnes. Like most of the Greek entries in the LCB, these appear to have been entered in the 1760s, when TJ was studying with George Wythe. The translations are from Edward P. Coleridge, *The Plays of Euripides*, 2 vols. (London, 1910). For further information, see Euripides in the Register of Authors.

TJ's diacritical marks are frequently ambiguous, such that it is not always readily apparent whether he intended an acute or a grave accent, or whether he intended an accent or a breathing. For the many marks of this sort, the Editor has adopted the reading of the Barnes text (which sometimes exhibits similar ambiguities). As the reader of Greek will recognize, TJ is surprisingly careless about diacritical marks, frequently ignores them, and sometimes dispenses with them altogether. TJ's line numbers correspond to Barnes; those given in the notes reflect modern numbering.

§85 Translation: A thankless race! all ye who covet honour from the mob for your oratory. Oh that ye were unknown to me! ye who harm your friends and think no more of it, if ye can but say a word to win the mob.

Euripides, *Hecuba*, 254-7.

§86 Translation: 'Tis never right that those in power should use it out of season, or when prosperous suppose they will be always so.

Same, 282-3.

§86.1 του] Barnes: τους.

§87 Translation: For the same argument, when proceeding from those of no account has not the same force as when it is uttered by men of mark.

Same, 294-5.

[88] Εν τῳδε γὰρ κάμνουςιν αἱ πολλαὶ πόλεις,
οταν τις ἐςθλός και πρόθυμος ων ανήρ,
μηδέν φέρηται των κακιόνων πλέον.
Id: v: 306.

[89] Καὶ μὴν ἐμοιγε ζῶντι μὲν καθ' ἡμέραν,
κ'ει σμίκρ' ἔχοιμι, πάντ' ἀν αρκούντας ἔχοι
τύμβον δέ βουλοίμην ἀν αξιούμενον
τὸν εμόν ὁρᾶςθαι. διά μακρου γὰρ ἡ χάρις
[Id: v: 317]

[90] Ὅς τις γὰρ ουκ εἴωθε γεύεςθαι κακῶν,
φέρει μὲν, αλγεῖ δ' αυχέν' ἐντιθεὶς ζυγῷ.
θανὼν δ' αν είη μᾶλλον ευτυχέςτερος,
ἡ ζων. Τὸ γὰρ ζῆν μὴ καλως μεγὰς πόνος.
Δεινὸς χαρακτὴρ, καπίςημος ἐν βροτοῖς,
εςθλῶν γενέςθαι. καπὶ μεῖζον ἐρχεται
τῆς ἐυγενείας τούνομα τοῖσιν αξίοις.
Id: v: 375.

[91] ——Ούκουν δεινόν, εἰ γῆ μὲν κακὴ,
τυχοῦσα καιροῦ θεόθεν, εὖ ςτάχυν φέρει,
χρηστὴ δ' ἁμαρτοῦς' ὧν χρεὼν αυτὴν τυχειν,
κακὸν δίδωςι καρπόν. ανθρώποις δ' αεὶ
ὁ μὲν πονηρὸς, ουδὲν άλλο πλὴν κακός.

§88 Translation: For herein is a source of weakness to most states, whene'er a man of brave and generous soul receives no greater honour than his inferiors. Same, 306-8.

§89 Translation: For myself, indeed, though in life my daily store were scant, yet would it be all sufficient, but as touching a tomb I should wish mine to be an object of respect, for this gratitude has long to run. Same, 317-20.

§90 Translation: For whoso is not used to taste of sorrow's cup, though he bears it, yet it galls him when he puts his neck within the yoke; far happier would he be dead than alive, for life of honour reft is toil and trouble. A wondrous mark, most clearly stamped, doth noble birth imprint on men, and the name goeth still further where it is deserved. Same, 375-81. The last sentence is spoken by the Chorus.

§91 Translation: Is it not strange that poor land, when blessed by heaven with a lucky year, yields a good crop, while that which is good, if robbed of needful care, bears but little increase; yet 'mongst men the knave is never other than a knave, the good man aught but good, never changing for the worse because of misfortune, but ever the same? Is then the difference due to birth or bringing up? Good training doubtless gives lessons in good conduct, and if a man have mastered this, he knows what is base by the standard of good. Same, 592-602. The last sentence is spoken by the Chorus.

ὁ δ' εϲθλὸς, εϲθλός. ουδὲ ϲυμφορᾶς ὕπο
φύϲιν διέφθειρ', αλλὰ χρηϲτός εϲτ αει·
ἆρ οἱ τεκόντες διαφέρουϲιν, η τροφαί;
ἔχει γε μέν τοι και τὸ θρεφθῆναι καλως,
δίδαξιν εϲθλοῦ. τοῦτο δ' ἥν τις εὖ μάθοι,
οἶδεν τό γ' αιϲχρόν, κανόνι τοῦ καλοῦ μαθών.

Id: v: 592

[92] ——Κεῖνος ολβιώτατος,
ὅτω κατ' ἦμαρ τυγχάνει μηδὲν κακόν.

Id: v: 627.

[93] εϲθλοῦ γὰρ ανδρός τῇ δίκῃ θ' υπηρετεῖν,
καὶ τοὺς κακοὺς δρᾶν πανταχοῦ κακῶς αεί.

Id: v: 844.

[94] Φεῦ, οὐκ έϲτ θνητῶν ὅς τις εϲτ' ελεύθερος.
ἡ χρημάτων γὰρ δοῦλός εϲτιν, ἢ τύχης,
ἢ πλῆθος αυτὸν πόλεος, ἢ νόμων γραφαὶ
είργουϲι χρῆϲθαι μὴ κατὰ γνώμην τρόποις.

Id: v: 864.

[95] Φευ, ουκ έϲτιν ουδὲν πιϲτόν, ούτ' ευδοξία,
ούτ' αὖ καλῶς πράϲϲοντα, μὴ πράξειν κακῶς.
φύρουϲι δ' αὖθ' οἱ θεοὶ πάλιν τε και πρόϲω,
ταραγμὸν εντιθέντες, ὡς αγνωϲίᾳ
ϲέβωμεν αυτούς.

Id: v: 956.

§92 Translation: He is happiest who meets no sorrow in his daily walk.
Same, 627-8.
§93 Translation: For 'tis ever a good man's duty to succour the right, and to punish evil-doers wherever found.
Same, 844-5. In his Legal Commonplace Book (§557), TJ used this extract as an illustrative footnote to a passage he commplaced from Lord Kames' *Historical Law Tracts*.
§94 Translation: Ah! there is not in the world a single man free; for he is either a slave to money or to fortune, or else the people in their thousands or the fear of public prosecution prevents him from following the dictates of his heart.
Hecuba, 864-7.
§95 Translation: Alas! there is naught to be relied on; fair fame is insecure, nor is there any guarantee that weal will not be turned to woe. For the gods confound our fortunes, tossing them to and fro, and introduce confusion, that our perplexity may make us worship them.
Same, 956-60.

[96] Τὸ γὰρ ὑπέγγυον
δίκᾳ καὶ θεοῖς, ου ξυμπιτνεῖ.
Id: v: 1029.

[97] Δράςαντι δ' αιςχρὰ, δεινὰ ταπιτίμια
δαίμων δέδωκεν. ⸺
Id: v: 1086.

[98] ⸺ἀνθρώποιςιν ουκ εχρῆν ποτὲ
τῶν πραγμάτων τήν γλωςςαν ιςχύειν πλέον.
αλλ' εἴτε χρῇςτ ἔδραςε, χρῇςτ' ἔδει λέγειν·
εἴτ' αὖ πονερὰ, τοὺς λόγους εἶναι ςαθρούς,
καὶ μὴ δύναςθαι τάδικ' εὖ λέγειν ποτέ.
ςοφοὶ μὲν οὖν εις' οἱ τάδ' ηκριβωκότες,
αλλ' οὐ δύνανται διὰ τέλους εἶναι ςοφοί,
κακῶς δ' απόλοντο, κού τις εξήλυξέ πω.
Id: v: 1187.

[99] ⸺Στεῤῥὰ γὰρ ανάγκη.
Id: v: 1293.

[100] Ουκ έςτιν ουδέν δεινὸν, ὦδ' ειπειν έπος,
ουδὲ πάθος, ουδέ ξυμφορά θεήλατος,
ἧς ουκ ἂν άραιτ' άχθος ανθρώπου φύςις.
Orestes. v: 1.

§96 Translation: Where liability to justice coincides with heaven's law. . . .
Same, 1028-9.
§97 Translation: A fearful penalty for thy foul deed hath the deity imposed.
. . .
Same, 1086-7.
§97.1 ταπιτίμια] Barnes: τα'πιτίμια
§98 Translation: Never ought words to have outweighed deeds in this
world. No! if a man's deeds had been good, so should his words have been; if,
on the other hand, evil, his words should have betrayed their unsoundness,
instead of its being possible at times to give a fair complexion to injustice.
There are, 'tis true, clever persons, who have made a science of this, but their
cleverness cannot last for ever; a miserable end awaits them; none ever yet es-
caped.
Hecuba, 1187-94.
§98.1 ἀνθρώποιςιν] *Ms.* TJ's mark over the alpha looks more like a cir-
cumflex but was probably intended to represent the smooth breathing in
Barnes.
§98.5 εὖ λέγειν] *Ms.* TJ has a faint λ between these words, which seems
to represent an erasure.
§99 Translation: For such is fate's relentless hest.
Hecuba, 1295. The last line of the play.
§100 Translation: There is naught so terrible to describe, be it physical pain

[101] Ὦ πότνια λήθη τῶν κακῶν, ὡς εἶ ϛοφή,
καὶ τοῖϛι δυϛτυχοῦϛιν εὐκταία θεός.
[Id: v: 213]

[102] ——Μεταβολὴ πάντων γλυκύ.
Id: v: 234.

[103] Επικουρίαι γὰϱ αἴδε τοῖς φίλοις καλαί.
Id: v: 300.

[104] Ὁ μέγας ὀλβος ου μόνιμος εν βϱοτοῖς.
ανά δέ λαῖφος ὧς τις ακάτου θοᾶς
τινάξας δαίμων, κατέκλυϛε,
δεινῶν πόνων, ὡς πόντου,
λάβϱοις ολεθϱίοιϛιν ἐν κύμαϛι.
Id: v: 340.

[105] Ὄνομα γὰϱ, ἔϱγον δ' ουκ ἔχουϛιν, οἱ φίλοι,
οἱ μὴ 'πὶ ταῖϛι ϛυμφοϱαῖς ὄντες φίλοι.
Id: v: 454.

[106] Ζηλωτὸς, ὅϛτις ηυτύχηϛεν εις τέκνα,
καὶ μὴ 'πιϛήμους ϛυμφοϱάς ἐκτήϛατο.
Id: v: 541.

---

or heaven-sent affliction, that man's nature may not have to bear the burden of it.
Orestes, 1-3. The opening lines of the play.
§101 Translation: All hail, majestic power, oblivious of woe! How wise this goddess is, and how earnestly invoked by every suffering soul!
Same, 213-14.
§102 Translation: Change is always pleasant.
Same, 234.
§103 Translation: For to help our friends like this is a gracious task.
Same, 300.
§104 Translation: Great prosperity abideth not amongst mankind; but some power divine, shaking it to and from like the sail of a swift galley, plunges it deep in the waves of grievous affliction, boisterous and deadly as the waves of the sea.
Same, 340-4.
§105 Translation: For such friends as desert us in the hour of adversity, are friends in name but not in reality.
Same, 454-5.
§106 Translation: His is an enviable lot, who is blest in his children, and does not find himself brought into evil notoriety.
Same, 542-3.

THE LITERARY COMMONPLACE BOOK

[107] Γάμοι δ' ὅςοις μέν εὖ καθεςτᾶςι ϐροτων,
μακάριος αιών· οἷς δὲ μὴ πίπτουςιν εὖ,
τά τ' ἔνδον ειςί, τάτε θύραζε δυςτυχεῖς.
Id: v: 601.

[108] ——Ἔςτι δ' οὖ ςιγὴ λόγου
κρείςςων γένοιτ' ἄν. ἔςτι δ' οὖ ςιγῆς λόγος.
Id: v: 637.

[109] Ἐν τοῖς κακοῖς χρὴ τοῖς φίλοιςιν ωφελεῖν.
Ὅταν δ' ὁ δαίμων εὖ διδῷ τί χρή φίλων;
Ἀρκεῖ γὰρ αυτὸς ὁ θεὸς, ωφελεῖν θέλων.
Id: v: 665.

[110] Σμικροῖςι γαρ τά μεγάλα πῶς ἕλοι τίς άν
πονοῖςιν; αμαθὲς και τὸ ϐούλεςθαι τάδε.
Id: v: 693.

[111] ——Πιςτὸς ἐν κακοῖς ανὴρ,
κρείςςων γαλήνης ναυτίλοιςιν εισορᾶν.
Id: v: 725.

[112] ——Που γὰρ ἂν δείξω φίλος,
εἴ ςε μὴ εν δειναῖςιν ὄντα ςυμφοραῖς επαρκέςω;
Id: v: 800

§107 Translation: A blessed life those mortals lead who make wise marriages; but those who wed unhappily are alike unfortunate in their public and private concerns.
Same, 602-4.
§107.3 τάτε] As per manuscript, following Barnes.
§108 Translation: There are occasions when silence would be better than speech; there are others when the reverse holds good.
Orestes, 638-9.
§109 Translation: Friends are bound to succour friends in trouble. But when fortune giveth of her best, what need of friends? for God's help is enough of itself when he chooses to give it.
Same, 666-8.
§110 Translation: For how can you win a great cause by small efforts? it were senseless even to wish it.
Same, 694-5.
§111 Translation: A trusty comrade is a more cheering sight in trouble than a calm is to sailors.
Same, 727-8.
§112 Translation: For how shall I prove my friendship if not by helping thee in sore distress?
Same, 802-3.

[113] Ὅταν γὰρ ἡδύς τοῖς λόγοις, φρονων κακῶς,
πείθῃ τὸ πλῆθος, τῇ πόλει κακὸν μέγα.
ὅςοι δὲ ςὺν νῷ χρηςτὰ ϐουλεύους' αεὶ,
κἂν μὴ παραυτίκ', αὖθίς εἰςι χρήςιμοι
[πόλει.]

[Id: v: 905]

[114] Ἰὼ, ἰὼ, πανδάκρυτ' εφαμέρων ἔθνη
πολύςτονά τε δὴ καὶ πολύπονα, λεύςςεθ' ὡς παρ'
ελπίδα.
μοῖρα ϐαίνει.
ἕτερα δ' ἑτέροις αμείϐεται
πήματ' ἐν χρονῳ μακρῷ
ϐροτων δ' ὁ πᾶς αςτάθμητας αιών.

Id: v: 974.

[115] ——Οὐκ ἔςτιν ουδέν κρεῖςςον, ἢ φίλος
ςαφής.
οὔ πλοῦτος, οὐ τυραννίς· αλόγιςτον δέ τι
τὸ πλῆθος, αντάλλαγμα γενναίου φίλου.

Id: v: 1155.

[116] Τέλος ἔχει δαίμων ϐροτοῖςι, τέλος ὄπα
θέλει.

Id: v: 1545.

[117] Φιλόψογον γάρ χρῆμα θηλείων ἐφυ·
ςμικρὰς δ' αφορμὰς ἢν λάϐωςι των λόγων,

§113 Translation: For when a man with a pleasing trick of speech, but of unsound principles, persuades the mob, it is a serious evil to the state; whereas all who give sound and sensible advice on all occasions, if not immediately useful to the state, yet prove so afterwards.
Same, 907-12.
§114 Translation: Woe to you! ye tribe of short-lived men, full of tears and born to suffering, see how fate runs counter to your hopes! All in time's long march receive in turn their several troubles; and man throughout his life can never rest.
Same, 976-81.
§115 Translation: There is nothing better than a trusty friend, neither wealth nor princely power; mere number is a senseless thing to set off against a noble friend.
Same, 1155-7.
§116 Translation: God holds the issue in his hand, to give to mortal men what end he will.
Same, 1545.
§117 Translation: Now the race of women by nature loves scandal; and if

πλείους επεισφέρουσιν. ἡδονὴ δέ τις
γυναιξὶ, μηδὲν ὑγιές αλλήλαις λεγειν.
                              Phoenissæ. v: 206.

[118]   τα χρημat' ανθρωποισι τιμιωτατα,
        δυναμιν τε πλειςτην των εν ανθρωποις εχει.
                              [Id: v: 442]

[119]   Απλους ὁ μυθος της αληθειας εφυ,
        κοῦ ποικιλων δει τα 'νδιχ' ἑρμηνευματων.
        εχει γαρ αυτα καιρον. ὁ δ' αδικος λογος
        νοςων εν αὑτῳ, φαρμακων δειται ςοφων·
                              Id: v. 472

[120]   Ουκ ευ λεγειν χρη μη 'πι τοις εργοις καλοις.
        ου γαρ καλον τουτ', αλλα τη δικη πικρον.
                              Id: v: 529.

[121]   ——ἡ 'μπειρια
        εχει τι λεξαι των νεων ςοφωτερον.
                              Id: v. 532.

[122]   ——Κεινο καλλιον, ——
        ιςοτητα τιμαν· ἡ φιλους αει φιλοις,
        πολεις τε πολεςι, ξυμμαχους τε ξυμμαχοις
        ςυνδει. το γαρ ιςον, νομιμον ανθρωποις εφυ.

they get some slight handle for their gossip they exaggerate it, for they seem to take a pleasure in saying everything bad of one another.
    Euripides, *Phoenissae*, 198-201.
    §118 Translation: Men set most store by wealth, and of all things in this world it hath the greatest power.
    Same, 439-40.
    §119 Translation: The words of truth are simple, and justice needs no subtle interpretations, for it hath a fitness in itself; but the words of injustice, being rotten in themselves, require clever treatment.
    Same, 469-72.
    §120 Translation: Fair words are only called for when the deeds they crown are fair; otherwise they lose their charm and offend justice.
    Same, 526-7.
    §121 Translation: Sometime the experience of old age can offer sager counsel than can youth.
    Same, 529-30.
    §122 Translation: Better far, . . . prize equality that ever linketh friend to friend, city to city, and allies to each other; for equality is man's natural law; but the less is always in opposition to the greater, ushering in the dayspring of dislike.
    Same, 535-40.

τω πλεονι δ' αιει πολεμιον καθιϛαται
τουλαϛϛον, εχθρας θ' ἡμερας καταρχεται.
Id: v. 538.

[123] ——τι δ' εϛι το πλεον; ονομ' εχει μονον·
επει ταγ' αρχουνθ' ἱκανα τοιϛι ϛωφροϛιν
Ουτοι τα χρηματ' ιδια κεκτηνται ϐροτοι,
τα των θεων δ' εχοντες επιμελουμεθα·
οταν δε χρηζως', αυτα 'φαιρουνται παλιν.
οδ' ολϐος ου βεϐαιος, αλλ εφημερος.
Id: v. 558.

[124] Παντα δ' ευπετη θεοις.
Id: v. 696.

[125] ει γαρ λαϐων ἑκαϛος ὁ, τι δυναιτο τις
χρηϛον, διελθοι τουτο, κεἰς κοινον φεροι
πατριδι, κακων αν αἱ πολεις ελαϛϛονων
πειρωμεναι, τολοιπον ευτυχοιεν αν.
Id: v. 1022.

[126] Χρηϛοιϛι δουλοις ξυμφορα τα δεϛποτων
κακως πιτνουντας, και φρενων ανθαπτεται.
Medæa. v. 54

[127] ——πας τις αὑτον του πελας μαλλον φιλει.
Id: v. 86.

§123 Translation: What advantage is it? 'tis but a name; for the wise find that enough which suffices for their wants. Man indeed has no possessions of his own; we do but hold a stewardship of the gods' property; and when they will, they take it back again. Riches make no settled home, but are as transient as the day.
Same, 553-8.
§124 Translation: For the gods all things are easy.
Same, 689.
§125 Translation: For if we each were to take and expend all the good within his power, contribute it to his country's weal, our states would experience fewer troubles and would for the future prosper.
Same, 1015-18.
§126 Translation: Our masters' fortunes when they go awry make good slaves grieve and touch their hearts.
Euripides, *Medea*, 54-5.
§127 Translation: Every single man cares for himself more than for his neighbour.
Same, 86.

[128] Το γαρ ειθιςθαι ζην επ' ιςοιςι,
κρειςςον εμοιγ' ουν, ει μη μεγαλως,
οχυρως τ' ειη καταγηραςκειν.
[Id: v. 122.]

[129] Σκαιοιςι μεν γαρ καινα προςφερων ςοφα,
δοξεις αχρειος, κου ςοφος πεφυκεναι.
Id: v. 298.

[130] Ω Ζευ, τι δη χρυςου μεν, ός κιβδηλος η,
τεκμηρι' ανθρωποιςιν ωπαςας ςαφη,
ανδρων δ,' ότω χρη τον κακον διειδεναι,
ουδεις χαρακτηρ εμπεφυκε ςωματι;
Id: v. 516.

[131] Πενητα φευγει πας τις εκποδων φιλος.
Id: v. 561.

[132] ——χρην γαρ αλλοθεν ποθεν βροτους
παιδας τεκνουςθαι, θηλυ δ' ουκ ειναι γενος.
όυτω δ' αν ουκ ην ουδεν ανθρωποις κακον.
Id: v. 573.

[133] Αχαριςτος ολοιθ', ότω παρεςται
μη φιλους τιμαν, καθαραν ανοιξαν—

§128 Translation: 'Tis better then to have been trained to live on equal terms. Be it mine to reach old age, not in proud pomp, but in security.
Same, 122-4.
§129 Translation: For if thou shouldst import new learning amongst dullards, thou will be thought a useless trifler, void of knowledge.
Same, 298-9.
§130 Translation: O Zeus! why hast thou granted unto man clear signs to know the sham in gold, while on man's brow no brand is stamped whereby to gauge the villain's heart?
Same, 516-19.
§131 Translation: For well I know that every whilom friend avoids the poor.
Same, 562.
§132 Translation: Yea, men should have begotten children from some other source, no female race existing; thus would no evil ever have fallen on mankind.
Same, 573-5. Cf. §146 and §241.
§133 Translation: May he perish and find no favour, whoso hath not in him honour for his friends, freely unlocking his heart to them. Never shall he be friend of mine.
Medea, 659-62.

τι κληϊδα φρενων·
καμοι φιλος ου ποτ' εςται.
Id: v. 659.

[134] Χρυςος δε κρειςςων μυριων λογων βροτοις.
[Id: v. 965]

[135] Κουφως φερειν χρη θνητον οντα ςυμφορας.
Id: v. 1018.

[136] Τα θνητα δ' ου νυν πρωτον ήγουμαι ςκιαν.
Id: v. 1224.

[137] Θνητων γαρ ουδεις εςτιν ευδαιμων ανηρ·
ολβου δ' επιρρυεντος, ευτυχεςτερας
αλλου γενοιτ' αν αλλος, ευδαιμων δ' αν ου.
Id: v. 1228.

[138] Πολλων ταμιας Ζευς εν ολυμπω,
πολλα δ' αελπτως κραινουςι θεοι.
και τα δοκηθεντ' ουκ ετελεςθη,
των δ' αδοκητων πορον ευρε θεος.
Id: v. 1415.

[139] ——Χρη δε ςυγγνωμην εχειν,
ει τις γ' ύφ' ήβης ςπλαγχνον εντονον φερων,
ματαια βαζει· μη δοκει τουτου κλυειν.
Hippolytus. v. 117.

§134 Translation: O'er men's minds gold holds more potent sway than
countless words.
Same, 965.
§135 Translation: Bear patiently thy troubles as a mortal must.
Same, 1018.
§136 Translation: Not now for the first time I think this human life a
shadow.
Same, 1224.
§137 Translation: For amongst mortals no man is happy; wealth may pour
in and make one luckier than another, but none can happy be.
Same, 1228-30.
§138 Translation: Many a fate doth Zeus dispense, high on his Olympian
throne; oft do the gods bring things to pass beyond man's expectation; that,
which we thought would be, is not fulfilled, while for the unlooked-for god
finds out a way.
Same, 1415-18. This is the last speech of the play, omitting the last line.
§139 Translation: But thou should'st pardon all, who, in youth's impetuous
heat, speak idle words of thee; make as though thou hearest not.
Euripides, *Hippolytus* 117-19.

[140] Πας δ' οδυνηρος βιος ανθρωτων,
κουκ εςτι πονων αναπαυςις·
αλλ' ὁ τι του ζην φιλτερον αλλο,
ςκοτος αμπιςχον κρυπτει νεφελαις.
δυςερωτες δη φαινομεθ' οντες
τουδ', ότι τουτο ςτιλβει κατα γην,
δι' απειροςυναν αλλου βιοτου,
κουκ αποδειξιν των ὑπο γαιας·
                                Id: v. 189.

[141] Ρᾳον δε νοςον μετα θ' ἡςυχιας
και γενναιου λημματος οιςεις·
μοχθειν δε βροτοιςιν, αναγκη.
                                Id: v. 205.

[142] Τα χρηςτ' επιςταμεςθα, και γιγνωςκομεν,
ουκ εκπονουμεν δ'. ὁι μεν αργιας ὑπο,
ὁιδ' ἡδονην προθεντες αντι του καλου
αλλην τιν'. ειςι δ' ἡδοναι πολλαι βιου,
μακραι τε λεςχαι, και ςχολη τερπνον κακον,
αιδως τε. —————-
                                Id: v. 380.

[143] ——το ςωφρον ὡς ἁπανταχου καλον,
και δοξαν εςθλην εν βροτοις κομιζεται.
                                Id: v. 431.

§140 Translation: Man's whole life is full of anguish; no respite from his woes he finds; but if there is aught to love beyond this life, night's dark pall doth wrap it round. And so we show our mad love of this life because its light is shed on earth, and because we know no other, and have naught revealed to us of all our earth may hide.
    Same, 189-96.
    §141 Translation: Lie still, be brave, so wilt thou find thy sickness easier to bear; suffering for mortals is nature's iron law.
    Same, 205-7.
    §142 Translation: By teaching and experience we learn the right but neglect it in practice, some from sloth, others from preferring pleasure of some kind or other to duty. Now life has many pleasures, protracted talk, and leisure, that seductive evil; likewise there is shame. . . .
    Same, 380-5.
    §143 Translation: How fair is chastity however viewed, whose fruit is good repute amongst men.
    Same, 431-2.

[144] ——καν βροτοις
αἱ δευτεραι πως φροντιδες ςοφωτεραι.
Id: v. 435

[145] Τολμα δ'ερωςα· θεος εβουληθη ταδε.
νοςουςα δ', ευ πως την νοσον καταςτρεφου.
Id: v. 476.

[146] Ω Ζευ, τι δη κιβδηλον ανθρωποις κακον,
γυναικας, εις φως ἡλιου κατωκιςας;
ει γαρ βροτειον ηθελες ςπειραι γενος,
ουκ εκ γυναικων χρην παραςχεςθαι τοδε
αλλ' αντιθεντας ςοιςιν εν ναοις βροτους
η χαλκον, η ςιδηρον, η χρυςου βαρος,
παιδων πριαςθαι ςπερμα, του τιμηματος
της αξιας ἑκαςτον· εν δε δωμαςι
ναιειν ελευθεροιςι, θηλειων ατερ.
νυν δ' εις δομους μεν πρωτον αξεςθαι κακον
μελλοντες, ολβον δωματων εκτινομεν.
τουτῳ δε δηλον, ως γυνη κακον μεγα·
προςθεις γαρ ὁ ςπειρας τε και θρεψας πατηρ
φερνας, απῳκις', ὡς απαλλαχθη κακου.
ὁ δ' αυ λαβων ατηρον εις δομους κακον,

§144 Translation: Second thoughts are often best even with men.
Same, 435-6.
§145 Translation: Face thy love; 'tis heaven's will thou shouldst. Sick thou art, yet turn thy sickness to some happy issue.
Same, 476-7.
§146 Translation: Great Zeus, why didst thou, to man's sorrow, put woman, evil counterfeit, to dwell where shines the sun? If thou wert minded that the human race should multiply, it was not from women they should have drawn their stock, but in thy temples they should have paid gold or iron or ponderous bronze and bought a family, each man proportioned to his offering, and so in independence dwelt, from women free. But now as soon as ever we would bring this plague into our home we bring its fortune to the ground. 'Tis clear from this how great a curse a woman is; the very father, that begot and nurtured her, to rid him of the mischief, gives her a dower and packs her off; while the husband, who takes the noxious weed into his home, fondly decks his sorry idol in fine raiment and tricks her out in robes, squandering by degrees, unhappy wight! his house's wealth. For he is in this dilemma; say his marriage has brought him good connections, he is glad then to keep the wife he loathes; or, if he gets a good wife but useless relations, he tries to stifle the bad luck with the good. But it is easiest for him who has settled in his house as wife a mere nobody. . . .
Same, 616-38. Cf. §132 and §241.
§146.23 μηδεν,] Ms. TJ wrote αλλ α (the next word in Euripides) after the comma, and then crossed it out.

γεγηθε, κοσμον προστιθεις αγαλματι
καλον κακιστῳ, και πεπλοισιν εκπονει,
δυστηνος, ολβον δωματων ὑπεξελων.
εχει δ' αναγκην, ὡστε κηδευσας καλοις
γαμβροισι, χαιρων σωζεται πικρον λεχος.
η χρηστα λεκτρα, πενθερους δ' ανωφελεις
λαβων, πιεζει ταγαθῳ, το δυστυχες.
ῥαστον δ' οτῳ το μηδεν, ———
                         Id: v. 616.

[147] Ολοιο και συ, χ' ῳστις ακοντας φιλους
προθυμος εστι μη καλως ευεργετειν.
                         Id: v. 693.

[148] Προς τας τυχας γαρ τας φρενας κεκτημεθα.
                         Id: v. 701.

[149] Φευ, χρην βροτοισι των φιλων τεκμηριον
σαφες τι κεισθαι, και διαγνωσιν φρενων,
ὁστις τ' αληθης εστιν, ὁστε μη φιλος·
δισσας δε φωνας παντας ανθρωπους εχειν,
την μεν δικαιαν, τηνδ' ὁπως ετυγχανεν·
ὡς ἡ φρονουσα ταδικ' εξηλεγχετο
προς της δικαιας, κουκ αν ηπατωμεθα.
                         Id: v. 925.

[150] Φευ, της βροτειας ποι προβησεται φρενος;
τι τερμα τολμης και θρασους γενησεται;

  §147 Translation: Perdition seize thee and every meddling fool who by dis-
honest means would serve unwilling friends!
  Hippolytus, 693-4.
  §148 Translation: The credit we get for wisdom is measured by our success.
  Same, 701.
  §149 Translation: Man needs should have some certain test set up to try his
friends, some touchstone of their hearts, to know each friend whether he be
true or false; all men should have two voices, one the voice of honesty, expe-
diency's the other, so would honest confute its knavish opposite, and then we
could not be deceived.
  Same, 925-31.
  §150 Translation: O the mind of mortal man! to what lengths will it proceed? What limit will its bold assurance have? for if it goes on growing as man's
life advances, and each successor outdo the man before him in villainy, the gods
will have to add another sphere unto the world, which shall take in the knaves
and villains.
  Same, 936-42.

ει γαρ κατ' ανδρος βιοτος εξογκωςεται,
οδ' ὑςτερας του προςθεν εις ὑπερβολην
πανουργος εςται, θεοιςι προςβαλειν χθονι
αλλην δεηςει γαιαν, ἡ χωρηςεται
τους μη δικαιους και κακους πεφυκοτας.
Id: v. 936.

[151] ――Όι γαρ εν ςοφοις
φαυλοι, παρ' οχλω μουςικωτεροι λεγειν.
Id: v. 988.

[152] Ταχυς γαρ ἀδης ῥαςτος ανδρι δυςτυχει.
Id: v. 1047.

[153] ――Τους γαρ ευςεβεις θεοι
θνηςκοντας ου χαιρουςι· τους γε μην κακους
αυτοις τεκνοιςι και δομοις εξολλυμεν.
Id: v. 1338.

[154] ――Ανθρωποιςι δε,
θεων διδοντων, εικος εξαμαρτανειν.
Id: v. 1433.

Homer's Iliad

[155] Ληϊςτοι μεν γαρ τε βοες και ιφια μηλα,
Κτητοι δε τριποδες τε, και ιππων ξανθα καρηνα·
Ανδρος δε ψυχη παλιν ελθειν ουτε ληϊστη,
Ουθ' ἑλετη, επει αρ κεν αμειψεται ἑρκος οδοντων.
Il: ι. v. 406.

§151 Translation: They, whom the wise despise, are better qualified to speak before a mob.
Same, 988-9.
§152 Translation: Death, that cometh in a moment, is an easy end for wretchedness.
Same, 1047.
§153 Translation: For when the righteous die, there is no joy in heaven, albeit we try to destroy the wicked, house and home.
Same, 1339-41.
§154 Translation: Men may well commit an error when gods put it in their way.
Same, 1433-4.
§§155-62 The handwriting of the English headings seems to belong to the first half of the 1760s, a period when TJ was studying with George Wythe,

[156] ──ὦδε που αμμι
Ζευς επι γεινομενοισιν ἱει κακοτητα βαρεῖαν.
Il: κ. v. 70.

[157] Ὦ πεπον, ει μεν γαρ πολεμον περι τονδε φυγοντες,
Αιει δη μελλοιμεν αγηρω τ' αθανατω τε
Εςςεςθ', ουτε κεν αυτος ενι πρωτοιςι μαχοιμην,
Ουτε κε σε ςτελλοιμι μαχην ες κυδιανειραν·
Νῦν δ', εμπης γαρ κῆρες εφεςτᾶςιν [θανατοιο]
Μυριαι, ἀς ουκ εςτι φυγειν βροτον, ουδ' ὑπαλυξαι,
[Ι]ομεν· ──
Il: μ. v. 322.

[158] Ου μεν γαρ τι που εςτιν οϊζυρωτερον ανδρος
Παντων, ὁςςα τε γαιαν επιπνειει τε και ἑρπει.
Il. ρ. v. 446.

and although the Greek entries are difficult to distinguish as to date, it seems likely that these belong to that period. Tending to confirm this finding is the fact that all but one of the Greek passages from the *Iliad* in this section are also present a few pages later in Pope's translation, where the handwriting is clearly assignable to the early 1760s. The conclusion that TJ placed these entries in the LCB for comparison seems inescapable, lending weight to the notion that they were entered contemporaneously. See §§397-8 for two entries from the *Iliad* that were entered later. Translations: Richmond Lattimore, *The Iliad of Homer* (London, 1951); *The Odyssey of Homer* (New York, 1967). For further information on TJ and Homer, see the Register of Authors.

§155 Translation:

> Cattle and fat sheep are things to be had for the lifting,
> and tripods can be won, and the tawny high heads of horses,
> but a man's life cannot come back again, it cannot be lifted
> nor captured again by force, once it has crossed the teeth's
>   barrier.

Homer, *Iliad* 9. 406-9. Cf. §199.

§156 Translation: Zeus cast on us as we were born this burden of evil. *Iliad* 10. 70-1. Cf. §200.

§157 Translation:

> Man, supposing you and I, escaping this battle,
> would be able to live on forever, ageless, immortal,
> so neither would I myself go on fighting in the foremost
> nor would I urge you into the fighting where men win glory.
> But now, seeing that the spirits of death stand close about us
> in their thousands, no man can turn aside nor escape them,
> let us go on . . .
>   *Iliad* 12. 322-8. Cf. §201.

§158 Translation:

> Among all creatures that breathe on earth and crawl on it
> there is not anywhere a thing more dismal than man is.

Iliad 17. 446-7. Cf. §196. Note similarities in §162.

[159] Στρεπτη δε γλῶσσ᾿ εςτι βροτῶν, πολεες δ᾿ενι μῦθοι,
Παντοῖοι᾿ επεων δε πολυς νομος ενθα και ενθα.
Ιλ. τ. ν. 248.

[160] Ου γαρ τις πρῆξις πελεται κρυεροῖο γοοιο.
Ὡς γαρ επεκλωσαντο θεοι δειλοῖςι βροτοῖςι,
Ζωειν αχνυμενους᾿ αυτοι δε τ᾿ ακηδεες εις.
Δοιοι γαρ τε πιθοι κατακειαται εν Διος ουδει
Δωρων, οἶα διδωςι, κακῶν, ἕτερος δε ἑαων·
Ὧ μεν καμμιξας δωη Ζευς τερπικεραυνος,
Αλλοτε μεν τε κακῷ ὁγε κυρεται, αλλοτε δ᾿ εςθλῷ·
Ὧ δε κε των λυγρῶν δωη, λωβητον εθηκε·
Και ἑ κακη βουβρωςτις επι χθονα δῖαν ελαυνει·
Φοιτᾷ δ᾿ ουτε θεοῖςι τετιμενος, ουτε βροτοῖςιν.
Ιλ. ω. ν. 524.

Homer's Odyssey.

[161] ——φαρμακον——
Νηπενθες τ᾿ αχολον τε, κακων επιληθον ἁπαντων.
Ός το καταβροξειεν επην κρητηρι μιγειη,
Ουκ᾿ αν εφημεριος γε βαλοι κατα δακρυ παρειων,

§159 Translation:

The tongue of man is a twisty thing, there are plenty of words there.

Iliad 20. 248-9.

§160 Translation:

Any advantage to be won from grim lamentation.
Such is the way the gods spun life for unfortunate mortals,
that we live in unhappiness, but the gods themselves have no sorrows.
There are two urns that stand on the door-sill of Zeus. They are unlike
for the gifts they bestow: an urn of evils, an urn of blessings.
If Zeus who delights in thunder mingles these and bestows them
on man, he shifts, and moves now in evil, again in good fortune.
But when Zeus bestows from the urn of sorrows, he makes a failure
of man, and the evil hunger drives him over the shining
earth, and he wanders respected neither of gods or mortals.

Same, 24. 524-33. Cf. §202

§161 Translation:

She drugged the wine with an herb that banishes all care,
sorrow, and ill humour. Whoever drinks wine thus drugged
cannot shed a single tear all the rest of the day, not even
though his father and mother both of them drop down dead, or
he sees a brother or a son hewn in pieces before his very eyes.

Homer, *Odyssey* 4. 220-6.

Ουδ' ει όι κατα τεθναιη μητης τε πατης τε,
Ουδ' ει όι προπαροιθεν αδελφεον η φιλον ύιον
Χαλκῷ δηϊῳεν, ὁ δ' οφθαλμοιςιν ὁρῷτο
Οδ. δ. v. 220.

[162] Ουδὲν ακιδνοτερον γαια τρεφει ανθρωποιο
Παντων, ὁςςα τε γαιαν επιπνειει τε και ἑρπει.
Ου μεν γαρ ποτε φηςι κακον πειςεςθαι οπιςςω,
Οφρ' αρετην παρουχωςι θεοι, και γουνατ' ορωρῃ·
Αλλ' οτε δε και λυγρα θεοι μακαρες τελε[ς]ωςι,
Και τα φερει αεκαζομενος τετληοτι θυμῳ.
Τοιος γαρ νοος εςτιν επιχθονιων ανθρωπων,
Οιον επ' ημαρ αγηςι πατηρ ανδρωντε θεωντε.
Οδ. ς. v. 129.

[163] Parcius ista viris tamen objicienda memento.
Virg. Ecl: 3. l: 7.

[164] Quid domini faciant, audent cum talia fures?
Id: l: 16.

[165] Improbe Amor, quid non mortalia pectora cogis[.]
Æn. 4. 412.

§162 Translation:

Man is the vainest of all creatures that have their being upon
earth. As long as heaven vouchsafes him health and strength,
he thinks that he shall come to no harm hereafter, and even
when the blessed gods bring sorrow upon him, he bears it as
he needs must, and makes the best of it; for God almighty
gives men their daily minds day by day.

Same, 18. 130-7. TJ was probably attracted to this passage by similarities
to a passage in the *Iliad* (see §157).

§§163-6 Translations from Virgil are from the Loeb Classical Library edition (§84n). For information on TJ and Virgil, see the Register of Authors.
§§163-4 were entered very early and probably belong to TJ's school days in
the 1750s. §165-6 may have been entered much later. Though the sentiments
seem more representative of TJ's teens, the handwriting appears to be from a
later time, possibly dating from the 1770s or 1780s.

§163 Translation: Yet have a care to fling these taunts more sparingly at
men.
Virgil, *Eclogues* 3. 7.

§164 Translation: What can owners do when thieves are so daring?
Same, 3. 16.

§165 Translation: O tyrant Love, to what dost thou not drive the hearts of
men!
Virgil, *Aeneid* 4. 412.

[166] Eia age, rumpe moras; varium & mutabile sempe[r]
Femina. ——

Æn. 4. 569.

Horat:

[167] Diffugere nives, redeunt jam gramina camp[is]
Arboribusque comæ.——

[168] Horrida tempestas cælum contraxit, et Imbres
Nivesque deducunt jovem.——

[169] O, matre pulchrâ, filia pulchrior.

[170] ——Sed levius fit patientia,
Quicquid corrigere est nefas.

Lib: 1. Ode: 24.

[171] Pallida mors æquo pulsat pede pauperum taburn[as]
Regumque turreis.——

Lib: 1. Ode: 4.

§166 Translation: Up ho! break off delay! A fickle and changeful thing is woman ever.
Same, 4. 569-70.
§§167-78 These entries from Horace, a lifelong favorite of TJ, are quite early (see notes below). §§167-72 may, in fact, be the earliest in the LCB. §§173-8 appear to be somewhat later than the previous entries and seem to be contemporaneous with the selections from Cicero's *Tusculan Disputations* (§§59-79). The likelihood is that all of these belong to TJ's school days late in the 1750s. The translations are from the Loeb Classical Library editions: Horace, *The Odes and Epodes*, ed. and trans. C. E. Bennett (New York, 1914); Horace, *Satires, Epistles and Ars Poetica*, ed. and trans. H. Rushton Fairclough (New York, 1926).
§167 Translation: The snow has fled; already the grass is returning to the fields and the foliage to the trees.
Horace, *Odes* 4. 7. 1-2.
§168 Translation: A dreadful storm has narrowed heaven's expanse, and rain and snow are bringing Jove to earth.
Horace, *Epodes* 13. 1-2.
§169 Translation: O maiden, fairer than thy mother fair. . . .
Horace, *Odes* 1. 16. 1.
§170 Translation: But by endurance that grows lighter which Heaven forbids to change for good.
Same, 1. 24. 19-20.
§171 Translation: Pale Death with foot impartial knocks at the poor man's cottage and at princes' palaces.
Same, 1. 4. 13-4.

[172] —Carpe diem, quam minimum credula postero.
Lib: 1. Ode: 12.

[173]   O fortes pejoraque passi
Mecum sæpe viri, nunc vino pellite curas:
Cras ingens iterabimus æquor.
Lib: 1. Ode. 7.

[174] ——Absentem qui rodit amicum,
Qui non defendit, alio culpante; solutos
Qui captat risus hominum, famamque dicacis
Fingere qui non visa potest, commissa tacere
Qui nequit, hic niger est: hunc tu Romane caveto[.]
Satyr: Lib: 1. Sat: 4. 1: 81.

[175] O rus quando ego te aspiciam? quandoque licebit
Nunc veterum libris, nunc somno & inertibus horis
Ducere sollicitæ jucunda oblivia vitæ?
Lib: 2. Sat: 6. v: 60.

[176]   ——terrestria quando
Mortales animas vivunt sortita, neque ulla est
Aut magno aut parvo lethi fuga: quo, bone, circa,

§172 Translation: Reap the harvest of to-day, putting as little trust as may
be in the morrow!
Same, 1. 11. 8.
§173 Translation: O ye brave heroes, who with me have often suffered worse
misfortunes, now banish care with wine! To-morrow we will take again our
course over the mighty main.
Same, 1. 7. 30-2.
§174 Translation: The man who backbites an absent friend; who fails to
defend him when another finds fault; the man who courts the loud laughter of
others, and the reputation of wit; who cannot keep a secret—that man is black
of heart; of him beware, good Roman.
Horace, *Satires* 1. 4. 81-5.
§174.4 *caveto* has been inserted with a caret to replace an illegible word.
§175 Translation: O rural home: when shall I behold you! When shall I be
able, now with books of the ancients, now with sleep and idle hours, to quaff
sweet forgetfulness of life's cares!
Satires 2. 6. 60-2.
§176 Translation: Inasmuch as all creatures that live on earth have mortal
souls, and for neither great nor small is there escape from death, therefore, good
sir, while you may, live among happy joys; live mindful ever of how brief your
time is!
Same, 2. 6. 93-7.

Dum licet, in rebus jucundis vive beatis:
Vive memor, quam sis ævi brevis.———
Id: v: 93.

[177] Quisnam igitur liber? Sapiens; sibi qui imperiosus
Quem neque pauperies, neque mors, neque vincula
terre[nt,]
Responsare cupidinibus, contemnere honores
fortis, & in seipso totus teres atque rotundus[,]
Externi ne quid valeat per læve morari;
In quem manca ruit semper fortuna. —
Sat: 7. v: 83. Lib. 2.

[178]   ———Adde quod idem
Non horam tecum esse potes, non otia recte
Ponere; teque ipsum vitas fugitivus & erro;
Jam vino quærens, jam somno fallere curam:
Frustra: nam comes atra premit, sequiturq: fugacem[.]
Id: v: lll.

[179] Dum in dubio est animus, paulo momento huc illuc
impell[itur.]
Ter. Andr.

§177 Translation: Who then is free? The wise man, who is lord over himself,
whom neither poverty nor death nor bonds affright, who bravely defies his
passions, and scorns ambition, who in himself is a whole, smoothed and
rounded, so that nothing from outside can rest on the polished surface, and
against whom Fortune in her onset is ever maimed.
Same, 2. 7. 83-8. In response to the request of a schoolmaster for something
in his own hand for the edification of students, TJ copied out this passage as
an alternative to one on the same theme from Cicero (§79), "if a poetical dress
will be more acceptable to the fancy of the juvenile student." TJ to Amos Cook,
21 Jan. 1816, L & B, XIV, 405.
§178 Translation: And again, you cannot yourself bear to be in your own
company, you cannot employ your leisure aright, you shun yourself, a runaway
and vagabond, seeking now with wine, and now with sleep, to baffle Care. In
vain: that black consort dogs and follows your flight.
Satires 2. 7. 111-15.
§178.5 *sequiturq:*] Abbreviation: *sequiturque*
§179-80 These extracts from Terence's first play were apparently entered
somewhat later than the other Terence entries (§390-1) in the LCB, most likely
in the 1770s. The translations are from the Loeb Classical Library edition:
John Sargeaunt, ed., *Terence*, 2 vols. (New York, 1912). See Terence in the
Register of Authors.
§179 Translation: When the mind is in the balance a straw will turn the
scale.
Terence, *Andria* 1. 5. 31.

[180] Facile omnes, cum valemus, recta consilia aegrotis
     damus.
ib.

Ovid: Epist:

[181] Leniter, ex merito quicquid patiare, ferendum est:
     Quæ venit indignæ poena, dolenda venit.
Oenon: Par: v. 7.

[182] Me miseram, quod Amor non est medicabilis herbis!
Id: 123.

[183] Quicquid erit, melius quam nunc erit. ——
Sappho Phaon:

[184] Sed male dissimulo: quis enim celaverit ignem,
     Lumine qui semper proditur ipse suo?
Par: Helen:

§180 Translation: When you're well it's easy to give sound advice to a sick man.
  Same, 2. 1. 9.
§181-4 These entries from Ovid's *Heroides*, imaginary letters from famous women to their husbands or lovers, are quite early and probably belong to TJ's school days in the 1750s. The line numbers and translations are from the Loeb Classical Library edition: Grant Showerman, ed. and trans., *Ovid with an English Translation: Heroides and Amores* (New York, 1925).
§181 Translation: Softly must we bear whatever suffering is our desert; the penalty that comes without deserving brings us grief.
  Ovid, *Heroides*, "Oenone to Paris," 5. 7-8.
§182 Translation: Alas, wretched me, that love may not be healed by herbs!
  Same, 5. 149.
§183 Translation: Whatever shall be, better 'twill be than now!
  Same, "Sappho to Phaon," 15. 177.
§184 Translation: But I can ill disguise; for who could conceal a fire that ever betrays itself by its own light.
  Same, "Paris to Helen," 16. 7-8.
§185-98 These entries from Alexander Pope's translation of Homer's *Iliad* (1715-1720) were made prior to 1763 and may well date from the 1750s. The edition TJ used is not known, but his use of capital letters for nouns conforms more closely to the original edition than to the duodecimo editions that were issued in the 1750s, one of which he later acquired for his library (Sowerby 4264).

Popes Translation of Homer.

[185] But should this Arm prepare to wreak our h[ate]
On thy lov'd Realms, whose Guilt demands their f[ate,]
Presume not thou the lifted Bolt to stay,
Remember *Troy*, & give the Vengeance way.
Iliad: 4. l: 61.

[186] 'Tis not in me the Vengeance to remove:
The Crime's sufficient that they share my Love.
Id: l: 79.

[187] Say, is it thus those Honours you requite?
The first in Banquets, but the last in Fight.
Id: l: 400.

[188] Who dares think one Thing, & another tell,
My heart detests him as the Gates of Hell.
Il: 9 l: 412.

[189] The Wife whom Choice & passion both approve,
Sure every wise & worthy Man will love.
Nor did my fair one less Distinction claim;
Slave as she was, my Soul ador'd the Dame.
Id: l: 450.

[190] There deaf for ever to the Martial Strife,
Enjoy the dear prerogative of Life.
Life is not to be bought with heaps of Gold.
Not all Apollo's Pythian Treasures hold,
Or Troy once held, in peace & pride of Sway,
Can bribe the poor possession of a Day!
Id: l: 523.

§185 Pope's *Iliad*, 4. 61-4.
§185.4 Troy] The italics indicate that the word is printed, rather than written cursively, by TJ.
§186 Pope's *Iliad*, 4. 79-80.
§187 Same, 4. 400-1.
§188 Same, 9. 412-13.
§189 Same, 9. 450-3.
§190 Same, 9. 522-7. Note that §199, entered at a later period, records the next four lines.

[191]   Yet hear one Word, & lodge it in thy Heart;
        No more molest me on Atrides' part:
        Is it for him these Tears are taught to flow,
        For him these Sorrows? for my mortal Foe?
        A Gen'rous Freindship no cold medium knows,
        Burns with one Love, with one Resentment glows,
        One should our Int'rests, & our passions be;
        My Friend must hate the Man that injures me[.]
                        Id: l: 721.

[192]   —— but at the Tyrant's Name
        My Rage rekindles, & my Soul's on flame:
        'Tis just Resentment, & becomes the brave;
        Disgrac'd, dishonour'd, like the vilest slave[!]
                        Id: l: 759.

[193]   Then none (said Nestor) shall his Rule withst[and,]
        For great Examples justify Command.
                        Il: 10. l: 148.

[194]   Death is the worst; a Fate which all must try;
        And, for our Country, 'tis a Bliss to die.
        The gallant Man tho' slain in Fight he [be,]
        Yet leaves his Nation safe, his Children free;
        Entails a Debt on all the gratefull State;
        His own brave Friends shall glory in his Fate;
        His wife live Honour'd, all his Race succeed;
        And late Posterity enjoy the Deed.
                        Il: 15. l: 582.

[195]   On Valour's Side the Odds of Combate lie,
        The brave live glorious, or lamented die;
        The Wretch that trembles in the Field of Fame[,]
        Meets Death, & worse than Death, eternal Shame.
                        Id: l: 670.

        §191 Pope's *Iliad*, 9. 721-8.
        §191.1 *Heart*] TJ seems to have first written *Breast*, the word immediately
        above in Pope's text, and then written *Heart* over it.
        §192 Pope's *Iliad*, 9. 759-62.
        §193 Same, 10. 148-9.
        §194 Same, 15. 582-9.
        §195 Same, 15. 670-3.

[196] For ah! what is there, of inferiour Birth,
       That breathes or creeps upon the Dust of Earth;
       What wretched Creature of what wretched Kind,
       Than Man more weak, calamitous, & blind?
       A miserable Race! —— Il: 17. l: 508.

[197] What art thou, speak, that on Designs unknown
       While others sleep, thus range the Camp alone?
       Seek'st thou some Friend or nightly Centinel?
       Stand off, approach not, but thy purpose tell.
                 Il: 10. l. 90.

[198] These shall I slight? And guide my wav'ring Mind
       By wan'dring Birds that flit with ev'ry Wind?
       Ye Vagrants of the Sky! your Wings extend[,]
       Or where the Suns arise, or where descend;
       To Right, to Left, unheeded take your Way
       While I the Dictates of high Heav'n obey.
       Without a Sign his Sword the brave Man draw[s,]
       And asks no Omen but his Country's Cause.
               Il: 12. l: 277.

[199] Lost herds and treasures, we by arms regain,
       And steeds unrivall'd on the dusty plain:
       But from our lips the vital spirit fled,
       Returns no more to wake the silent dead.
               Il: 9. v. 528.

[200] To labour is the lot of man below;
       And when Jove gave us life, he gave us woe.
               Il: 10. v. 78.

     §196 Same, 17. 508-12. Cf. §158.
     §197 Same, 10. 90-3.
     §197.3 *Ms.* The word *nightly* has been written above the line and inserted with a caret.
     §198 Pope's *Iliad*, 12: 277-84.
     §199-202 These entries were written later than the previous entries from Pope's translation of Homer, and belong to the period 1762-1765, when TJ was working on his Greek. Note that all four of these entries are translations of passages TJ entered about the same time in Greek (§§155-7, 160).
     §199 Pope's *Iliad*, 9. 528-31. See §155 for this passage in Greek. Note that §190, entered at an earlier period, records the six preceding lines.
     §200 Same, 10. 78-9. See §156 for this passage in Greek.

[201]   Could all our care elude the gloomy grave,
        Which claims no less the fearful than the brave,
        For lust of fame I should not vainly dare
        In fighting fields, nor urge thy soul to war.
        But since, alas! ignoble age must come,
        Disease, and death's inexorable doom;
        The life which others pay let us bestow,
        And give to fame what we to nature owe;
                        Il: 12. v. 387.

[202]   —— Let reason mitigate our care:
        To mourn, avails not: man is born to bear.
        Such is, alas! the gods severe decree;
        They, only they, are blest, and only free.
        Two urns by Jove's high throne have ever stood,
        The source of evil one, and one of good;
        From thence the cup of mortal man he fills,
        Blessings to these, to those distributes ills;
        To most, he mingles both: the wretch decreed
        To taste the bad, unmix'd, is curst indeed;
        Pursu'd by wrongs, by meagre famine driv'n,
        He wanders, outcast both of earth and heav'n.
        The happiest taste not happiness sincere,
        But find the cordial draught is dash'd with care.
                        B. 24. v. 659.

Pope's Essay on Man.

[203] If to be perfect in a certain Sphere
       What matters soon, or late, or here, or there,

§201 Same, 12. 387-94. See §157 for this passage in Greek.
§202 Pope's *Iliad,* 24. 659-72. See §160 for this passage in Greek. TJ quotes from this passage in a letter to John Adams, 1 Aug. 1816 (Cappon, p. 483).
§§203-13 As is evident from the inclusion of variant readings, these entries were copied from the edition of *The Works of Alexander Pope,* edited by Pope's designated editor, Bishop William Warburton, first published in 1751. The full title of the poem here commonplaced is given as "An Essay on Man, in Four Epistles, to H. St. John, Lord Bolingbroke." These extracts were entered several years before the extracts from Bolingbroke's *Philosophical Works* (§§4-34, 36-54), which are chiefly essays addressed to Pope. For further information, see Pope in the Register of Authors.
§203 Pope, "Essay on Man," 1: ff.73. These lines are printed by Warburton

The blest to Day is as completely so,
As who began a Thousand Years ago.
                    Ep: 1. v: 73.

[204] For more Perfection than this State can bear
In vain we sigh; Heaven made us as we are.
As Wisely sure a modest Ape might aim
To be like Man. ——
                    Ep: 2. v: 19.

[205] Fools who from hence into the Notion fall
That Vice or Virtue there is none at all.
If white, & black, blend, soften & Unite
A thousand Ways; is there no black or White?
Ask your own Heart, & Nothing is so plain;
'Tis to mistake them, costs the Time & pain.
                    Ep: 2. v: 211.

[206] What we resolve, we can: but here's the Fault,
We ne'er resolve to do the Thing we ought.

[207] Heaven forming each on other to depend,
A Master, or a Servant, or a Friend,
Bids each on other for assistance call,
'Till one Man's Weakness grows ye Strength of all.
                    Ep: 2. v: 249.

[208] Whate'r the Passion, Knowledge, Fame or Pelf[,]
Not one will change his Neighbour for himself.
The learn'd is happy Nature to explore,

---

as variations. For an account of how they were used by Pope in various versions
of the poem, see Maynard Mack, ed., *An Essay on Man*, in John Butt, ed.,
Twickenham Edition of the Poems of Alexander Pope (London, 1950), vol. 3, pt.
1.

§204 "Essay on Man," 2: ff.18. Warburton prints these lines and several
more that follow as manuscript variations that were not included by Pope in
the finished poem.

§205 "Essay on Man," 2: 211-16.

§206 Same, 2: ff.194. These are the last of 18 lines printed by Warburton as
variations from the manuscript. As this passage comes at the bottom of the page
in the manuscript and TJ omitted the usual citation below the entry, Chinard
printed §206 and §207 as a single entry.

§207 "Essay on Man," 2: 249-52.

§208 Same, 2: 261-82.

The Fool is happy that he knows no more,
The Rich is happy in the plenty Given,
The Poor contents him with the Care of Hea[v'n.]
See the blind Beggar dance, the Cripple sing,
The Sot a Hero, Lunatic a King;
The starving Chymist in his golden Views
Supremely blest, The Poet in his Muse,
See some strange Comfort ev'ry State attend.
And pride bestow'd on all, a common Friend[;]
See some fit passion ev'ry Age supply,
Hope travels thro', nor quits us when we die.
Behold the Child, by Nature's kindly Law,
Pleas'd with a Rattle, tickl'd with a Straw[:]
Some livelier Plaything gives his Youth Delight[,]
A little louder, but as empty quite:
Scarfs, Garters, Gold, amuse his riper Stage,
And Beads & Prayer-books are the Toys of Age:
Pleas'd with this Bauble still, as that before;
'Till tir'd he sleeps, & Life's poor Play is o'er.
                    Ep: 2. v: 261.

[209] Say not "Heav'n's here profuse, there poorly saves,
       "And for one Monarch makes a Thousand Slaves."
       You'll find, when Causes & their Ends are known,
       Twas for the Thousand Heav'n has made that one.
                    Ep: 4. v: 53

[210] Fortune her Gifts may variously dispose,
       And these be happy call'd, unhappy those;
       But Heaven's just Balance equal will appear,
       While those are plac'd in Hope, & these in Fear:

---

§208.2 *change his Neighbour for himself*] Warburton: *charge his Neighbour with himself*. In the Twickenham edition (87), Maynard Mack prints: *change his neighbor with himself*.

§208.13 *Ms*. TJ first wrote "strange" as the third word in the line, then struck it out.

§208.14 *Hope travels thro', nor quits us when we die*.] Quoted by TJ in "Thoughts on English Prosody" of Homer: "He like 'Hope travels on nor quits us when we die.'" L & B, XVIII, 448.

§209 "Essay on Man," 4: ff.52. Warburton printed these lines as manuscript variations, originally written to follow line 52 but not included by Pope in the final version of the poem.

§210 "Essay on Man," 4: 67-72.

Not present Good or Ill, the Joy or Curse,
But future Views of better, or of worse.
Ep: 4. v: 67.

[211] Honour & Shame from no Condition rise;
Act well your Part, there all the Honour lies[.]
Fortune in Men has some small Difference made[,]
One flaunts in Rags, one flutters in in Brocade.
The Cobler apron'd, & the Parson gown'd,
The Friar hooded, & the Monarch crown'd.
"What differ more, you say, than Crown & Cowl."
I'll tell you Friend.—A wise Man & a Fool.
Ep: 4. v: 193.

[212] Go; if your antient, but ignoble Blood
Has crept thro' Scoundrels ever since the Flood;
Go! & pretend your Family is Young;
Nor own, your Fathers have been Fools so long[.]
What can ennoble Sots, or Slaves, or Cowards?
Alas! not all the Blood of all the *Howards*.
Ep: 4. v: 211.

[213] Not one looks backward, onward still he go[es,]
Yet ne'er looks forward further than his N[ose.]
Ep: 4. v. 223.

[214] Tho' we with blacks & blues are suggil'd,
Or, as the vulgar say, are cudgel'd:
He that is valiant & dares fight
Tho' drubb'd, can lose no honor by't.
Hudibr. 3. 1039.

§211 Same, 4: 193-200.
§211.4 *in in*] Warburton: *in.*
§211.7 *"What differ more, you say,*] Warburton: *"What differ more (you cry).*
§212 "Essay on Man," 4: 211-16.
§212.1 *antient*] Warburton: *ancient.*
§212.6 Howards] The italics indicate that this word is printed, rather than written cursively, by TJ.
§213 "Essay on Man," 4: 223-4.
§213.2 *further*] Warburton: *farther.*
§214-17 These entries from Samuel Butler's *Hudibras* (1662-1678) were entered much later than those that precede and follow them. Though difficult to date with any precision, they were certainly entered no earlier than the mid-1770s.
§214 *Hudibras*, Part I, Canto III, ll. 1039-42.

[215] If he that is in battle slain
      Be in the bed of honor lain;
      He that is beaten, may be said
      To lie in honour's truckle bed
                  id. 3. 1047.

[216] For Wedlock, without love, some say,
      Is but a lock without a key.
              id. part. 2. Canto l. 321.

[217] Those that fly may fight again,
      Which he can never do that's slain.
                ib. 243.

Milton's Paradise lost.

[218] ——Round he threw his baleful Eyes
      That witness'd huge Affliction & Dismay.
            Lib: 1. 1. 56.

[219] ——What tho the Field be lost?
      All is not lost; the unconquerable Will,
      And Study of Revenge, immortal Hate
      And Courage never to submit or yield:
      And what is else not to be overcome?

§215 Same, 1047-50.
§215.1 *is in battle*] Butler: *in the field is*
§216 *Hudibras*, Part II, Canto I, ll. 321-2.
§217 Same, Part III, Canto III, ll. 243-4.
§§218-46 These entries from John Milton's *Paradise Lost* seem to have been made from at least three different sources or copy-texts, as indicated below. The evidence for this lies in the close conformity of TJ's text to those cited in distinctive editorial details, chiefly punctuation. Though following his copy-text fairly closely in all other respects, TJ here capitalized many more nouns than were warranted by his sources, as he did with all English poetry entered in the period prior to 1763.
§§218-32 These entries were apparently copied from: John Milton, *Paradise Lost, A Poem in Twelve Books* (Glasgow, 1750). According to the preface, this edition from the Foulis press was intended to be completed in two volumes, of which only the first (containing Books 1-6) is known to have been published.
§218 *Paradise Lost*, I: 56-7.
§218.1 *threw*] Milton: *throws*.
§219 *Paradise Lost*, I: 1056. The first four lines of this passage are cited by TJ in a letter to George W. Lewis, 25 Oct. 1825, L & B, XVI, 127.

That Glory never shall his Wrath or Might
Extort from me. To bow & Sue for Grace
With suppliant Knee, & deifie his Po[wer,]
Who from the Terrour of this Arm: so late
Doubted his Empire, that were low ind[eed,]
That were an Ignominy, & Shame benea[th]
This Downfall. ——
Id: l. 105.

[220]   —— But of this be sure
To do ought Good never will be our Tas[k,]
But ever to do Ill our sole Delight,
As being contrary to his high Will
Whom we resist. ——
I[d: l. 158.]

[221] Here we may reign secure, & in my Choice
To reign is worth Ambition tho' in Hell,
Better to reign in Hell, than serve in Heaven.
Lib: 1. l: 261.

[222]   —— But he his wonted pride
Soon recollecting, with high words that bore
Semblance of Worth, not Substance, gently rais'd
Their fainting Courage, & dispell'd their Fears.
Id: l: 527.

[223]   ——Our better Part remains
To work in close Design, by Fraud or Guile,
What Force effected not: that he no less
At length from us may find, who overcomes
By Force, hath overcome but half his Foe.
Lib: 1. v. 645.

[224]   —— though in this vast Recess,
Free, & to none accountable, preferring

§220 *Paradise Lost*, I: 158-62.
§221 Same, 261-3.
§222 Same, 527-30.
§223 Same, 645-9.
§224 Same, II: 254-7.

Hard Liberty before the easy Yoke
Of servile Pomp.
Lib: 2. v. 254.

[225] Nor gentle purpose, nor endearing smiles
Wanted, nor youthful dalliance as beseems
Fair couple, linkt in happy nuptial league,
Alone as they.—
Milt. Par. L. 4. 337.

[226] ——if I must contend, said he
Best with the best; the sender not the sent,
Or all at once; more glory will be won,
Or less be lost.—Milt. Par. L. 4. 851.

[227] ——well we may afford
Our givers their own gifts, & large bestow
From large bestow'd.
id. 5. 316.

[228] ——but in those hearts
Love unlibidinous reign'd, nor jealousy
Was understood, the injur'd lover's hell.
id. 5. 448.

§§225-9 From the crossed-out notation at the bottom of the page on which it appears—*For a Continuation Vol. 2. page 27*—§224 would appear to be the last *Paradise Lost* entry in what was then the first volume of TJ's commonplace book. The next four entries are in a later hand and may have been copied into the manuscript at the time it was being assembled for the binder, perhaps as late as the early 1780s. This later hand is also present in the first three lines of §229, which, like the remaining *Paradise Lost* entries, seems originally to have been written contemporaneously with §§218-24. These first three lines of §229 are squeezed onto the top of the page, which originally began with the fourth and final line of the entry. The disruption of the pagination at this juncture and the beginning of a new pagination series at 31 rather than 27 on the page where §229 appears suggests that §§225-8 may have been copied from the four pages that do not appear.

§225 *Paradise Lost*, IV: 337-40.

§226 Same, 851-4.

§227 Same, V: 316-18. *Ms*. TJ first wrote *Well we may afford our givers their own gifts* as though it were a single line of verse, then crossed it out and wrote the entry as shown.

§228 Same, 548-50. *Ms*. As in the previous entry, TJ wrote *But in th* at the beginning of the line, then struck it out and wrote the entry as shown.

[229]   —— One who brings
          A mind not to be chang'd by place or time.
          The mind is it's own place, & in itself
          Can make a Heav'n of Hell, a Hell of Heav'n.
                    Milt. Par. L. B: 1. l: 252.

[230] Reign thou in Hell thy Kingdom, let me serve
       In Heav'n God ever blest, & his divine
       Behests obey, worthiest to be obey'd,
       Yet Chains in Hell, not Realms expect. ——
                    B: 6: l: 183.

[231] Nameless in dark Oblivion let them dwell.
                    Id: l: 380.

[232] Nor long shall be our Labour, yet e'er Dawn[,]
       Effect shall end our Wish. Mean while revive;
       Abandon Fear; to Strength & Counsel join'd
       Think Nothing hard, much less to be dispair'd.
                    Id: l: 492.

[233] But apt the Mind or Fancy is to rove
       Uncheckt, & of her roving is no End;
       Till warn'd, or by Experience taught, she learn
       That not to know at large of Things remote
       From Use, obscure & suttle, but to know
       That which before us lies in daily Life,
       Is the prime Wisdom, what is more, is Fume,
       Or Emptiness, or fond Impertinence,
       And renders us in Things that most concern
       Unpractis'd, unprepar'd, & still to seek.
       Therefore from this high Pitch let us descend

§229 Same, I: 252-5. TJ wrote the first two words of this entry on the same page as the preceding three entries, then crossed them out. See note on §228 above.

§230 Same, VI: 183-6.

§231 Same, 380.

§232 Same, 492-5.

§233 Same, VIII: 188-200.

§233.5 suttle] *Ms.* It is very difficult to decide from the manuscript whether TJ intended to write this word with a *b* or with two *t*'s, and both are found in eighteenth-century editions. On the basis that the letter in question does not closely resemble any of the other *b*'s in the Milton section, it has been rendered as a *t*.

A lower Flight, & speak of Things at Hand
Useful. ——B: 8. l: 188.

[234] Among Unequals what Society
Can sort, what Harmony or true Delight?
Which must be mutual, in Proportion due
Giv'n & receiv'd; but in Disparity
The one intense, the other still remiss
Cannot well suit with either, but soon prove
Tedious alike: ——Id: l: 383.

[235] ——here Passion first I felt,
Commotion strange, in all Enjoyments else
Superior & unmov'd, here only weak
Against the Charm of Beautie's powerful Glan[ce.]
Or Nature fail'd in me, & left some Part
Not Proof Enough such Object to sustain,
Or from my Side subducting, took perhaps
More than enough; at least on her bestow'd
Too much of Ornament, in outward Shew
Elaborate: ——Id: l: 530.

[236] For what admir'st thou, what transports thee s[o?]
An Outside? fair no Doubt, & worthy well
Thy cherishing, thy honouring, & thy Love,
Not thy Subjection: weigh with her thyself;
Then value: Oft-times nothing profits more
Than Self-esteem, grounded on just & right
Well manag'd; of that Skill the more thou know['st]
The more she will acknowledge thee her Head,
And to Realities yield all her Shows:
Made so adorn for thy Delight the more,
So awful, that with Honour thou may'st love
Thy Mate, who sees when thou art seen least wise[.]
Id: l: 567.

[237] For he who tempts, though in vain, at least asperses
The tempted with Dishonour foul, suppos'd

§234 *Paradise Lost*, VIII: 383-9.
§235 Same, 530-9.
§236 Same, 567-78.
§237 Same, IX: 296-9.

Not incorruptible of Faith, not Proof
[Against Temptation. —B: 9. l. 296.]

[238]   ——Thus it shall befal
Him who to Worth in Women overtrusting
Lets her Will rule; restraint she will not brook,
And left to herself, if Evil thence ensue,
She first his weak Indulgence will accuse.
                          Id: l: 1182.

[239] But past who can recall, or done undo?
Not God omnipotent, nor Fate. ——
                          Id: l: 926.

[240] Be it so! for I submit; His Doom is fair,
That Dust I am, & shall to Dust return.
O welcome Hour whenever! Why delays
His Hand to execute, what His Decree
Fix'd on this Day? Why do I over-live?
Why am I mock'd with Death, & lengthen'd out
To deathless Pain? How gladly would I meet
Mortality my Sentence, & be Earth
Insensible! How glad would lay me down,
As in my Mother's Lap! There I should rest
And sleep secure: His dreadful Voice no more
Would thunder in my Ears: ——
                          B: 10. l: 769.

[241]   ——imagin'd wise,
Constant, mature, proof against all Assaults:
And understood not all was but a Shew,
Rather than solid Virtue; all but a Rib,
Crooked by Nature, bent (as now appears)
More to the Part sinister from me drawn;
Well if thrown out, as supernumerary
To my just Number found!—O! why did God[,]
Creator wise! that Peopl'd highest Heav'n

§238 Same, 1182-6.
§239 Same, 926-7.
§§240-246 These entries conform closely in spelling and punctuation to the
text edited by Elijah Fenton, first published in 1725 and frequently reprinted.
§240 *Paradise Lost*, x: 769-80.
§241 Same, 881-98. Cf. §132 and §146.

With Spirits masculine, create at last
This Novelty on Earth, this fair Defect
Of Nature? And not fill the World at once
With Men, as Angels, without feminine?
Or find some other Way to generate
Mankind? This Mischeif had not then befall['n,]
And more that shall befal: innumerable
Disturbances on Earth through female Snares,
And straight Conjunction with this Sex!——
                    [Id: l: 881]

236482.

[242]   ——let us make short,
Let us seek *Death*:—or, he not found, supply
With our own Hands his Office on ourselves.
Why stand we longer shivering under Fears,
That shew no End but Death; & have the Pow'r
Of many Ways to die, the shortest chusing,
Destruction with Destruction to Destroy?
                    Id: l: 1000.

[243] But have I now seen Death? is this the Way
I must return to native Dust? O Sight
Of Terror, foul, & ugly to behold,
Horrid to think, how horrible to feel.
                    B: 11. l: 462.

[244] At length a reverend Sire among them came,
And of their Doings great Dislike declar'd,
And testify'd against their Ways: he oft
Frequented their Assemblies, whereso met,
Triumphs, or Festivals; & to them preach'd
Conversion & Repentance;——
                    Id: l: 719.

[245]   ——Let no Man seek
Henceforth to be foretold, what shall befall
Him or his Children: Evil he may be sure:
Which neither his foreknowing can prevent,

§242 Same, 1000-6.
§243 Same, XI: 462-5.
§244 Same, 719-24.
§245 Same, 770-5.

And he the future Evil shall no less
In Apprehension, than in Substance, feel;
Id: l: 770.

[246]   ——since with Sorrow, & Heart's Distress
Wearied I fell asleep: but now, lead on!
In me is no Delay; with thee to go,
Is to stay here; without thee here to stay,
Is to go hence unwilling: thou to me
Art all Things under Heav'n; all places thou[;]
B: 12. l: 613

[247] Youth is not rich in time, it may be, poor;
Part with it as with money, sparing; pay
No moment but in purchase of it's worth;
And what it's worth, ask death-beds; they can tell.
Part with it as with life, reluctant; big
With holy hope of nobler time to come.
Young's N. T. night. 2.

[248] Time's use was doom'd a pleasure: waste, a pain;
That man might feel his error if unseen:
And, feeling, fly to labor for his cure;
Not, blund'ring, split on idleness for ease.
Life's cares are comforts; such by heav'n design'd;
He that has none must make them or be wretched.
Cares are emploiments; and without employ

§246 Same, xii: 613-18.
§§247-67 These excerpts from Edward Young's *Night-Thoughts* were entered at two different periods. §§247-57 and §§262-7 were entered late in the
1760s, whereas the intervening entries, §§258-61, belong to the period prior
to 1763, possibly dating from TJ's school days in the 1750s. Because of the
order of the later entries, it seems likely that TJ began entering his second
round of commonplacing from *Night-Thoughts* immediately after the previous
entries from that work (§§258-61). Then, having used up the available space
between these entries and the Shakespeare section, he entered the remaining
extracts on empty pages preceding the earlier entries.
Young's poem was published as *The Complaint: or, Night-Thoughts on Life,
Death, and Immortality* in nine parts, or "Nights," between 1742 and 1746.
The edition cited in the notes by volume and page number is *The Works of the
Author of Night-Thoughts*, 4 vols. (London, 1757). For further information, see
Young in the Register of Authors.
§247 *Night-Thoughts*, "Night the Second on Time, Death, Friendship,"
Works, iii: 23.
§248 Same, 26.

The soul is on a rack; the rack of rest,
To souls most adverse; action all their joy.
                Id. Ib.

[249]   Speech ventilates our intellectual fire;
        Speech burnishes our mental magazine;
        Brightens for ornament; and whets for use.
        What numbers, sheath'd in erudition, lie,
        Plung'd to the hilts in venerable tomes,
        And rusted in; who might have borne an edge,
        And play'd a sprightly beam, if born to speech;
        If born blest heirs of half their mother's tongue!
        Tis thought's exchange, which, like th' alternate push
        Of waves conflicting, breaks the learned scum,
        And defecates the student's standing pool.
                Id. Ib.

[250]   Nature, in zeal for human amity,
        Denies, or damps, an undivided joy.
        Joy is an import; joy is an exchange;
        Joy flies monopolists: it calls for two;
                Id. Ib.

[251]   O! lost to virtue, lost to manly thought,
        Lost to the noble sallies of the soul!
        Who think it solitude to be alone.
        Communion sweet! communion large and high!
        Our reason, guardian angel, and our god!
        Then nearest these, when others most remote;
        And all, ere long, shall be remote, but these.
                Id. Night. 3.

[252]   Woes cluster; rare are solitary woes;
        They love a train, they tread each other's heel;
                Id. Ib.

[253]   Ye that e'er lost an angel! pity me.
                Id. Ib.

§249 Same, 37.
§250 Same, 38.
§251 Same, "Night the Third. Narcissa," *Works*, III: 47.
§25 Same, 49.
§253 Same, 51.

[254] For what live ever here? with lab'ring step
To tread our former footsteps? pace the round
Eternal? to climb life's worn, heavy wheel,
Which draws up nothing new? to beat, and beat
The beaten track? to bid each wretched day
The former mock? to surfeit on the same,
And yawn our joys? or thank a misery
For change, tho' sad? To see what we have seen?
Hear, till unhear'd the same old slabber'd tale?
To taste the tasted, and at each return
Less tasteful? o'er our palates to decant
Another vintage? strain a flatter year
Thro' loaded vessels, and a laxer tone?
                              Id. Ib.

[255] A truth it is, few doubt, but fewer trust,
'He sins against this life, who slights the next.'
                              Id. Ib.

[256] A languid, leaden, iteration reigns
And ever must, o'er those, whose joys are joys
Of sight, smell, taste: the cuckow seasons sing
The same dull note to such as nothing prize,
But what those seasons, from the teeming earth,
To doating sense indulge. but nobler minds,
Which relish fruits unripen'd by the sun,
Make their days various; various as the dyes
On the dove's neck, which wanton in his rays.
                              Id. Ib.

[257] Why start at death? where is he? death arriv'd,
Is past; not come, or gone, he's never here.
Ere hope, sensation fails; black-boding man
Receives, not suffers, death's tremendous blow.
The knell, the shroud, the mattock, and the grave;
The deep damp vault, the darkness, and the worm;

§254 Same, 58. TJ adapted this passage in two different ways in letters to
Abigail and John Adams. See TJ to Abigail Adams, 11 Jan. 1817; TJ to John
Adams, 1 June 1822 (Cappon, p. 504, 577).
§255 *Night-Thoughts*, "Night the Third," *Works*, III: 60.
§256 Same.
§257 Same, "Night the Fourth. The Christian Triumph," *Works*, III: 69-70.

These are the bugbears of a winter's eve,
The terrors of the living, not the dead.
Imagination's fool, and error's wretch,
Man makes a death which nature never made;
Then on the point of his own fancy falls;
And feels a thousand deaths in fearing one.
Id. Night. 4.

[258] Death! great Proprietor of all! tis thine
To tread out Empire, & to quench the Stars.
The Sun himself by thy Permission shines;
And, one Day, thou shalt pluck him from his Sphere
Amid such mighty Plunder, why exhaust
Thy partial Quiver on a Mark so mean?
Why thy peculiar Rancour wreck'd on me?
Insatiate Archer could not one suffice?
Thy Shaft flew thrice, & thrice my Peace was slain
And thrice, e'er thrice yon Moon had fill'd her Hor[n.]
L: D: & Immortality.

[259] Know'st thou, Lorenzo! what a Freind contai[ns?]
As Bees mixt Nectar draw from fragrant Flow['rs,]
So Men from Freindship, Wisdom & Delight;
Twins ty'd by Nature; if they Part they die.
Hast thou no Freind to set thy Mind abroach[?]
Good Sense will stagnate, Thoughts shut up, want Air[,]
And spoil like Bales unopen'd to the Sun.
T: D: Freindship

[260] A Soul immortal spending all her Fires;
Wasting her Strength in strenuous Idleness,
Thrown into Tumult, raptur'd, or alarm'd,
At ought this Scene can threaten, or indulge,
Resembles Ocean into Tempest wrought,
To waft a Feather, or to drown a Fly.
L: D: Immort:

§258 Same, "Night the First. On Life, Death, and Immortality," *Works*, III: 10. The page on which this entry appears carries the heading "Young's Night-Thoughts" in a pre-1763 hand.
§259 *Night-Thoughts*, "Night the Second on Time, Death, Friendship," *Works*, III: 36-7.
§260 Same, "Night the First. On Life, Death, and Immortality," *Works*, III: 8.

[261] What Numbers once in Fortune's Lap high-fed,
Sollicit the cold Hand of Charity!
To shock us more, sollicit it in vain!
Id:

[262] Tir'd nature's sweet restorer, balmy sleep!
He, like the world, his ready visit pays
Where fortune smiles; the wretched he forsakes;
Swift on his downy pinion flies from woe,
And lights on lids unsullied with a tear.
Id. ib.

[263] The cobweb'd cottage, with it's ragged wall
Of mould'ring mud, is royalty to me!
The spider's most attenuated thread
Is cord, is cable, to man's tender tie
On earthly bliss; it breaks at every breeze.
Id. Ib.

[264] Misfortune, like a creditor severe,
But rises in demand for her delay;
She makes a scourge of past prosperity,
To sting thee more, and double thy distress.
Id. Ib.

[265] By nature's law, what may be, may be now;
There's no prerogative in human hours.
In human hearts what bolder thought can rise,
Than man's presumption on tomorrow's dawn?
Where is tomorrow? in another world.
For numbers this is certain; the reverse
Is sure to none; and yet on this *perhaps*,
This *peradventure*, infamous for lies,
As on a rock of adamant we build
Our mountain hopes; spin out eternal schemes,

§261 Same, 12.
§262 Same, 3. The opening lines of the poem.
§263 Same, 9.
§264 Same, 14.
§265 Same, 16.
§265.7 perhaps] Printed, rather than written cursively.
§265.8 peradventure] Printed, rather than written cursively.

As we the fatal sisters could outspin,
And, big with life's futurities, expire.

Id. Ib.

[266] Be wise today; tis madness to defer;
Next day the fatal precedent will plead;
Thus on till wisdom is push'd out of life.
Procrastination is the thief of time;
Year after year it steals, till all are fled,
And to the mercies of a moment leaves
The vast concerns of an eternal scene.
If not so frequent, would not this be strange?
That tis so frequent, this is stranger still.
  Of man's miraculous mistakes, this bears
The palm, 'that all men are about to live',
For ever on the brink of being born.

Id. Ib.

[267] All promise is poor dilatory man,
And that thro' every stage: when young, indeed,
In full content we, sometimes, nobly rest,
Unanxious for ourselves; and only wish,
As duteous sons, our fathers were more wise.
At thirty man supects himself a fool;
Knows it at forty, and reforms his plan;
At fifty chides his infamous delay,
Pushes his prudent purpose to resolve;
In all the magnaminity of thought
Resolves; and re-resolves; then dies the same.
  And why? because he thinks himself immortal.
All men think all men mortal, but themselves;
Themselves, when some alarming stroke of fate
Strikes thro' their wounded heart the sudden dread;
But their hearts wounded, like the wounded air,
Soon close; where past the shaft no trace is found.
As from the wing no scar the sky retains;
The parted wave no furrow from the keel;

§266 *Night-Thoughts*, "Night the First," *Works*, iii: 16-17.
§267 Same, 17-18.
§267.14 *stroke*] *Works: shock.*
§267.15 *heart*] *Works: hearts.*

So dies in human hearts the thought of death.
Ev'n with the tender tear which nature sheds
O'er those we love, we drop it in their grave.
Young's N. T. night. 1.

Shakespear ——

[268] Cowards die many Times before their Deaths;
The valiant never taste of Death but once.
Of all the Wonders that I yet have heard,
It seems to me most strange that Men should fear
Seeing that Death, a necessary End,
Will come when it will come.——
Julius Caesar. Act. 2. Scene 4.

[269] Must I give Way & Room to your rash Choler?
Shall I be frighted when a Madman stares?

——Fret 'till your proud Heart break:
Go, shew your Slaves how choleric you are,
And make your Bond-men tremble. Must I budge?
Must I observe you? Must I stand & crouch
Under your testy Humour? By the Gods,
You shall digest the Venom of your Spleen,
Tho' it do split you: For from this Day forth,
I'll use you for my Mirth, yea, for my Laughter,
When you are waspish.——
Id: Act: 4. S: 3.

[270] Do not presume too much upon my Love;
I may do that I shall be sorry for.
Id:

§268-80 Certain distinctive readings and scene numberings make it clear that TJ's copy-text for these entries was Sir Thomas Hanmer's edition of Shakespeare's plays, first published in 1744 and frequently reprinted. The scene numbering given in the notes reflects modern editorial practice.
§268 *Julius Caesar*, II: 2. Hanmer's edition: II: 4.
§269 Same, IV: 1.
§270 Same.

[271] I cannot tell, what you & other Men
       Think of this Life; but for my single self,
       I had as lief not be, as live to be
       In Awe of such a Thing as I myself.
       I was born free as Caesar, so were you;
       We both have fed as well; & we can both
       Endure the Winter's cold as well as he.

       ———   ———This Man
       Is now become a God; & Cassius is
       A wretched Creature, & must bend his Body,
       If Caesar carelessly but nod on him.
                     Id: Act: 1. Sc: 3.

[272]   ———Hold my Hand:
       Be factious for Redress of all these Griefs,
       And I will set this Foot of mine as far,
       As who goes farthest.
                     Id: Sc: 7.

[273] That we shall die, we know; 'tis but the Time,
       And drawing Days out, that Men stand upon.
           And he that cuts off twenty Years of Life,
       Cutts of so many Years of fearing Death.
           Grant that & then is Death a Benefit.
                     Id: Act. 3. Sc: 2.

[274] If we are mark'd to die, we are enow
       To do our Country Loss; & if to live,
       The fewer Men, the greater Share of Honour.
       God's Will! I pray thee wish not one Man more.
                     Shakespear.

[275] But if it be a Sin to covet Honour,
       I am the most offending Soul alive.
                     Id:

§271 Same, I: 2. Hanmer's edition: I: 3.
§272 Same, I: 3. Hanmer's edition: I: 7.
§273 Same, III: 1. Hanmer's edition: III: 2.
§274 *Henry V*, IV: 3.
§275 Same.

[276]   ——Honour pricks me on. But how if Honour prick
me off, when I come on? how then? Can Honour set a
Leg? No: or an Arm? No: Or take away the Greif of a
Wound? No: Honour hath no Skill in Surgery then?
No: What is Honour? A Word: What is that Word
Honour? Air; a trim Reckoning—Who hath it? He that
died a Wednesday. Doth he feel it? No: Doth he hear
it? No: Is it insensible then? yea, to the Dead: But will
it not live with the Living? No. Why? Detraction will
not suffer it. Therefore I'll none of it; Honour is a meer
Scutcheon, & so ends my Catechism.
                          Henry 4th. Part. 1st. Act: 5. Sc: 2.

[277]   ——Extremity was the Trier of Spirits,
That common Chances common Men could bear;
That when the Sea was calm, all Boats alike,
Shew'd Mastership in floating; Fortune's Blows
When most struck Home, being greatly warded, crave
A noble Cunning.
                          Coriolanus. Act. 4. Sc: 1.

[278] I wish the Gods had nothing else to do,
But to confirm my Curses——Id: Sc: 2.

[279] He was not taken well, he had not din'd.
The Veins unfill'd, Our Blood is cold, & then,
We pout upon the Morning, are unapt
To give, or to forgive; but when we've stuff'd
These Pipes, & these Conveyances of Blood
With Wine & Feeding, we have suppler Souls
Than in our Priest-like Fasts.——
                          Id: Act: 5. Sc: 1.

[280]   ——Shall remain?
Hear you this Triton of the Minnows? mark you
His absolute Shall? ——

§276 *Henry* iv, Part i, v: 1. Hanmer's edition: v: 2.
§277 *Coriolanus*, iv: 1.
§277.4 *greatly warded*] This is Hanmer's distinctive reading in a much-dis-
puted passage.
§278 *Coriolanus*, iv: 2.
§279 Same, v: 1.
§280 Same, iii: 1. In an original treatment of this passage, Hanmer restruc-

———Shall?
O! good, but most unwise Patricians, why,
You grave but reckless Senators, have you thus
Given Hydra here to chuse an Officier,
That with his peremptory Shall, being but
The Horn & Noise o'th' Monsters, wants not Spirit
To say he'll turn your Current in a Ditch,
And make your Channel his? if they have Power
Let them have Cushions by you: if none, awake
Your dang'rous Lenity: if you are learned,
Be not as common Fools: if you are not,
Then vail your Ignorance. ———
———They chuse their Magistrate,
And such a one as he, who puts his Shall,
His popular Shall, against a graver Bench
Than ever frown'd in Greece.

Id: Act: 3. Sc. 1.

[281] What stronger Breast-plate than a Heart untainted?
Thrice is he arm'd that has his Quarrel just;
And he but naked though lock'd up in Steel,
Whose Conscience with Injustice is corrupted.

Hen: VIth.

[282]   ———In struggling with Misfortunes
Lies the true Proof of Virtue. On smooth Seas
How many Bawble Boats dare set their Sails,
And make an equal Way with firmer Vessels:
But let the Tempest once enrage the Sea,
And then behold the strong ribb'd Argosie
Bounding between the Ocean & the Air,
Like Perseus mounted on his Pegasus;
Then where are those weak Rivals of the Main?

---

tured the speech so that the phrase "Let them have cushions by you" took the
position occupied in earlier texts by the phrase "Then vail your ignorance,"
and vice versa.

§281-2 These entries were apparently taken from *Thesaurus Dramaticus* , a
collection of excerpts from popular British plays used by TJ. See §§286-96n.

§281 *Henry VI, Part 2*, III: 2. This entry is repeated, perhaps inadvertently,
as §291.

§282 Not by Shakespeare. TJ presumably found this passage from John
Dryden's version of Shakespeare's *Troilus and Cressida*, Act 1, Scene 1, 13-25,
under the heading "Fortitude" in *Thesaurus Dramaticus*, where it is attributed
to Shakespeare.

Or to avoid the Tempest, fled to port,
Or made a Prey to Neptune. Even thus
Do empty Shew & true-priz'd Worth divide
In Storms of Fortune. ——
Troilus & Cressida.

Thomson's Seasons.

[283] Even love itself is bitterness of soul,
A pleasing anguish pining at the heart.
Spring v. 338.

[284]   ——Ah then, ye fair!
Be greatly cautious of your sliding hearts;
Dare not th'infectious sigh; the pleading eye,
In meek submission drest, deject, and low,
But full of tempting guile. Let not the tongue,
Prompt to deceive, with adulation smooth,
Gain on your purpos'd will. Nor in the bower,
Where woodbines flaunt, and roses shed a couch
While evening draws her crimson curtains round,
Trust your soft minutes with betraying man.
   And let th'aspiring youth beware of love,
Of the smooth glance beware; for 'tis too late,
When on his heart the torrent softness pours.
Then wisdom prostrate lies; and fading fame
Dissolves in air away: while the fond soul
Is wrapt in dreams of ecstacy, and bliss;
Still paints th'illusive form; the kindling grace;
Th'inticing smile; the modest-seeming eye,

§§283-5 These entries from "Spring," the first of James Thomson's four-part cycle, *The Seasons*, were copied by TJ early in the 1760s from the first collected edition of the poem (1730). Line numbers used in the notes below are from that edition, followed parenthetically by the line numbers of the final version from the variorum edition of Thomson's poems: J. Logie Robertson, ed., *The Complete Poetical Works of James Thomson* (London, 1908). *Ms.* TJ's heading originally read *Thompson's Seasons*, reflecting the way he usually spelled the poet's name, but the *p* has at some point been stricken.

For another extract from "Spring," see §349. For further information, see Thomson in the Register of Authors.

§283 James Thomson, "Spring," *The Seasons*, 338-9 (288-9).

§284 Same, 887-96 (973-5).

§284.7 *will*] 1730: *wills*.

Beneath whose beauteous beams, belying heaven,
Lurk searchless cunning, cruelty and death:
And still, false-warbling in his cheated ear,
Her syren voice, enchanting draws him on,
To guileful shores, and meads of fatal joy.
Id: v. 887.

[285] But absent, what fantastick pangs arrous'd,
Rage in each thought, by restless musing fed,
Chill the warm cheek, and blast the bloom of life!
Neglected fortune flies; and sliding swift,
Prone into ruin, fall his scorn'd affairs.
'Tis nought but gloom around. The darken'd sun
Loses his light. The rosy bosom'd Spring
To weeping fancy pines; and yon bright arch
Of heav'n, low bends into a dusty vault.
All nature fades extinct; and she alone
Heard, felt, and seen, possesses every thought,
Fills every sense, and pants in every vein.
Books are but formal dulness, tedious friends,
And sad amid the social band he sits,
Lonely, and inattentive. From the tongue
Th'unfinish'd period falls: while, born away
On swelling thought, his wafted spirit flies
To the vain bosom of his distant fair;
And leaves the semblance of a lover, fix'd
In melancholy site, with head declin'd,
And love-dejected eyes. Sudden he starts,
Shook from his tender trance, and restless runs
To glimmering shades, and sympathetic glooms,
Where the dun umbrage o'er the falling stream
Romantic hangs; there thro' the pensive dusk
Strays, in heart-thrilling meditation lost,
Indulging all to love: or on the bank
Thrown, amid drooping lillies, swells the breeze
With sighs unceasing, and the brook with tears.
Thus in soft anguish he consumes the day,
Nor quits his deep retirement, till the moon

§285 "Spring," 918-92 (1004-75).
§285.60 *yeilding*] 1730: *yielded.*
§285.71-3 These lines were omitted by Thomson beginning with the 1744
edition.

Peeps thro' the chambers of the fleecy east,
Enlighten'd by degrees, and in her train
Leads on the gentle hours; then forth he walks,
Beneath the trembling languish of her beams,
With soften'd soul, and wooes the bird of eve
To mingle woes with his: or while the world,
And all the sons of care, lie hush'd in sleep,
Associates with the midnight shadows drear;
And sighing to the lonely taper, pours
His idly-tortur'd heart into the page,
Meant for the moving messenger of love;
Where rapture burns on rapture, every line
With rising frenzy fir'd. But if on bed
Delirious flung, sleep from his pillow flies.
All night he tosses, nor the balmy power
In any posture finds; till the grey morn
Lifts her pale lustre on the paler wretch,
Exanimate by love: and then perhaps
Exhausted nature sinks a while to rest,
Still interrupted by distracted dreams,
That o'er the sick imagination rise,
And in black colors paint the mimic scene.
Oft with th'enchantress of his soul he talks;
Sometimes in crouds distress'd; or if retir'd
To secret-winding, flower-enwoven bowers,
Far from the dull impertinence of man,
Just as he, credulous, his thousand cares
Begins to lose in blind oblivious love,
Snatch'd from her yeilding hand, he knows not h[ow,]
Through forests huge, and long untravel'd heath
With desolation brown, he wanders waste,
In night and tempest wrapt; or shrinks aghast
Back, from the bending precipice; or wades
The turbid stream below, and strives to reach
The farther shore; where succorless, and sad,
Wild as a Bacchanal she spreads her arms,
But strives in vain, born by th'outrageous flood
To distance down, he rides the ridgy wave,
Or whelm'd beneath the boiling eddy sinks.
Then a weak, wailing, lamentable cry
Is heard, and all in tears he wakes, again

To tread the circle of revolving woe.
These are the charming agonies of love,
Whose misery delights. ——
Id: v: 918.

[286]   ——It wounds indeed
To bear Affronts, too great to be forgiven,
And not have Power to punish.——
Dryd: Sp: Fryar.

[287] Fortune takes Care that Fools should still be seen;
She places them aloft, o'th'topmost Spoke
Of all her Wheel. Fools are the daily Work
Of Nature, her Vocation. If she form
A Man, she loses by it; 'tis too expensive;
'Twould make ten Fools: A Man's a Prodigy.
Dryd: Oedip:

[288] That I could reach the Axle where the Pins are
Which bolt this Frame; that I might pull 'em out,
And pluck all into Chaos with myself!
Who would not fall with all the World about him?
Johnson's Catal: Consp:

[289] I thank the Gods, no secret Thoughts reproach me:
No, I dare challenge Heaven, to turn me outward,
And shake my Soul quite empty in your Sight;
[Dryd: Oedip:]

§§286-96 These entries appear to have been copied from a particular collection of extracts from English plays. First published in 1724 as *Thesaurus Dramaticus. Containing all the Celebrated Passages, Soliloquies, Similies, Descriptions, and other Poetical Beauties in the Body of English Plays, Ancient and Modern*, it was reissued in 1737 and 1756 as *The Beauties of the English Stage*. A comparison of texts indicates that TJ probably used as his copy-text the 1724 edition, though some deviations appear. As the subtitle makes abundantly clear, it was intended to serve as a compendium of the most noteworthy passages in English drama, all of which were placed in appropriate categories, such as "Love," "Misery," and so forth. In the notes that follow, the category under which the passage was classified is given, as well as the author and title indicated.

§286 "Affronts," *The Spanish Friar* by John Dryden.
§287 "Fool," *Oedipus* by John Dryden.
§288 "Imprecations," *The Cataline Conspiracy* by Ben Jonson.
§289 "Innocence," *Oedipus* by John Dryden.

[290] There is no Courage but in Innocence;
No Constancy but in an honest Cause.
South: Fate of Cap:

[291] What stronger Breast-plate than a Heart untainted,
Thrice is he arm'd that has his Quarrel just;
And he but naked though lock'd up in Steel,
Whose Conscience with Injustice is corrupted.
Shak: Hen: VI.

[292] 'Tis not for Nothing that we Life pursue;
It pays our Hopes with something still that's New,
Each Day's a Mistress unenjoy'd before:
Like Travellers, we're pleas'd with seeing more.
Dr: Auren:

[293] How vainly would dull Moralists impose
Limits on Love, whose Nature brooks no Laws.
Love is a God, & like a God, should be
Inconstant, with unbounded Liberty;
Rove as he list.
Otw: D. Carlos.

[294]   ——What so hard, so stubborn, or so fierce,
But Music for the Time will change its Nature?

§290 "Innocence," *The Fate of Capua* by Thomas Southerne.
§291 "Innocence," *Henry VI* by William Shakespeare.
§292 "Life," *Aurengzeb*e by John Dryden.
§293 "Inconstancy," *Don Carlos* by Thomas Otway.
§294 "Musick," *The Merchant of Venice* by William Shakespeare. A rewriting of Shakespeare's play by George Granville, Lord Landsdowne (1667-1735), *The Jew of Venice*, was more popular in the eighteenth century than the original, which may account for the title TJ assigns. The text of this entry is also anomalous, as will be seen from the annotation. Note that where they differ, the text of *Thesaurus* is that of Shakespeare, except at line 5.
§294.1 ——*What so hard, so stubborn, or so fierce,*] Having decided to omit the first 11 lines of his copy-text, TJ may have invented this line to lead into the succeeding lines, for no such line is evident in this passage in *Thesaurus*, and the line which follows it does not form a question in the original, as TJ makes it do.
§294.2 *will*] *Thesaurus*: *doth.*
§294.3 *his Soul*] *Thesaurus*: *himself.*
§294.4 *touch'd*] *Thesaurus*: *mov'd.*
§294.5 *Stratagems*] *Thesaurus*: *Villanies*; Shakespeare: *stratagems.*
§294.6 *Mind*] *Thesaurus*: *Spirit.*

The Man who has not Music in his Soul,
Or is not touch'd with Concord of sweet Sounds,
Is fit for Treasons, Stratagems, & Spoils,
The Motions of his Mind are dull as Night,
And his Affections dark as Erebus:
Let no such Man be trusted. ——
                              Shak: Jew of Ven:

[295] Music has Charms to sooth a savage Breast,
To soften Rocks, or bend a knotted Oak.
I've read that Things inanimate have mov'd,
And, as with living Souls, have been inform'd
By magic Numbers & persuasive Sound.
                              Congr: Mourn: Br:

[296] Let there be Music, let the Master touch
The sprightly String, & softly breathing Lute,
Till Harmony rouse ev'ry gentle Passion,
Teach the cold Maid to lose her Fears in Love,
And the fierce Youth to languish at her Feet.
Begin: ev'n Age itself is chear'd with Music,
It wakes a glad Remembrance of our Youth,
Calls back past joys, & warms us into Transport.
                              Rowe's F: Penit:

[297] We break no Laws either of Gods or Men:
So, if we fall, it is with Reputation;
A Fate which Cowards shun, & brave Men seek.
If Cæsar punish Men for speaking Truth,
My honest Tongue shall dare his utmost Doom.
               Buck: Jul: Cæs: altered from Shak:
                         Act: 1. Sc: 2.

§295 "Musick," *The Mourning Bride* by William Congreve.
§295.1 *Breast*] *Thesaurus: Beast.*
§296 "Musick," *The Fair Penitent* by Nicholas Rowe.
§296.2 *Lute*] *Thesaurus: Flute.*
§297-300 These four entries are from a rewriting of Shakespeare's *Julius Caesar* by John Sheffield, Duke of Buckingham, who rewrote the work as two plays, *The Tragedy of Julius Caesar, Altered* and *The Death of Marcus Brutus.* See Buckingham in Register of Authors. Compare these entries with §§268-73 from Shakespeare's version.
§297 Buckingham, *Julius Caesar*, I: 2.

[298] I know where I shall wear this Dagger then:
Cassius from Bondage will deliver Cassius.
Herein the Poor are rich, the Weak most strong;
By this the wretched mock at base Oppression;
The meanest are victorious o'er the mighty.
Not Tow'rs of Stone, Nor Walls of harden'd Brass,
Nor airless Dungeons, the poor Strength of Tyrants!
Not all their strongest Guards, nor heaviest Chains,
Can in the least controul the mighty Spirit.
For noble Life, when weary of itself,
Has allways Power to shake it off at Pleasure,
Since I know this, know all the World besides,
That Part of Tyranny prepar'd for me,
I can & will defy.—

                          And so can I.
Thus ev'ry Bondman in his own Hand bears
The Pow'r to cancel his Captivity.
   And why should Cæsar be a Tyrant then?
Poor Man! I know he would not be a Wolf,
But that he sees the Romans are but Sheep:
He were no Lion if we were not Lambs.
                    Id: Sc: 5.

[299] ——where does Nature or the Will of Heav'n
Subject a Creature to one like itself?
Man is the only Brute enslaves his Kind.
                    Buck: Death of Marc: Brut: Act. 1.
                    Sc: 3.

[300]   ——If hearing Lyes
With greedy Ears, & soon beleiving them;
If misinterpreting whate'er I do,
And representing Things in foulest Colours,
Can be call'd wronging, who was e'er so wrong'd?
                    Id: Act: 4. Sc: 3.

§298 Same, I: 5. This passage consists of two speeches by Cassius (ll. 1-14, 18-21) and an intervening speech by Casca.
§299 Buckingham, *Marcus Brutus*, I: 3.
§300 Same, IV: 3.

[301]   ——Wed her!
No! were she all Desire could wish, as fair
As would the vainest of her Sex be thought,
With Wealth beyond what Woman's Pride could waste,
She should not cheat me of my Freedom. Marry!
When I am old & weary of the World,
I may grow desparate,
And take a Wife to mortify withal.
                        Otway's Orph: Act: 1.

[302]   ——Your Sex
Was never in the Right; y'are allways false,
Or silly, ev'n your Dresses are not more
Fantastic than your Appetites; you think
Of Nothing twice: Opinion you have none.
To Day y'are nice, tomorrow not so free;
Now smile, then frown; now sorrowful, then glad;
Now pleas'd, now not; And all you know not why?
Virtue you affect, Inconstancy's your Practice;
And when your loose Desires once get Dominion,
No hungry Churl feeds coarser at a Feast;
Ev'ry rank Fool goes down.——
                        Id:

[303] Who'd be that sordid foolish Thing call'd Man,
To cringe thus, fawn, & flatter for a Pleasure,
Which Beasts enjoy so very much above him?

§§301-15, 320-3 It seems quite possible that the five plays by Thomas Otway and Nicholas Rowe commonplaced in these entries were read at about the
same time in an anthology of plays. Dating from the Restoration and early in
the eighteenth century, these plays were all very popular in TJ's time and were
widely anthologized. A contemporary anthology that includes all the plays in
question, and therefore a prime candidate for TJ's source, is *A Select Collection
of English Plays*, 6 vols. (Edinburgh, 1755), to which the LCB text has been
compared in the notes below. Other such collections are listed in George Wat-
son, ed., *The New Cambridge Bibliography of English Literature* (Cambridge,
1971), II, 701. It should be pointed out, however, that in the case of the plays
by Rowe, TJ's text conforms at least as closely to that of a contemporary edition, *The Works of Nicholas Rowe, Esq.*, 2 vols. (London, 1756).

§301 Thomas Otway, *The Orphan: Or, The Unhappy Marriage*, I: 158-65.
Line numbers are supplied from J. C. Ghosh, ed., *The Works of Thomas Otway:
Plays, Poems, and Love-letters*, 2 vols. (Oxford, 1932). For information on Ot-
way, see the Register of Authors.

§302 Otway, *The Orphan*, I: 340-51.

§303 Same, 362-7.

The lusty Bull ranges through all the Field,
And from the Herd singling his Female out,
Enjoys her, & abandons her at Will.
Id:

[304] No Flattery, Boy! an honest Man can't live by't,
It is a little sneaking Art, which Knaves
Use to cajole & soften Fools withal.
If thou hast Flattery in thy Nature, out with't,
Or send it to a Court, for there 'twill thrive.
Id: Act. 2.

[305]   ——shun
The Man that's singular, his Mind's unsound
His Spleen o'erweighs his Brains; but above all,
Avoid the politic, the factious Fool,
The busy, buzzing, talking, harden'd Knave,
The quaint smooth-rough, that sins against his Reason,
Call saucy loud Suspicion, public Zeal,
And Mutiny, the Dictates of his Spirit;
Be very careful how you make new Freinds.
Otw: Orph: Act: 3.

[306] I'd leave the World for him that hates a Woman.
Woman the Fountain of all human Fraility!
What mighty ills have not been done by Woman?
Who was't betray'd the Capitol? A Woman.
Who lost Marc Anthony the World? A Woman.
Who was the Cause of a long ten years War,
And laid at last old Troy in ashes? Woman.
Destructive, damnable, deceitful Woman!
Woman to Man first as a Blessing giv'n,
When Innocence & Love were in their Prime;
Happy a while in Paradise they lay,
But quickly Woman long'd to go astray;

§304 Same, II: 15-19.
§305 Same, III: 76-84.
§305.6 *quaint smooth-rough*] Otway (Ghosh ed.): *quaint, smooth Rogue* Evidence that TJ was here copying from *A Select Collection of English Plays* (see above) is the fact that it prints *quaint smooth rough*.
Ms. smooth-rough has been inserted with a caret.
§306 *The Orphan*, III: 579-94.

Some foolish new Adventure needs must prove,
And the first Devil she saw, she chang'd her Love;
To his Temptations lewdly she inclin'd
Her Soul, & for an Apple damn'd Mankind.
Id:

[307] ——All the Heav'n they hope for is Variety.
One Lover to another still succeeds,
Another, & another after that,
And the last Fool is welcome as the former,
'Till, having lov'd his Hour out, he gives Place
And mingles with the Herd that goes before him.
Rowe's Fair Penit: Act. 1.

[308] You blast the Fair with Lies because they scorn you[,]
Hate you like Age, like Ugliness & Impotence;
Rather than make you bless'd they would die Virgi[ns,]
And stop the Propagation of Mankind.
Id: Act: 2.

[309] Can there in Women be such glorious Faith?
Sure all ill Stories of thy Sex are false!
O Woman! lovely Woman! Nature made thee
To temper Man: we had been Brutes without you:
Angels are painted fair to look like you:
There's in you all that we beleive of Heav'n,
Amazing Brightness, Purity & Truth,
Eternal joy, & everlasting Love.
Otw: Ven: preserv: Act: 1.

[310] Cowards are scar'd with Threatnings; Boys are whipt
Into Confessions: but a steady Mind
Acts of itself, ne'er asks the Body Counsel.
Give him the Tortures! Name but such a Thing
Again, by Heav'n I'll shut these Lips for ever.

§307 Nicholas Rowe, *The Fair Penitent*, I, 386-91. Line numbers are supplied from: Nicholas Rowe, *The Fair Penitent*, ed. Malcolm Goldstein (Lincoln, 1969). For information on Rowe, see the Register of Authors.
§308 Rowe, *The Fair Penitent*, II: 2, 97-100.
§309 Thomas Otway, *Venice Preserved, Or, A Plot Discover'd*, I: 335-42. Line numbers supplied from Ghosh edition (see §302n).
§310 Otway, *Venice Preserved*, IV: 152-8.

Not all your Racks, your Engines, or your Wheels,
Shall force a Groan away, that you may guess at.
Id: Act. 4.

[311]   ———You want to lead
My Reason blindfold, like a Hamper'd Lion,
Check'd of its nobler Vigour; then when bated
Down to obedient Tameness, make it couch,
And shew strange Tricks, which you call Signs of Faith.
So silly Souls are gull'd, & you get Money.
Away; no more:—
Id. Act. 5.

[312] Look round, how Providence bestows alike
Sunshine & Rain, to bless the fruitful Year,
On different Nations, all of different Faiths;
And (tho' by several Names & Titles worship'd)
Heav'n takes the various Tribute of their Praise;
Since all agree to own, at least to mean,
One best, one greatest, only Lord of all.
Rowe's Tamerl: Act. 3. Sc: 2.

[313] ———to subdue th'unconquerable Mind,
To make one Reason have the same Effect
Upon all Apprehensions; to force this,
Or this Man, just to think, as thou & I do;
Impossible! unless Souls were alike
In all, which differ now like human Faces.
Ib:

[314] Yet ere thou rashly urge my Rage too far,
I warn thee to take Heed; I am a Man,
And have the Frailties common to Man's Nature;
The fiery Seeds of Wrath are in my Temper,
And may be blown up to so fierce a Blaze
As Wisdom cannot rule. Know, thou hast touch'd me
Ev'n in the nicest, tenderest Part, my Honour.
My Honour! which, like Pow'r, disdains being question'd;
Id: Act: 4. Sc: 1.

§311 Same, v: 384-90.
§312 Nicholas Rowe, *Tamerlane: A Tragedy*, iii: 2.
§313 Same.
§314 Same, iv: 1.

[315] Women, like summer Storms, awhile are cloudy,
       Burst out in Thunder, & impetuous Show'rs;
       But straight the Sun of Beauty dawns abroad,
       And all the fair Horison is serene.
                              Id: Act. 5. Sc: 1.

[316]   ——Say now Melissa
       Is there among the Daughters of Affliction
       One so forlorn as poor Eurydice?
                       Mallet's Euridice. Act: 1. Sc. 1.

[317] Would Tears, my gracious Mistress, aught avail us
       Methinks these aged Eyes could number Drops
       With falling Clouds, or the perpetual Stream.
                              Ib: Sc: 4.

[318]   ——By Heav'n my Soul can form
       No Wish, no Thought but her. I tell thee, Medor
       With Blushes tell thee, this proud Charmer reign[s]
       Unbounded o'er my Reason. I have try'd
       Each Shape, each Art of varied Love to win her;
       Alternate Prayers, & Threats, the soothing Skill
       Of passionate Sincerity, The Fire
       Of rapturous Vows, but all these Arts were vain.
       Her rooted Hate is not to be remov'd.
       And 'twas my Soul's first Aim, the towering Poi[nt]
       Of all my Wishes, to prevail in this.
                              Id: Sc: 6.

[319] What is the blooming Tincture of a Skin,
       To Peace of Mind, to Harmony within?
       What the bright Sparkling of the finest Eye,
       To the soft soothing of a calm Reply?
       Can Comeliness of Form, or Shape, or Air,

---

§315 Same, v: 1.
§316 David Mallet, *Eurydice, A Tragedy*, i: 1. The source of this and the
following two entries from Mallet was probably *The Works of David Mallet*
(London, 1743). In the three-volume edition of Mallet's works published in
1759, the scene is much revised and this passage omitted. For information on
Mallet, see the Register of Authors.
§317 Mallet, *Eurydice*, i: 4.
§318 Same, i: 6.
§319 [Robert Dodsley], *Beauty: Or The Art of Charming. A Poem* (London,
1735), 9.

With Comeliness of Words, or Deeds, compare?
No; —those at first th'unwary Heart may gain;
But these, these only can that Heart retain.
The Art of charming.

[320]   ——Whatsoever
Fortune decrees, still let us call to Mind
Our Freindship, & our Honour. And since Love
Condemns us to be Rivals for one Prize,
Let us contend as Freinds & brave Men ought,
With Openness & justice to each other;
That he who wins the fair one to his Arms,
May take her as the Crown of great Desert:
And if the wretched Loser does repine,
His own Heart & the World may all condemn him.
Rowe's Jane Gray. Act. 1.

[321] I had beheld, ev'n her whole Sex, unmov'd,
Look'd o'er 'em like a Bed of gaudy Flowers,
That lift their painted Heads, & live a Day,
Then shed their trifling Glories unreguarded:
My Heart disdain'd their Beauties, till she came
With ev'ry Grace that Nature's Hand could give.
Id: Act: 3.

[322]   ——Thy narrow Soul
Knows not the God-like Glory of forgiving:
Nor can thy cold, thy ruthless Heart conceive,
How large the Power, how fix'd the Empire is,
Which Benefits confer on generous Minds:
Goodness prevails upon the stubbon'st Foes,
And conquers more than ever C[æ]sar's Sword did.
Id: Act. 5. Sc: 1.

[323] And canst thou tell? who gave thee to explore
The secret Purposes of Heav'n, or taught thee
To set a Bound to Mercy unconfin'd?
But Know, thou proud, perversely judging Wincheste[r,]
Howe'er you hard imperious Censures doom,

§320 Nicholas Rowe, *Lady Jane Gray: A Tragedy*, I.
§321 *Jane Gray*, III.
§322 Same, V: 1.
§323 Same, V: 2.

And portion out our Lot in Worlds to come;
Those who with Honest Hearts pursue the Right,
And follow faithfully Truth's sacred Light,
Tho' suffering here shall from their Sorrows cease,
Rest with the Saints, & dwell in endless Peace.
                    Ib: Act: 5. Sc: last.

[324] Retiring from the popular Noise, I seek
This unfrequented place to find some Ease,
Ease to the Body some, none to the Mind
From restless Thoughts, that like a deadly swarm
Of Hornets arm'd, no sooner found alone
But rush upon me thronging, & present
Times past, what once I was, & what am now.
                    Milton's Samson Agonistes. v: 16

[325] But what is Strength without a doubles Share
Of Wisdom, vast, unweildy, burdensome,
Proudly secure, yet liable to fall
By weakest Subtleties, not made to rule,
But to subserve where Wisdom bears Command.
                    Id: v: 53.

[326] Suffices that to me Strength is my Bane,
And proves the Source of all my Miseries;
So many, & so huge, that each apart
Would ask a Life to wail;——
                    Id: v: 63.

[327] Scarce Half I seem to live, dead more than Half
O! dark, dark, dark, amid the Blaze of Noon,
Irrecoverably dark, total Eclipse
Without all Hopes of Day!——
                    Id: v: 79

[328] For him I reckon not in high Estate
Whom long Descent of Birth
Or the Sphere of Fortune raises;
                    Id: v: 170.

§324 John Milton, *Samson Agonistes*, 16-22.
§325 Same, 53-7.
§326 Same, 63-6.
§327 Same, 79-82.
§328 Same, 170-2.

[329] ——apt Words have Pow'r to swage
The Tumours of a troubled Mind,
And are as Balm to fester'd Wounds.
Id: v: 184.

[330] ——for I learn
Now of my own Experience, not by Talk,
How counterfeit a Coin they are who Freinds
Bear in their Superscription, (of the most
I would be understood); in prosp'rous Days
They swarm, but in adverse withdraw their hea[d,]
Not to be found, thoug sought.——
Id: v: 187

[331] ——tell me, Freinds,
Am I not sung & proverb'd for a Fool
In ev'ry Street? do they not say, how well
Are come upon him his Deserts?——
Id: v: [202]

[332] Dejected not then so overmuch thyself,
Who hast of Sorrow thy full Load besides;
Id: v: 213.

[333] ——who think not God at all
If any be, they walk obscure;
For of such Doctrine never was there School,
But the Heart of the Fool,
And no Man therein Doctor but himself.
Id: v: 295.

[334] Nothing of all these Evils hath befall'n me
But justly; I myself have brought them on,
Sole Author I, sole Cause; if ought seem vile,
As vile hath been my Folly ——
Id: v: 374.

§329 Same, 184-6.
§330 Same, 187-93.
§331 Same, 202-5.
§332 Same, 213-14.
§333 Same, 295-9.
§334 Same, 374-7.

[335]   ——thou bear'st
Enough, & more, the Burden of that Fault,
Bitterly hast thou paid, & still art paying
That rigid Score. ——
                         Id: v: 430.

[336] So much I feel my genial Spirits droop,
My Hopes all flat, Nature within me seems
In all her Functions weary of herself,
My Race of Glory run, & Race of Shame,
And I shall shortly be with them that rest.
                         Id: v: 594.

[337]   ——If Weakness may excuse,
What Murderer, what Traitor, Parricide,
Incestuous, sacrilegious, but may plead it?
All Wickedness is Weakness: That Plea therefore
With God or Man will gain thee no Remission.
                         Id: v: 831.

[338] Nor think me so unwary or accurs'd,
To bring my Feet again into the Snare
Where once I have been caught.——
                         Id: v: 930

[339] Fame, if not double-fac'd, is double-mouth'd,
And with contrary Blast proclaims most Deeds
On both his Wings, one black, the other white,
Bears greatest Names in his wild airy Flight.
                         Id: v 971

[340] It is not Virtue, Wisdom, Valour, Wit,
Strength, Comeliness of Shape, or amplest Merit,
That Woman's Love can win or long inherit;
But what it is, hard is to say,
Harder to hit,

§335 Same, 430-3.
§336 Same, 594-8.
§337 Same, 831-5.
§338 Same, 930-2.
§339 Same, 971-4.
§340 Same, 1010-17.

(Which way soever Men refer it)
Much like thy Riddle Samson in one Day
Or sev'n, though one should musing sit.

Id: v: 1010.

[341] Is it for that such outward Ornament
Was lavish'd on their Sex, that inward Gifts
Were left for Haste unfinished, judgment scant,
Capacity not rais'd to apprehend
Or value what is best
In Choice, but oftest to affect the Wrong?
Or was too much of Self-Love mix'd,
Of Constancy no Root infix'd,
That either they love Nothing, or not long?
   Whate'er it be to wisest Men & best
Seeming at first all-heav'nly under Virgin Vail.
Soft, modest, meek, demure,
Once join'd, the contrary she proves, a Thorn
Intestine, far within defensive Arms
A cleaving Mischeif, in his Way to Virtue
Adverse & turbulent, or by her Charms
Draws him away inslav'd
With Dotage, & his Sense deprav'd
To Folly & shameful Deeds which Ruin ends.
What Pilot so expert but needs must wreck,
Imbark'd with such a Steersmate at the Helm?
   Favour'd of Heav'n who finds
One virtuous rarely found,
That in domestic Good combines:
Happy that House! his Way to Peace is smoo[th]
But Virtue which breaks through all Opposition
And all Temptations can remove,
Most shines, & most is acceptable above.
   Therefore God's universal Law
Gave to Man despotic Power
Over his Female in due Awe,
Nor from that Right to part an Hour,
Smile she or lour:
So shall he least Confusion draw

§341 Same, 1025-60.
§341.17 *away*] Milton: *awry*.
§341.36 *no*] Milton: *not*.

On his whole Life, no sway'd
By female Usurpation, or dismay'd.
Id: v: 1025.

[342]   ——Who but rather turns
To heav'n's broad fire his unconstrained view,
Than to the glimmering of a waxen flame?
Who that, from Alpine heights his lab'ring eye
Shoots round the wide horizon to survey
The Nile or Ganges roll his wasteful tide
Thro' mountains, plains, thro' empires black with shade
And continents of sand; will turn his gaze
To mark the windings of a scanty rill
That murmurs at his feet? the high born soul
Disdains to rest her heav'n aspiring wing
Beneath it's native quarry.
Pleasures of Imagn. B. 1. v. 174.

[343] Does beauty ever deign to dwell where health
And active use are strangers? is her charm
Confess'd in ought, whose most peculiar ends
Are lame and fruitless? or did nature mean
This awful stamp the herald of a lie?
To hide the shame of discord and disease,
And catch with fair hypocrisy the heart
Of idle faith?
id. B. 1. v. 350.

[344] Oh! blest of heaven, whom not the languid songs
Of luxury, the syren! not the bribes
Of sordid wealth, nor all the gaudy spoils

    §§342-5 These entries from Mark Akenside's long poem, *The Pleasures of Imagination* (1744), were made late in the 1760s. For further information on Akenside, see the Register of Authors.
    §342 *Pleasures of Imagination*, I: 174-85. According to the Argument, this passage belongs to the section on "The pleasure from greatness."
    §342.3 *heights*] *Ms.* Inserted above the line with a caret.
    §343 *Pleasures of Imagination*, I: 350-7. According to the Argument, this passage belongs to the section on "Pleasures from beauty."
    §344 *Pleasures of Imagination*, III: 568-633; lines 582-92 and 610-12 are omitted. This passage forms the conclusion of the poem in its original version (the one commonplaced here) and is intended, according to the Argument, to be "an account of the natural and moral advantages resulting from a sensible and well-form'd imagination."

Of pageant honor can seduce to leave
Those ever blooming sweets, which from the store
Of nature fair imagination culls
To charm th' inliven'd soul! What tho' not all
Of mortal offspring can attain the heights
Of envied life; tho' only few possess
Patrician treasures or imperial state;
Yet nature's care, to all her children just,
With richer treasures and an ampler state
Endows at large whatever happy man
Will deign to use them.——
———Not a breeze
Flies o'er the meadow, not a cloud imbibes
The setting sun's effulgence, not a strain
From all the tenants of the warbling shade
Ascends, but whence his bosom can partake
Fresh pleasure unreprov'd.   nor thence partakes
Fresh pleasure only: for th'attentive mind,
By this harmonious action on her pow'rs
Becomes herself harmonious: wont so long
In outward things to meditate the charm
Of sacred order, soon she seeks at home
To find a kindred order, to exert
Within herself this elegance of love,
This fair inspired delight: her temper'd pow'rs
Refine at length, and every passion wears
A chaster, milder, more attractive mien.
But if to ampler prospects——
———the mind
Exalt her daring eye, then mightier far
Will be the change, and nobler. Would the forms
Of servile custom cramp her gen'rous pow'rs?
Would sordid policies, the barb'rous growth
Of ignorance and rapine bow her down
To tame pursuits, to indolence and fear?
Lo! she appeals to nature, to the winds
And rolling waves, the sun's unwearied course,
The elements and seasons: all declare
For what th'eternal maker has ordain'd
The pow'rs of man: we feel within ourselves
His energy divine: he tells the heart
He meant, he made us to behold and love

What he beholds and loves. The gen'ral orb
Of life and being; to be great like him
Beneficent and active. Thus the men
Whom nature's works can charm, with God himself
Hold converse; grow familiar day by day,
With his conceptions; act upon his plan;
And form to his the relish of their souls.
Pl. of Imagn. B. 3. v. 568.

[345]   ——On my strain
Perhaps ev'n now, some cold fastidious judge
Casts a disdainful eye; and calls my toil,
And calls the love and beauty which I sing
The dream of folly. Thou grave censor! say,
Is beauty then a dream, because the glooms
Of dulness hang too heavy on thy sense
To let her shine upon thee?
id. v. 443.

[346] Te flagrantis atrox hora Caniculæ
Nescit tangere: tu frigus amabile
Fessis vomere tauris
Præbes, et pecori vago.
Fies nobilium tu quoque fontium.
Hor. L. 3. ode. 13.

[347] Τροχὸς ἅρματος γαρ οἷα
Βιοτος τρεχει κυλιϛθεις.
Ολιγη δε κειϛομεϛθα
Κονις, οϛτεων λυθεντων.
Anac. od. 4.

§345 *Pleasures of Imagination*, III: 443-50. The section of the poem from which this passage was taken is described in the Argument as "The benevolent order of the world illustrated in the arbitrary connection of these pleasures with the objects which excite them."

§346 Translation: Thee the fierce season of the blazing dog-star cannot touch; to bullocks wearied of the ploughshare and to the roaming flock thou dost offer gracious coolness. Thou, too, shalt be numbered among the far-famed fountains. . . .

Horace, "To the Fountain Bandusia," *Odes* III. 13. 9-13. Translation: Loeb (see §167-78n).   For other entries from Horace, see §§167-78.

§§347-8 These entries are from the *Anacreontea*, a collection of verses written in imitation of the meter and characteristic manner of the sixth-century Greek poet Anacreon, which, in TJ's day, were thought to have been by Anac-

[348] Φθονον ουκ οιδ᾽ εμον ητορ,
Φθονον ου δειδια δηκτην·
Φιλολοιδοροιο γλωττης
Φευγω 6ελεμνα κουφα.

Anacr. ode. 42.

[349] ——Now from the town
Buried in smoke, and sleep, and noisome damps,
Oft let me wander o'er the dewy fields
Where freshness breathes, and dash the trembling drops
From the bent bush, as thro' the verdant maze
Of sweet-brier hedges I pursue my walk;
Or taste the smell of daisy; or ascend
Some eminence,——
And see the country far diffus'd around,

---

reon himself. The translations are taken from Thomas Moore, *Odes of Anacreon, Translated into English Verse* (London, 1800). TJ later knew and admired the poetry of Moore, whose translations of Anacreon he procured for his library. (See Sowerby 4406.) The numbering of poems and verses in the notes follows the Loeb Classical Library edition: J. E. Edmund, ed. and trans., *Elegy and Iambus*, 2 vols. (New York, 1931). It is indicative of the way TJ selected material for his commonplace book that these extracts from the *Anacreontea*, so poignantly philosophical in isolation, are from revelrous drinking songs that celebrate wine and amorous dalliance as a means to banish care.

§347 Translation:

Swift as the wheels that kindling roll,
Our life is hurrying to the goal:
A scanty dust, to feed the wind,
Is all the trace 'twill leave behind.

Anacreontea 32. 7-10. Late in life TJ used these verses in the document in which he left his self-composed epitaph. Before setting down the famous inscription for his tombstone, he wrote: "could the dead feel any interest in Monuments or other remembrances of them, when as Anacreon says Ολιγη δε κειςομεσθα / Κονις, οςτεων λυθεντων / the following would be to my Manes the most gratifying" (TJ Papers, DLC).

§348 Translation:

My soul to festive feelings true,
One pang of envy never knew;
And little has it learn'd to dread
The gall that Envy's tongue can shed.

Anacreontea 42. 9-12.

§349 James Thomson, "Spring," *The Seasons*, 101-13. Unlike the passages from "Spring" entered earlier (§§283-5), these lines were copied from one of the later editions of *The Seasons*, incorporating changes made after 1738.

§349.7 daisy] Thomson: *dairy*.

§349.8 TJ has eliminated the last part of this line, which in its entirety reads: *Some eminence, Augusta, in thy plains,*

One boundless blush, one white-empurpled show'r
Of mingling blossoms; where the raptur'd eye
Hurries from joy to joy, and, hid beneath
The fair profusion, yellow Autumn spies.
                    Thompson's Spring. 101.

[350] Let us, Amanda, timely wise,
      Improve the hour that swiftly flies
      And, in soft raptures, waste the day
      Among the shades of Endermay.

      For soon the winter of the year
      And age, life's winter, will appear:
      At this, thy living bloom must fade;
      As that will strip the verdant shade,
      Our taste of pleasure then is o'er;
      The feather'd songsters love no more:
      And when they droop and we decay
      [Adieu the shades of Endermay!   Mallet's poems]

[351] O scap'd from life! O safe on that calm shore,
      Where sin, and pain, and passion are no more!
                          Mallet's Poems.

[352] In lonely walks and awful cells,
      Secluded from the light and vain,
      The cherub peace with virtue dwells
      And solitude and silence reign.

 §§350-1, 353-5 These passages by David Mallet were probably copied from *The Works of Mallet* (London, 1743), the edition from which TJ had, about 10 years earlier, copied extracts from Mallet's *Eurydice* (§§316-18) and which was to find a place in his great library. He probably recommended the expanded edition of 1759 to Robert Skipwith in 1771 because it was the most readily obtainable (see Mallet in Register of Authors). Page numbers refer to the 1743 edition.

 §350 "Song. To a Scotch Tune, *The Birks of Endermay*," lines 5-16, p. 205-6.

 §350.2 *Improve the hour that swiftly flies*] Mallet: *Like them improve the hour that flys;* This line was apparently altered because, in omitting the first four lines of the poem, the antecedent of "them" ("tuneful birds") had been eliminated.

 §351 "Epitaph on a Young Lady," lines 5-6, p. 210.

 §352 This is the first "Air" in *The Nun: A Cantata* by Edward Moore. TJ's text differs markedly from that printed in Moore's *Poems, Fables, and Plays* (London, 1756), p. 201, as noted below.

 §352.1 *lonely*] *Poems, Fables, and Plays*: hallow'd.

 §352.3 *cherub peace*] *Poems, Fables, and Plays*: chaste-ey'd maid.

The babbler's voice is heard not here
To heav'n the sacred pile belongs
Each wall returns the whisper'd pray'r,
And echoes but to holy songs.
                    Song by Moore.

[353] Hail midnight shades! hail venerable dome!
By age more venerable; sacred shore,
Beyond time's troubled sea, where never wave,
Where never wind of passion or of guilt,
Or suffering, or of sorrow, shall invade
The calm, sound night of those who rest below.
The weary are at peace: the small and great,
Life's voiage ended, meet and mingle here.
Here sleeps the prisoner safe, nor feels his chain,
Nor hears th'oppressor's voice. The poor and old,
With all the sons of mourning, fearless now
Of want or woe, find unalarm'd repose.
Proud greatness too, the tyranny of power,
The grace of beauty, and the force of youth,
And name and place, are here, for ever lost!
                    Mallet's Excursion.

[354] Thyrsis—tis he! the wisest and the best!
Lamented shade! whom ev'ry gift of heav'n
Profusely blest: all learning was his own.
Pleasing his speech, by nature taught to flow,
Persuasive sense and strong, sincere and clear.
His manners greatly plain; a noble grace

§352.5 *babbler's*] *Poems, Fables, and Plays*: *wanton's*.
§353 Mallet, "The Excursion," 245.
§354 "The Excursion," 245-6. This passage, entered late in the 1760s, was
later adapted by TJ in drafting possible inscriptions for the tomb of his
brother-in-law and dearest friend, Dabney Carr, who died in 1773. This version, which was written soon after Carr's death, appears on a leaf of what seems
to have been an early notebook, possibly a precursor of TJ's Garden Book. It
is preserved in the Manuscript Department, ViU, and reads as follows:

Lamented shade [whom every] gift of heav'n
Profusely blest: a temper winning mild;
Nor pity softer, nor was truth more bright.
Constant in doing well, he neither sought
Nor shunn'd applause. [No] bashful merit sigh'd
Near him neglected: sympathizing he
Wip'd off the tear from Sorrow's clouded eye
With kindly hand and taught her heart to smile.

Self-taught, beyond the reach of mimic art,
Adorn'd him: his calm temper winning mild;
Nor Pity softer, nor was truth more bright.
Constant in doing well, he neither sought
Nor shun'd applause. No bashful merit sigh'd
Near him neglected: sympathizing he
Wip'd off the tear from Sorrow's clouded eye
With kindly hand, and taught her heart to smi[le.]
                    Mallet's Excursion

[355]   ——a place of tombs
Waste, desolate, where Ruin dreary dwells,
Brooding o'er sightless sculls and crumbling bones.
Ghastful he sits, and eyes with stedfast glare
                    the falling roof,
The time-shook arch, the column grey with moss,
The leaning wall, the sculptur'd stone defac'd.
                    Mallet's Excursion.

[356] I have turn'd o'er the catalogue of woes,
Which sting the heart of man, and find none equal;
It is the Hydra of calamities;
The seven fold death: the jealous are the damn'd.
O jealousy, each other passion's calm
To thee, thou conflagration of the soul!
Thou king of torments! thou grand counterpoise
For all the transports beauty can inspire!
                    Young's Revenge. act. 2.

[357] What is the world?—thy school, O misery!
Our only lesson is to learn to suffer;
And he who knows not that, was born for nothing.

§355 "The Excursion," 244. TJ has omitted a line and a half occurring parenthetically between *stedfast glare* and *the falling roof*:

> *(Sad trophies of his power, where ivy twines*
> *Its fatal green around)*

§§356-65 TJ entered these excerpts from two plays by Edward Young, the
author of *Night-Thoughts* (§§247-67, 366), in a handwriting style distinctive
to the late 1760s. *The Revenge: A Tragedy* was first performed in 1721; *The
Brothers: A Tragedy* was written in the 1720s but not performed until 1753.
Volume and page numbers refer to *The Works of the Author of Night-Thoughts*,
4 vols. (London, 1757).
§356 *The Revenge, Works*, II, 126.
§357 Same, 133-4.

Tho' deep my pangs, and heavy at my heart,
My comfort is, each moment takes away
A grain at least from the dead load that's on me
And gives a nearer prospect of the grave.
But put it most severely—should I live —
Live long—alas! there is no length in time;
Not in thy time, O man! what's fourscore years?
Nay, what indeed the age of time itself,
Since cut from out eternity's wide round?
Young's Revenge. act. 2.

[358] This hand is mine. O what a hand is here!
So soft, souls sink into it, and are lost.
Young's Revenge act. 4.

[359] Why did I leave my tender father's wing,
And venture into love? that maid that loves,
Goes out to sea upon a shatter'd plank.
And puts her trust in miracles for safety.
Id. Ib.

[360] This vast and solid earth, that blazing sun,
Those skies thro' which it rolls, must all have end.
What then is man? the smallest part of nothing.
Day buries day; month, month; and year the year:
Our life is but a chain of many death.
Can then death's self be fear'd? our life much rather;
Life is the desart, life the solitude;
Death joins us to the great majority;
Tis to be born to Platos and to Cæsars;
Tis to be great for ever;
Tis pleasure, tis ambition, then, to die.
Id. Ib.

[361] I am no gewgaw, for the throng to gaze at:
Some are design'd by nature but for shew;
The tinsel and the feather of mankind.
Young's Brothers. act. 1.

§358 Same, 164.
§359 Same, 165.
§360 Same, 166.
§360.5 *death*] *Works*: *deaths*.
§361 *The Brothers*, *Works*, II, 208.

[362]   We run our fates together; you deserve
        And she can judge; proceed we then like friends,
        And he who gains the heart, and gains it fairly
        Let him enjoy his gen'rous rival's too.
                       Id. Ib.

[363]   The days of life are sisters; all alike;
        None just the same; which serves to fool us on
        Thro' blasted hopes, with change of fallacy;
        While joy is, like tomorrow, still to come;
        Nor ends the fruitless chace but in the grave.
                       Id. Ib.

[364]   Thrice happy they, who sleep in humble life,
        Beneath the storm ambition blows, 'tis meet
        The great should have the fame of happiness;
        The consolation of a little envy;
        Tis all their pay for those superior cares,
        Those pangs of heart their vassals ne'er can feel.
                       Id. Ib.

[365]   How vain all outward effort to supply
        The soul with joy! the noontide sun is dark,
        And music discord, when the heart is low.
                     Id. act. 2.

[366]   Fate! drop the curtain; I can lose no more!
                    Young's Night Thoughts.

[367]   Jepthes.   'O grata sortis infimæ securitas!
                  Felice natum sidere illum existimo,
                  Procul tumultu qui remotus exigit
                  Ignotus ævum tuta per silentia.

§362 Same, 210.
§362.3 *the heart*] *Works: her heart.*
§363 *The Brothers, Works*, II: 211.
§364 Same, 213-14.
§365 Same, 227.
  §366 *Night-Thoughts*, "Night the First. On Life, Death, and Immortality,"
Works (1757), III, 4.
  §§367-72 These entries are taken from *Jephtes, sive Votum* (*Jephtha, or The
Vow*), a tragedy in Latin verse by the Scottish humanist, George Buchanan
(1506-1582), based on the biblical account of Jephtha, the commander of the
army of Israel against the Ammonites (*Judges* 11:29-40). Having promised to

Symmachus. At ego beatum potius illum duxero,
            Cui vera virtus peperit aeternum decus:
            Quem de tenebris erutum popularibus
            Splendore, vulgo et separatum a deside,
            Gloria futuris merita seclis consecrat.
            At qui sepori deditus et ignaviae est,
            Et vitam inertem pecudis insta transigit,
            Nil interesse opinor, an sit mortuus,
            An morte vitam obscuriorem duxerit,
            Quum par utrumque supprimat silentium.
            . . . .

Jephthes. Praeclara dictu res honor, victoria,
            Decus, trimumphus, parta bello gloria:
            At quae videntur fronte prima suavia,
            Eadem intuere propius, et intelliges
            Condita fellis acri amaritudine.
            Fortuna nulli sic refulsit prospera,
            Adversa ut illam lance non penset pari:
            Tristia secundis, et secunda tristibus
            Vicissitudo acerba sortis temperat.
            Buchanani Jephthes.

---

make a burnt offering of the first thing that emerges from his house if victorious, Jephtha is obliged to sacrifice his own daughter. Buchanan's version is patterned after classical tragedy and expands the story to include additional characters, such as Symmachus, and a Chorus. TJ had on his desiderata list of paintings to acquire in Europe a representation of "Jephtha meeting his daughter." See Fiske Kimball, "TJ and the Arts," American Philosophical Society, *Proceedings*, LVII (1943), 242. For more information on Buchanan, see Register of Authors. Translations: adapted from Chinard.

§367 Translation: *Jephtha*: Oh happy security of a modest condition. He is happy indeed who far from disturbances spends his years unknown in a secure obscurity.

Symmachus: But I would rather consider him happy whose virtue has begotten an eternal honor, whom taken from the obscurity of the ordinary people and freed of vulgar indolency a well deserved glory consecrates in centuries to come. But the man who gives himself up to slumbering a worthless existence and spends an inert life like an animal, there is no difference in my opinion whether he is dead or lives a life more obscure than death, since in both cases he is buried under the same oblivion. . . .

Jephtha: Honor, victory, marvelous words to tell, as well as distinction, triumph and glory acquired in war. But these things which in appearance are so sweet, if you examine them more exactly conceal in themselves the bitterness of gall. Has ever good fortune shone so constantly for any man that bad fortune has not compensated in on an even scale. The cruel changes of fate temper unhappiness with happy things and happiness and sadness.

Buchanan, *Jephtes*.

§367.10 *sepori*] Buchanan: *sopori*. In forming his letters, TJ may have inadvertently caused the *o* to resemble an *e*.

[368] Acerba laetis sors utrinque miscuit:
　　　Sed illa certe existimanda est optima,
　　　Quæ multa paucis laeta condit tristibus.
　　　　　　　　　　Id. Ib.

[369] Heu mutatio subitæ sortis!
　　　Ut perpetua serie laetum
　　　Nil mortalibus usque relictum est!
　　　　　　　　　　Id. Ib.

[370] Consilia dubiis remedium rebus ferunt.
　　　Qui consulit, quum nullus auxilio est locus,
　　　Addit miseriis sponte stultitiam suis.
　　　　　　　　　　Id. Ib.

[371] Auctore magno desipere, pene sapere est.
　　　　　　　　　　Id. Ib.

[372] Hæc nimirum est addita nostrae
　　　Vitae sors, ut tristia laetis
　　　Vicibus subeant, tenebrae ut soli,
　　　Ut veri aspera bruma tepenti.
　　　Nulla est adeo pura voluptas,
　　　Quam non tetro felle dolores
　　　Vitient: levitas perfida sortis
　　　Vice saeva res hominum miscet.
　　　　　　　　　　Id. Ib.

　　§368 Translation: Fate has always mingled sadness with joy and this fate forsooth is to be considered the best of all when only a few sad things are hidden under many happy ones.
　　Same.
　　§369 Translation: Alas, sudden change of fortune. How in the interrupted series of events absolutely nothing pleasant has been left to the mortals.
　　Same.
　　§370 Translation: Advice brings remedy to things which are in doubt. But he who seeks advice when there is no possibility of help, adds only stupidity to his misery.
　　Same.
　　§371 Translation: To act foolishly on good authority is hardly to be sensible.
　　Same.
　　§372 Translation: Such is the fortune of our life that unhappy things succeed happy ones as darkness follows daylight and rough weather the pleasant spring. There is no pure pleasure that pains do not spoil with their bitter gall; the perfid inconstancy of fortune introduces terrible turns in the lives of men.
　　Same; scene following the one above.

[373] Fortuna fortes metuit; ignavos premit.
Senecae Medea. 159.

[374] Qui statuit aliquid parte inaudita altera,
Aequum licet statuerit, haud aequus fuit.
Id. Ib. 199.

[375] Ut flos in septis secretis nascitur hortis
Ignotus pecori, nullo contusus aratro.
Quem mulcent aurae, firmat sol, educat imber,
Multi illum pueri, multae cupiere puellae.
Idem, cum tenui carptus defloruit ungui,
Nulli illum pueri, nullae cupiere puellae.
Sic virgo, dum intacta manet, dum cara suis: sed
Cum castum amisit, polluto corpore, florem,
Nec pueris jucunda manet, nec cara puellis.

[376] Yet shall thy grave with rising flow'rs be drest,
And the green turf lie lightly on thy breast:
There shall the morn her earliest tears bestow,

§373-4 These are the only two entries from Seneca in the LCB. Translations
are from the Loeb Classical Library edition: Frank Justus Miller, ed. and
trans., *Seneca's Tragedies*, 2 vols. (New York, 1927). See Seneca in the Register of Authors.

§373 Translation: Fortune fears the brave, the cowardly overwhelms.
Seneca, *Medea*, 159.

§374 Translation: He who has judged aught, with the other side unheard,
may have judged righteously, but was himself unrighteous.
Same, 199-200.

§375 Translation: As a flower springs up secretly in a fenced garden, unknown to the cattle, torn up by no plough, which the winds caress, the sun
strengthens, the shower draws forth, many boys, many girls, desire it; when
the same flower fades, nipped by a sharp nail, no boys, no girls, desire it; so a
maiden, whilst she remains untouched, so long she is dear to her own; when
she has lost her chaste flower with sullied body, she remains neither lovely to
boys nor dear to girls.
Catullus 62. 39-47. The translation is from Francis Warre Cornish, trans.,
The Poems of Gaius Valerius Catullus (Cambridge, 1904).

§376 Alexander Pope, "Elegy to the Memory of an Unfortunate Lady," 63-
74. TJ was almost certainly using the edition of Pope's works edited by William Warburton (1751). In manuscript notes on possible inscriptions for the
tomb of his dearest friend, Dabney Carr, written in 1773, TJ included the first
six lines of this passage, probably copied from his Commonplace Book:

send for a plate of copper to be nailed on the tree at the foot
of his grave with this inscription

Still shall thy grave with rising flow'rs be dresss'd
And the green turf lie lightly on thy breast:

There the first roses of the year shall blow;
While Angels with their silver wings o'ershade
The ground now sacred by thy reliques made.
So peaceful rests without a stone, a name,
What once had beauty, titles, wealth and fame.
How lov'd, how honour'd once, avails thee not,
To whom related, or by whom begot;
A heap of dust alone remains of thee,
Tis all thou art, and all the proud shall be!

Pope. elegy. v. 63.

[377]   Adieu, ye vales, ye mountains, streams and groves.
Adieu ye shepherds' rural lays and loves;
Adieu, my flocks; farewell, ye sylvan crew;
Daphne, farewell; and all the world adieu!

Pope. Past. 4. v. 89.

[378]   Beatus ille, qui procul negotiis
    Ut prisca gens mortalium
Paterna rura bobus exercet suis,
    Solutus omni foenore:
Forumque vitat, et superba civium
    Potentiorum limina.
Libet jacere modo sub antiqua ilice
    Modo in tenaci gramine:

There shall the morn her earliest tears bestow,
There the first roses of the year shall blow:
While angels with their silver wings o'ershade
The ground now sacred by thy reliques made. (ViU)

For another entry relating to the death of Dabney Carr, see §354n.

§377 Alexander Pope, "Winter. The Fourth Pastoral, or Daphne," 89-92, the last four lines of the fourth and final pastoral. Pope's note reads: "These four last lines allude to the several subjects of the four Pastorals, and to the several scenes of them, particularized before in each." Warburton edition, I, 75

§378 Translation: Happy the man who, far away from business cares, like the pristine race of mortals, works his ancestral acres with his steers, from all money-lending free; he avoids the Forum and proud thresholds of more powerful citizens. 'Tis pleasant, now to lie beneath some ancient ilex-tree, now on the matted turf. Meanwhile the rills glide between their high banks; birds warble in the woods; the fountains splash with their flowing waters, a sound to invite soft slumbers. But when the wintry season of thundering Jove brings rains and snow, with his pack of hounds one either drives fierce boars from here and there into the waiting toils, or on polished pole stretches wide-meshed nets, a snare for greedy thrushes. But if a modest wife shall do her part in tending home and children dear, piling high the sacred hearth with seasoned

Labuntur altis interim rivis aquae;
  Queruntur in silvis aves;
Fontesque lymphis obstrepunt manantibus,
  Somnos quod invitet leves.
At cum tonantis annus hibernus Jovis
  Imbres nivesque comparat
Aut trudit acres hinc et hinc multa cane
  Apros in obstantes plagas;
Aut amite levi rara tendit retia,
  Turdis edacibus dolos;
Quod si pudica mulier in partem juvans
  Domum et dulces liberos,
Sacrum vetustis exstruat lignis focum
  Lassi sub adventum viri,
Claudensque textis cratibus laetum pecus,
  Distenta siccet ubera;
Et horna dulci vina promens dolio,
  Dapes inemptas adparet.
Has inter epulas, ut juvat pastas oves
  Videre properantes domum!
Videre fessos vomerem inversum boves
  Collo trahentes languido;
Positosque vernas, ditis examen domus,
  Circum renidentes lares!
Hor. epod. 2.

---

firewood against the coming of her weary husband, penning the frisking flock
in wattled fold, draining their swelling udders, and drawing forth this year's
sweet vintage from the jar, prepare an unbought meal, amid such feasts, what
joy to see the sheep hurrying homeward from pasture, to see the wearied oxen
dragging along the upturned ploughshare on their tired necks, and the home-
bred slaves, troop of a wealthy house, ranged around the gleaming Lares!

Horace, *Epodes* 2. 1-4, 7-8, 23-34, 39-40, 43-8, 61-6. TJ condensed a poem
of 70 lines to 32 and eliminated the ironic ending, in which it is revealed that
these are the words of a money-lender whose enchantment with the country
life is shortlived. In his pocket Memorandum Book for 1771, TJ quoted from
these lines in projecting a landscape design for the north spring at Monticello:

near the spring also inscribe on stone, or a metal plate fastened to a tree,
these lines: 'Beatus ille qui procul negotiis, Ut prisca gens mortalium, Paterna rura bobus exercet suis, solutus omni foenore; Forumque vitat et
superba civium Potentiorum limina. Liget jacere modo sub antiqua ilice,
modo in tenaci gramine: Labuntur altis interim ripis aquae; Queruntur in
silvis aves; Fontesque lymphis obstrepunt manantibus, somnos quod invitet leves.' (*Garden Book*, 26)

[379] An unfrequented vale, o'ergrown with trees;
Mossy and old, within whose lonesome shade
Ravens and birds ill-omen'd only dwell:
No sound to break the silence, but a brook,
That bubbling, winds among the weeds: no mark
Of any human shape that had been there,
Unless a skeleton of some poor wretch,
Who had long since, like me by love undone,
Sought that sad place out, to despair and die in.
Rowe's Fair penitent.

[380] Be juster heaven; such virtue punish'd thus,
Will make us think that Chance rules all above,
And shuffles with a random hand, the lots
Which man is forc'd to draw—

[381] The cheif like a whale of ocean, whom all his billows follow,
poured valor forth as a stream, rolling his might along the
shore.
Fingal. B. 1.

§379 Nicholas Rowe, *The Fair Penitent*, II: 21-9. Line numbers supplied
from Goldstein edition (see §307n). While some earlier entries from the
Rowe's *Fair Penitient* (§§307-8) seem to have been taken from the play itself,
TJ may have taken this passage, along with the one from Dryden's *All for Love*
which follows it, from *Thesaurus Dramaticus*, where it appears under the heading "Despair." (See §§286-96n.) TJ sketched a plan for a graveyard at Monticello in his pocket Memorandum Book for 1771, in which he adapted this
passage from Rowe to suggest the atmosphere he wanted to create by means of
a landscape design:

> choose out for a Burying place some unfrequented vale in the park, where
> is 'no sound to break the stillness but a brook, that bubbling winds among
> the weeds; no mark of any human shape that had been there, unless the
> skelton of some poor wretch, Who sought that place out to despair and die
> in.' let it be among antient and venerable oaks; intersperse some gloomy
> evergreens. (*Garden Book*, 25)

§380 John Dryden, *All for Love*, V: 1, 1-4. First produced in 1677, *All for
Love* was based on the story of Mark Antony and Cleopatra and, while not a
re-writing of Shakespeare's play, was proclaimed by the author as "Written in
Imitation of *Shakespeare's* Stile." (See the California edition, Maximillian E.
Novak, George R. Guffey, and Alan Roper, eds., *The Works of John Dryden*
[Berkeley, 1984], XIII.) TJ may have taken this passage, like the one from
Rowe which precedes it, from *Thesaurus Dramaticus*, where it appears under
the heading "Fate." (See §§286-96n.)

§§381-9, 399-403 These 14 entries are from the poetry of Ossian, which
was put forth in the 1760s as the work of an ancient Celtic bard but was ac-

[382] *As two dark streams from high rocks meet, and mix and roar on the plain; loud, rough, and dark in battle me[et] Lochlin and Innis-fail: †chief mixed his strokes with chief, and man with man; steel clanging sounded on steel, helmets

---

tually that of Scottish writer James Macpherson (1736-1796). For information on Macpherson, see the Register of Authors. Comparison of TJ's entries with the variorum edition of Ossian makes it clear that TJ's copy-text for these entries was Macpherson's second volume of Ossianic material, *Fingal, An Ancient Epic Poem* (1762). See Otto L. Jiriczek, ed., *James Macpherson's Ossian: Faksimile-Newdruck der Erstausgabe von 1762/63 mit Belgleitband: Die Varianten*, 3 vols. (Heidelberg, 1940). The page references given below correspond both to the 1762 *Fingal* and to Volume I of the Jiriczek edition, which reproduces the 1762 text in facsimile.

§381 *Fingal*, Book I, p. 10.

§382 Translations:

> *As when rivers in winter spate running down from the mountains
> throw together at the meeting of streams the weight of their water
> out of the great springs behind in the hollow stream-bed,
> and far away in the mountains the shepherd hears their thunder;
> such, from the coming together of men, was the shock and the shouting.

> †they dashed their shields together and their spears, and the strength
> of armoured men in bronze, and the shields massive in the middle
> clashed against each other, and the sound grew huge of the fighting.

> locking spear by spear, shield against shield at the base, so buckler
> leaned on buckler, helmet on helmet, man against man

> . . . foot fast with foot, and man massed with man.

> Then shield thrusts against shield, boss upon boss, threatening sword on
>   sword, foot against foot and lance on lance.

Fingal, Book I, p. 12-13. The asterisk (*) and dagger (†) indicate footnoted passages from classical epic poetry that exemplify poetic devices similar to those employed in Ossian. TJ is here loosely following the lead of Macpherson, who frequently cites in footnotes Ossianic parallels to Homer, Virgil, Milton, and others.

TJ's first footnote (*), a passage from Homer, comes at a point in the text where Macpherson, in his footnote, quotes not the Greek but the English rendering of Pope. TJ's quotation of the Greek seems to have been prompted by Macpherson's footnote to an earlier passage, part of which TJ copied out as §381. To further complicate this confusing state of affairs, Macpherson's footnote quotes only the first three lines of the Greek text; the concluding two are added by TJ (*Iliad* 4. 452-6).

The second and third passages from Homer (*Iliad* 4. 447-9, *Iliad* 13. 130-1), together with the passages from Virgil (*Aeneid* 10. 361) and Statius (*Thebiad*, 8: 398-9), constitute TJ's second footnote (†). Only the Statius is suggested by Macpherson's footnote to this passage (p. 13); TJ apparently found the Virgil and the second of the two passages from Homer on his own. Translations: *Iliad* (see §§155-62n); *Aeneid* (see §184n); Statius, J. H. Mozley, ed. and trans., *Statius*, 2 vols. (New York, 1928).

§382.5 *cleft on high*;] *Ms.* TJ originally abridged this passage by replacing the period in the copy-text after *high* with semicolon, skipping three and a half sentences, and continuing: *as the last peel of the thunder of heaven.* He then struck this out and copied the passage as shown.

are cleft on high; blood bursts and smokes around. Strings murmur on the polished yews. Darts rush along the sky[.] spears fall like the circles of light that gild the stormy face of the night. As the troubled noise of the ocean when roll the waves on high; as the last peal of the thunder of heaven, such is the noise of the battle. Tho' Corm[ac's] hundred bards were there to give the war to song; feeb[le] were the voices of a hundred bards to send the deaths [to] future times. For many were the falls of the heroes[;] and wide poured the blood of the valiant.

Fingal B. 1.

*Ὣς δ' οτε χειμαρροι ποταμοι κατ' ορεϛφι ῥεοντες
Εϛ μιϛγαγκειαν ϛυμβαλλετον οβριμον ὑδωρ.
Κρουνων εκ μεγαλων, κοιλης εντοϛθε χαραδρης,
Των δε τε τηλοϛε δουπον εν ουρεϛι εκλυε ποιμην·
Ὡϛ των μιϛγομενων γενετο ιαχη τε φοβος τε.

Iliad. 4. 452

†Συν ῥ' εϐαλον ῥινους, ϛυν δ' εγχεα, και μενε' ανδρων
Χαλκεοθωρηκων· αταρ αϛπιδες ομφαλοεϛϛαι
Επληντ' αλληληϛι· πολυς δ' ορυμαμγδος ορωρει.

Iliad. 4. 447

Φραξαντες δορυ δουρι, ϛακος ϛακει προθελυμνω·
Αϛπις αρ' αϛπιδ' ερειδε, κορυς κορυν, ανερα δ' ανηρ.

[Iliad 13. 130]

——haeret pede pes, densusque viro vir.

Æneid. 9. 361.

Jam clypeus clypeis, umbone repellitur umbo,
Ense minax ensis, pede pes, et cuspide cuspis.

Statius.

[383] As roll a thousand waves to the rocks, so Swaran's host came on: as meets a rock a thousand waves, so Inis-fail met Swaran.

Fingal. B. 1.

§383 *Fingal*, Book I, p. 14. Cf. TJ's dramatic description of the coming together of the Shenandoah and Potomac rivers, written about 10 years after this was entered. See *Notes on Virginia*, p. 19.

[384] He had seen her like a beam of light that meets the sons of the cave when they revisit the feilds of the sun, and bend their aching eyes.

Fingal.

[385] The vanquished, if brave, are renowned; they are like the sun [i]n a cloud when he hides his face in the south, but looks again on [t]he hills of grass.

Fingal B. 6.

[386] Oh that I could forget my friends till my footsteps cease to be [s]een! till I come among them with joy! and lay my aged limbs [i]n the narrow house!

Ossian's Conlath and Cuthona.

[387] The dark and narrow house—the maid of the tearful eye. The son of songs, Carril of other times.—Grudar the youth of her secret soul.— he was the stolen sigh of her soul.—said Connal's voice of wisdom.—said the mouth of the song.— The chief of the little soul.—the ages of old, and the days of other yea[rs]

Ossian. passim.

[388] Raise the song of mourning, O bards, over the land of strangers. they have but fallen before us: for one day we must fall. Why dost thou build the hall, son of the winged days? Thou lookest from thy towers to day; yet a few years, and the blast of the desart comes; it houls in thy empty court, and whistles round thy half-worn sheild. and let the blast of the desart come! we shall be renowned in our day. the mark of my ar[m] shall be in the battle, and my name in the song of bards. raise the song; send round the shell; and let joy be

§384 *Fingal*, Book VI, p. 76-7.
§385 Same, p. 80.
§386 *Conlath and Cuthona*, p. 126. These are the concluding lines of the poem.
§387 This entry is a collection of phrases from Ossian, concentrated for the most part in *Fingal*, Book II: *The dark and narrow house*, p. 23; *the maid of the tearful eye*, p. 9; *The son of songs*, p. 72; *Grudar the youth of her secret soul*, p.17; *Carril of other times*, p. 32; *he was the stolen sigh of her soul*, p. 37; *said Connal's voice of wisdom*, p. 24; *said the mouth of the song*, p. 27; *the chief of the little soul*, p. 29; *the ages of old, the days of other years*, p. 32.
§388 *Carthon*, p. 132.

heard [in] my hall. when thou, Sun of heaven, shalt fail! if thou sha[lt] fail, thou mighty light! if thy brightness is for a season, [like] Fingal, our fame shall survive thy beams. such was the song of Fingal, in the day of his joy.

Ossian's Carthon.

[389]   O thou that rollest above, round as the sheild of my father[s!] whence are thy beams, o sun! thy everlasting light? thou comest forth in thy awful beauty and the stars hide themselves in the sky; the moon, cold and pale, sinks in the western wave. but thou thyself movest alone; who can be [a] companion of thy course! the oaks of the mountains fall: th[e] mountains themselves decay with years; the ocean shrinks and grows again: the moon herself is lost in heaven; but thou! art for ever the same; rejoicing in the brightness of th[y] course. when the world is dark with tempests; when thunder rolls, and lightning flies; thou lookest in thy beauty from the clouds, and laughest at the storm. but to Ossian thou lookest in vain; for he beholds thy beams no more; wh[e]ther thy yellow hair flows on the eastern clouds, or thou tremblest at the gates of the west. but thou art perhaps like me, for a season, and thy years will have an end. thou shalt sleep in thy clouds, careless of the voice of the morning. exult then o sun! in the strength of thy youth! age is dark and unlovely; it is like the glimmering light of the moon, when it shines thro' broken clouds, and the mist is on the hills; the blast of North is [on] the plain, the traveller shrinks in the midst of his journey.

[Ossian's Carthon.]

[390]   ——facile omnes perferre ac pati;
Cum quibus erat cunque una, iis sese dedere;

§389 *Carthon*, p. 141-2. These are the concluding lines of the poem.

§390 Translation: He fell in easily with the ways of all his acquaintances, gave himself up to his company, and joined heartily in their pursuits; never opposed anyone, never put himself ahead of anybody. That keeps clear of jealousy and is the simplest way of getting a good name and making friends.

Sosia: A wise start in life. Nowadays it's complaisance that makes friends and truthfulness is the mother of unpopularity.

Terence, *Andria* I. 1. 35-41. For two more entries from this work, see §§179-80. The translation is adapted from the Loeb Classical Library edition (see §§179-80n).

§390.5 *laudem*] Ms. This word is badly obscured in the manuscript.

§390.6 *So.*] Abbr. for Sosia, a character in the play.

Eorum obsequi studiis; advorsus nemini:
Numquam praeponens se illis. Ita facillume
Sine invidia laudem invenias, et amicos pares.
So. sapienter vitam instituit: namque hoc tempore,
Obsequium amicos, veritas odium parit.

Terent. Andr. act. 1. sc. 1. 35.

[391]   ————ingenium est omnium
Hominum ab labore proclive ad lubidinem.

ib. v. 50.

[392] Oh ciel! que tes rigueurs seroient peu redoutables,
Si la foudre d'abords accabloit les coupables!
Et que tes chatimens paroissent infinis,
Quand tu laisses la vie a ceux que tu punis!

Racine. Freres ennemis. act. 1 sc. 2

[393] Les autres ennemis n'ont que de courtes haines;
Mais quand de la nature on a brisé les chaines,
Cher Attale, il n'est rien qui puisse rëunir
Coeux que des noeuds si forts n'ont pas sû retenir.
L'on hait avec excès lors que l'on hait un frere.

ib. acte 3. sc. 6.

§391 Translation: . . . the human mind always runs downhill from toil to pleasure.

Andria I. 1. 50-1. Translation: Loeb edition.

§392-5 These four entries in the handwriting of the late 1760s are from the first two tragedies of Jean Racine (1639-1699), *La Thébaide, ou Les Frères Ennemis* (1664) and *Alexandre Le Grand* (1665); translations are from Jean Racine, *Complete Plays*, trans. Samuel Solomon, 2 vols (New York, 1967).

§392 Translation:

How much less dire, Heaven, were thy victims' plight
If thy bolt crushed the guilty ones outright!
How infinite thy chastisements appear
When thou let'st live those writhing in thy fear!

La Thébaide, III: 2.

§393 Translation:

The hates of other foes may not endure;
But when the bonds of nature once are broken,
Dear Attalus, nothing can bind again
Those whom such ties were powerless to restrain:
One hates a brother with a hate that's dire:

Same, III: 6.

[394] L'amour eut peu de part a cet hymen honteux,
Et la seule fureur en alluma les feux.
                    ib. acte 1. sc. 3.

[395] Son courage sensible a vos justes douleurs
Ne veut point de lauriers arrosez de vos pleurs.
                    ib. Alexandre. acte. 2. sc. 1.

[396] Sun of the soul whose chearful ray
          Darts o'er this gloom of life a smile;
    Sweet *Hope*, yet further gild my way,
          Yet light my weary steps awhile,
    Till thy fair lamp dissolve in endless day.
    O come! & to my pensive eye
    Thy far foreseeing tube apply,
    Whose kind deception steals us o'er
    The gloomy waste that lies before;
    Still opening to the distant sight
    The sunshine of the mountain's height;
    Where scenes of fairer aspect rise
    Elysian groves & azure skies.

        Life's ocean slept—the liquid gale
    Gently mov'd the waving sail.
    Fallacious *Hope*! with flattering eye
    You smiled to see the streamers fly.

> §394 Translation:
>
>> Love scarce had part in that most shameful match,
>> And burning hatred only lit its torch.
>
> Same, I: 3.
> §395 Translation:
>
>> His heart, susceptible to your just fears,
>> Will have no laurels watered by your tears.
>
> *Alexandre Le Grand*, II: 1.
> §396 John Langhorne, "A Hymn to Hope," stanzas I (1-5), III (6-13), VI
> (14-21), VII (22-35), VIII (36-45), IX (46-57), X (58-65), XIV (66-71). The
> excisions, amounting to 71 lines, reduce the poem to exactly half its original
> length. TJ's copy-text follows the revised version printed in *The Poetical Works
> of John Langhorne*, 2 vols. (London, 1766), which differs somewhat from the
> original version published in 1761.
> §396.31 *the captive's war-worne chain*] *Poetical Works*: *the war-worn Cap-
> tive's Chain*
> §396.55 *the bosom*] *Poetical Works*: *the blue bosom*

The thunder bursts, the mad wind raves
From slumber wake the 'frighted waves:
You saw me, fled me thus distrest,
And tore your anchor from my breast.
   Yet come, fair fugitive, again!
I love thee still, though false & vain.
Forgive me, gentle *Hope*, and tell
Where, far from me, you deign to dwell.
To soothe ambition's wild desires;
To feed the lover's eager fires;
To swell the Miser's mouldy store;
To gild the dreaming chymist's ore;
Are these thy cares? or more humane,
To loose the captive's war-worne chain,
And bring before his languid sight
The charms of liberty & light;
The tears of drooping grief to dry;
And hold thy glass to Sorrow's eye?
Or dost thou more delight to dwell
With silence in the hermit's cell?
To teach devotion's flame to rise,
And wing her vespers to the skies;
To urge, with still returning care,
The holy violence of prayer;
In rapt'rous visions to display
The realms of everlasting day,
And snatch from time the golden key,
That opens all eternity?

   Perchance on some unpeopled strand,
Whose rocks the raging tide withstand,
Thy soothing smile, in desarts drear,
A lonely mariner may chear,
Who bravely holds his feeble breath,
Attack'd by famine, pain, & death.
With thee he bears each tedious day
Along the dreary beach to stray:
Whence their wild way his toil'd eyes strain
O'er the bosom of the main;
And meet where distant surges rave,
A white sail in each foaming wave.
   Doom'd from each native joy to part,

Each dear connection of the heart,
You the poor exile's steps attend,
The only undeserting friend.
You wing the slow-declining year;
You dry the solitary tear;
And oft, with pious guile, restore
Those scenes he must behold no more.
———go,
Vain *Hope*, thou harbinger of woe.
Ah no!—that thought distracts my heart:
Indulge me, *Hope*, we must not part.
Direct the future as you please;
But give me, give me present ease.
Langhorne's Hymn to Hope. Stanz.
1. 3. 6. 7. 8. 9. 10. 1[4]

[397]   Αξυλον δ' αρ επεφνε δοην αγαθος Διομηδης,
Τευθρανιδην, ός εναιενεϋκτιμενη εν Αριςδη.
Αφνειος διοτοιο, φιλος δ' ην ανθρωποιςι·
Παντας γαρ φιλεεςκεν, όδῳ επι οικια ναιων.
Il. ζ. 12.

[398]   Όιη περ φυλλων γενεη, τοιηδε και ανδρων·
Φυλλα τα μεν τ' ανεμος χαμαδις χεει, αλλα δε θ' ὑλη
Τηλεθοωςα φυει, εαρος δ' επιγινεται ὡρη·
Ὡς ανδρων γενεη, ή μεν φυει, ή δ' απολήγει.
Il. ζ. 146.

§§397-8 For other entries from Homer and information on the translations,
see §§155-62 and §§185-202 (Pope's translations). Also see Homer in the
Register of Authors.
§397 Translation:

> Diomedes of the great war cry cut down Axylos,
> Teuthras' son, who had been a dweller in strong-founded Arisbe,
> a man rich in substance and a friend to all humanity
> since in his house by the wayside he entertained all comers.

Homer, *Iliad* 6. 12-15.
§397.2 εναιενεϋκτιμενη] As per manuscript.
§398 Translation:

> As is the generation of leaves, so is that of humanity.
> The wind scatters the leaves on the ground, but the live timber
> burgeons with leaves again in the season of spring returning.
> So one generation of men will grow while another dies.

Iliad 6. 146-9.

[149]

[399] Daughter of heaven, fair art thou! the silence of thy face [is] pleasant. thou comest forth in loveliness: the stars attend thy blue steps in the east. the clouds rejoice in thy presence O moon, and brighten their dark brown sides. who is like thee in heaven, daughter of the nig[ht?] the stars are ashamed in thy presence, and turn aside their green sparkling eyes. Whither dost thou retire from thy course, when t[he] darkness of thy countenance grows? hast thou thy hall like Ossian dwellest thou in the shadow of grief? have thy sisters fallen fr[om] heaven? are they, who rejoiced with thee, at night, no more? Yes[!] they have fallen, fair light! and thou dost often retire to mo[urn] but thou thyself shalt fail one night; and leave thy blue pa[th] in heaven. the stars will then lift their green heads: they wh[o] were ashamed in thy presence will rejoice. Thou are now clothed with thy brightness: look from thy gates in the sky. [Burst] the cloud, O wind, that the daughter of night may look forth[,] that the shaggy mountains may brighten, and the ocean roll it's blue waves in light.

Ossian's Darthula.

[400] Where have ye been, ye Southern winds! when the sons of my love were deceived? but ye have been sporting on plains, a[nd] pursuing the thistle's beard. O that ye had been rustling in the sails of Nathos, till the hills of Etha rose! till they rose in their clouds, and saw their coming cheif! long hast thou been absent, Nathos! and the day of thy return is past.

Ossian's Darthulah.

[401] How long shall we weep on Lena; or pour our tears in Ulli[n?] the mighty will not return. Oscar shall not rise in his strength[.] the valiant must fall one day, and be no more known on h[is] hills. where are our fathers, O warriors! the cheifs of the tim[es] of old? they have set like stars that have shone, we only hear the sound of their praise. but they were renowned in their day, and the terror of other times. thus

§399 *Darthula*, p. 155-6. This is the opening passage of the poem.
§400 Same, p. 157.
§401 *Temora*, p. 183. This work, which Macpherson here represents as "little more than the opening of the poem," was expanded and published as a full-length epic in 1763. TJ quoted from it in drafting possible inscriptions for the tomb of his friend and brother-in-law, Dabney Carr (see Macpherson in Register of Authors).

shall we pass, o warriors, in the day of our fall. then let us be renowned whe[n] we may; and leave our fame behind us, like the last beams [of] the sun, when he hides his red head in the west.

Ossian's Temora.

[402] Dost thou force me from my place, replied the hollow voice[?] the people bend before me. I turn the battle in the feild of the valiant. I look on the nations and they vanish: my nostrils pou[r] the blast of death. I come abroad on the winds: the tempests a[re] before my face. but my dwelling is calm, above the clouds. the feilds of my rest are pleasant.—he lifted high his shad[owy] spear; and bent forward his terrible height. but the king, advancing, drew his sword; the blade of dark-brown Luno. the gleaming part of the steel winds thro' the gloomy ghost[.] the form fell shapeless into air, like a column of smoke, whic[h] the staff of the boy disturbs, as it rises from the half-extinguish[ed] furnace. the spirit of Loda shrieked as, rolled into himself, he rose on the wind. Inistore shook at the sound. the waves heard it on the deep: they stopped in their course with fear.

Ossian's Carric-thura.

[403] Nor slept the sword by thy side, thou last of Fingal's race[!] Ossian rushed forward in his strength, and the people fell before him; as the grass by the staff of the boy, when he whistles along the feild, and the grey beard of the thistle falls. but careless the youth moves on; his steps are towards the desert.

Ossian's Lathmon.

[404]

The Beggar.

——inopemque paterni
Et Laris, et fundi.—Hor.

Pity the sorrows of a poor old man!
Whose trembling limbs have borne him to your door;
Whose days are dwindled to the shortest span,

§402 *Carric-thura*, p. 199–200. The dash indicates the omission of ten lines.
§402.9 *part*] Macpherson: *path*.
§403 *Lathmon*, p. 236.
§404 Thomas Moss, "The Beggar." First published anonymously in *Poems on Several Occasions* (1769). Popular in its day, this poem appeared in the "Poets Corner" of the *Virginia Gazette* (Purdie & Dixon), 28 Feb. 1771, but

Oh! give relief—and heav'n will bless your store.
    These tatter'd clothes my poverty bespeak,
These hoary locks proclaim my lengthen'd years,
And many a furrow in my grief-worn cheek
Has been the channel to a stream of tears.

    Yon house erected on the rising ground,
With tempting aspect drew me from my road,
For plenty there a residence has found,
And grandeur a magnificent abode.

    (Hard is the fate of the infirm & poor!)
Here craving for a morsel of their bread,
A pamper'd menial forced me from the door,
To seek a shelter in an humbler shed.

    Oh! take me to your hospitable dome,
Keen blows the wind, & piercing is the cold!
Short is my passage to the friendly tomb,
For I am poor, and miserably old.

    Should I reveal the source of ev'ry grief,
If soft humanity e'er touch'd your breast,
Your hand would not withold the kind relief,
And tears of pity could not be represt.

Heav'n sends misfortunes—why should we repine?
'Tis heav'n has brought me to the state you see:
And your condition may be soon like mine,
The child of sorrow, & of misery.

    A little farm was my paternal lot,
Then like the lark, I sprightly hail'd the morn;
But ah oppression forc'd me from my cot,
My cattle died, and blighted was my corn.

    My daughter, once the comfort of my age!

---

the absence of the Latin epitaph, as well as other textual differences, make it
unlikely that this could have been TJ's copy-text. The page of the manuscript
on which this poem was written has been cut off immediately below the last
line given in the present text, making it appear that the last two quatrains of
the poem may originally have been present and later cut out. The last quatrain
is a repeat of the first; the penultimate quatrain reads:

> My tender Wife—sweet Soother of my Care!
> Struck with sad Anguish at the stern Decree,
> Fell—ling'ring fell a Victim to Despair,
> And left the World to Wretchedness and me.

TJ's loss of his wife, Martha, in 1782 was emotionally shattering, but whether
he originally copied this stanza into the LCB and whether he or his daughter
or some other member of his family later cut it out are unknown.

Lur'd by a villain from her native home,
Is cast, abandon'd, on the world's wide stage,
And doom'd in scanty poverty to roam.

[405] Sweet are the jasmine's breathing flowers
Sweet the soft falling vernal showers
Sweet is the gloom the grove affords
And sweet the notes of warbling birds.
But not the grove, nor rain, nor flowers
Nor all the feathered songsters' powers
Can ever sweet & pleasing be
Oh lovely *Freedom*, without thee

[406] ——Dum quaerimus, aevum
Perdimus, et nullo votorum fine beati,
Victuros agimus semper, nec vivimus unquam.
                              Manilius.

[407]   αυταρ εγωγε
Ὑϛερον ουκ αλεγω, και ει παρα ποϛϛιν ολεθρος
Σημερον ἡμετερῃϛι πελει λυγρος· ουτι γαρ ανθρες
Ζωομεν ηματα παντα· ποτμος δ᾽ επι παϛι τετυκται.
                    Q. Calaber. 6. 431.

§405 Author and source unknown.
§406 Translation: Even as we seek to extend life we are losing it, unblessed by any limit to our wishes, always intending to live but never actually living.
Manilius, *Astronomica* 4. 3-5. The translation, as well as the book and line numbers, are from the Loeb Classical Library edition: G. P. Goold, ed. and trans., *Manilius: Astronomica* (Cambridge, 1977).
§407 Translation:

what shall betide
Hereafter, care I not—yea, though this day
Death's doom stand by my feet; no man may live
For ever; each man's fate is foreordained.

Quintus Smyrnaeus, *The Fall of Troy*, 6: 431-4. The evidence of the handwriting suggests that this entry, which seems clearly intended as a valedictory, was made in TJ's later years. For further information, see Quintus Smyrnaeus in the Register of Authors. The translation is from the Loeb Classical Library edition: Arthur S. Way, ed. and trans., *Quintus Smyrnaeus: The Fall of Troy* (New York, 1913).
§407.3 ανθρες] Loeb: ανδρες

REGISTER OF AUTHORS

The notes that follow provide only brief biographical information on the authors represented in Jefferson's Literary Commonplace Book. Authors who were important to the young man who kept this notebook but are now very little known have been identified somewhat more fully, and some attempt has been made to suggest the standing they occupied in the eighteenth century. But for the most part, these notes are intended to report, author by author, on what might be called Jefferson's literary relations, as discernible in his reading and commonplacing, his library holdings, his recommended reading lists, and his remarks in his correspondence and elsewhere on the writers in question. Omitted from this register are authors who are represented in the Literary Commonplace Book only in excerpts that were found in another work: Jonson, Southerne, Congreve (*Thesaurus Dramaticus*), and Statius (*Fingal*).

Mark AKENSIDE (1721-1770), English physician and poet. Akenside is principally remembered as the author of a long, didactic poem in Miltonic blank verse, *The Pleasures of Imagination*, first published in 1744. It was popular and influential in its day, and even Dr. Samuel Johnson, who did not approve of Akenside's dissenting views, allowed that the poem "has undoubtedly a just claim to very particular notice as an example of great felicity of genius and uncommon amplitude of acquisitions. . . ."[1]

Jefferson acquired an edition of *The Pleasures of Imagination* sometime before 3 Oct. 1764, when he paid 3/9 to have it bound.[2] It was thus one of the earliest books to find a place in his library, a place it seems not to have retained. For although Jefferson was to inscribe some 80 lines from Akenside's poem in his Commonplace Book (§§342-5) at the end of the decade, he does not seem to have replaced that poet's book when his Shadwell library burned in 1770, and he did not include Akenside on the select list of books he recommended to Robert Skipwith in 1771. Nonetheless, the physician-poet would again be represented on Jefferson's shelves when he acquired Bell's edition of the British poets in Paris in the 1780s.[3]

ANACREON (6th century B.C.), Greek poet. Though the work copied into the Literary Commonplace Book over his name (§347-8) was not actually by Anacreon, it was thought to be his work in the eighteenth century and was so regarded by Jefferson, whose great library contained a number of editions and translations of this early Greek poet (Sowerby 4404-8).

Henry Saint-John, Viscount BOLINGBROKE (1678-1751), English statesman and philosopher. Jefferson copied the extracts from Bolingbroke (§§4-34, 36-58) about 1765 from a five-volume set of his *Philosophical Works*, consisting mainly of four long essays and 81 "Fragments." "The foregoing Essays, if they may deserve even that name, and the Fragments or minutes that follow," wrote Bolingbroke, "were thrown upon paper in Mr. [Alexander]

[1] *Lives of the English Poets*, III, 416-17.
[2] Virginia Gazette Daybook (ViU).
[3] Leavitt, 609.

Pope's lifetime, and at his desire."[4] Pope was much interested in Bolingbroke's ideas during the time he was composing his "Essay on Man," a poem
carefully studied by Jefferson and whose four parts, or Epistles, are addressed
to Bolingbroke, just as Bolingbroke's Essays and Fragments are addressed to
Pope. It was the posthumous publication of these essays in 1754 by Bolingbroke's literary executor, David Mallet, that drew from Dr. Samuel Johnson
the famous remark that Bolingbroke was a scoundrel and a coward: "a scoundrel for charging a blunderbuss against religion and morality; a coward, because he had not resolution to fire it off himself, but left half a crown to a
beggarly Scotchman, to draw the trigger after his death."[5]

That these essays made an important impression on the young Jefferson is
manifest in at least two ways. The first is the extraordinary amount of material
from this source that Jefferson retained in his Commonplace Book—something in excess of 10,000 words. Though less than the amount originally
commonplaced (as is clear from the presence of several fragmentary entries
not included in their entirety), these 54 entries represent six times as many
words as he included from any other single author and constitute nearly 40
percent of the contents of the Literary Commonplace Book. The other telling
circumstance is the remarkable extent to which the major tenets of Bolingbroke's philosophical program were ultimately adopted by Jefferson as his
own: a thorough going materialism; a rejection of metaphysics and all speculation that ventures beyond the reach of human apprehension; an uncompromising commitment to reason as the final arbiter of knowledge and valid-
ity; a disposition to regard churchmen and theologians as the corrupters of
Christianity; a distaste for the doctrines of Plato and his influence on Christian teachings; and a strong skepticism regarding the historicity of biblical
accounts.

As Merrill D. Peterson has observed, the discovery that Jefferson was an
avid reader of Bolingbroke "comes as a shock to modern students" since in
our time "he is not only seldom read but his works are seldom admitted into
the literary canon of the Enlightenment." And yet, for Jefferson and John
Adams, "as for Voltaire, Alexander Pope, Jonathan Swift, and many others,
Bolingbroke was one of the century's giants."[6] Moreover, Jefferson's taste for
Bolingbroke's writings seems to have been more than a youthful enthusiasm.
He included them in a number of recommended reading lists[7] and reportedly
named Bolingbroke as one of his favorite prose writers.[8] Many commentators
have pointed out that his famous advice to his nephew, Peter Carr, on sub-
mitting religion to rational scrutiny and treating the Bible as any other historical account, comes straight from Bolingbroke: "Fix reason firmly in her
seat, and call to her tribunal every fact, every opinion. . . . Read the bible
then, as you would read Livy or Tacitus."[9] In old age, when his grandson

[4] *Phil. Works*, III, 334.

[5] H. T. Dickinson, *Bolingbroke* (London, 1970), p. 298.

[6] Merrill D. Peterson, "Thomas Jefferson and the Enlightenment: Reflections on Literary Influence," XI, *Lex et Scientia*, 103.

[7] See, for example, reading lists sent to the following: Robert Skipwith, 3 Aug. 1771,
Papers, 1: 78-81; Peter Carr, 10 Aug. 1787, same, 12: 18-19; John Garland Jefferson,
11 June 1790, same, 16: 481.

[8] John Bernard, *Retrospection of America 1797-1811*, ed. Mrs. Bayberry Bernard
(New York, 1887), p. 238.

[9] TJ to Peter Carr, 10 Aug. 1787, *Papers*, 12: 15. Cf. Bolingbroke, §58.

wrote from college and asked his opinion of Bolingbroke, Jefferson replied in a manner that suggests continued familiarity and admiration: "He was called indeed a tory: but his writings prove him a stronger advocate for liberty than any of his countrymen, the whigs of the present day. . . . Ld. Bolingbroke's . . . is a style of the highest order: the lofty, rythmical, full-flowing eloquence of Cicero. Periods of just measure, their members proportioned, their close full and round. His conceptions too are bold and strong, his diction copious, polished and commanding as his subject. His writings are certainly the finest samples in the English language of the eloquence proper for the senate. His political tracts are safe reading for the most timid religionist, his philosophical, for those who are not afraid to trust their reason with discussions of right and wrong."[10]

George BUCHANAN (1506-1582), Scottish humanist and historian. Buchanan was in his day perhaps the most highly regarded man of learning in Scotland. Educated at St. Andrews and in Paris, he gained fame both as a writer and a teacher, numbering among his pupils Montaigne, Mary Queen of Scots, and James VI, later James I of England.

The play from which the excerpts in the Literary Commonplace Book were taken, *Jephtha, Or The Vow*, was written when Buchanan was a college teacher in Bordeaux (1537-1544) to be performed by the students, one of whom was the future essayist, Montaigne.[11] Though based on an incident in the Bible, the play is deliberately cast in a classical mold, and the passages Jefferson copied out have much in common with those he excerpted from the plays of Euripides and Seneca.

Buchanan's presence in Jefferson's Literary Commonplace Book is explained by his eminence as a writer of Latin verse, which had a great vogue in the eighteenth century. Alexander Pope, who helped popularize the Latin poetry of the Renaissance humanists, was known to be an admirer of Buchanan's, and Dr. Johnson, whose scorn for the Scots was notorious, praised his Latin verses and allowed that Buchanan was "the only man of genius his country had ever produced."[12] This vogue had particular appeal for a young Latinist of Jefferson's abilities and inclinations, and though his Commonplace Book contains only excerpts from one of the verse dramas, the evidence of his library and his letters indicates that he knew Buchanan's other works, including his well-known translations of the Psalms.[13] In his retirement, Jefferson said of Buchanan: "his latinity is so pure as to claim a place in school reading."[14]

John Sheffield, Duke of BUCKINGHAM (1648-1721), English statesman and poet. Sheffield succeeded to the title Earl of Mulgrave, and, in the course of a brilliant career in the military and in politics, was created Marquis of Normandy and Duke of Buckingham. He enjoyed a reputation as a poet and

[10] TJ to Francis Wayles Eppes, 19 Jan. 1821, *Family Letters*, p. 438.

[11] Donald Stone, Jr., ed., *Four Renaissance Tragedies* (Cambridge, 1966), p. x.

[12] Cited from Boswell's *Life of Johnson* in I. D. McFarlane, *Buchanan* (London, 1981), p. 482.

[13] Jefferson's great library contained an edition of Buchanan's *Opera*, his translations of the Psalms, and his history of Scotland (Sowerby 433, 4399, 434). He refers to the translations of the Psalms in a letter, TJ to John Adams, 12 Oct. 1813, Cappon, p. 386.

[14] TJ to Rev. Samuel Knox, 12 Feb. 1810, L & B, XII, 360.

critic in his own time, his verse essays on poetry and satire being widely read and singled out for praise by Dryden, whom he patronized, and Pope, who edited his works for publication in 1723. Though his poems and plays were still being reprinted in the 1750s, his reputation eventually waned, so that Dr. Johnson would write of him in *Lives of the English Poets*: "if we credit the testimony of his contemporaries, he was a poet of no vulgar rank. But favour and flattery are now at an end; criticism is no longer softened by his bounties or awed by his splendour, and, being able to take a more steady view, discovers him to be a writer that sometimes glimmers, but rarely shines. . . ."[15]

Among Buckingham's works are two plays that derive from Shakespeare's *Julius Caesar*. Unpublished in his lifetime and never performed, these works are part of the pervasive impulse of the Restoration and eighteenth century to "improve" Shakespeare's plays by rewriting them.[16] *The Tragedy of Julius Caesar Altered* and *The Death of Marcus Brutus* represent a calculated attempt to improve upon Shakespeare's supposedly inspired but flawed original by preserving the classical unities, eliminating the low comedy, reforming the excesses of language, and enhancing the love interest. Jefferson read and commonplaced these plays (§297-300) in his teens at about the same time he commonplaced Shakespeare's original (§268-73), and seems to have been attracted by the same things in Buckingham as in Shakespeare—the strident note of defiance and the insistence that death is preferable to infringements of one's honor or liberty.

Many years later, perhaps as late as the 1780s or 1790s, Jefferson entered a four-line version of Buckingham's self-composed epitaph (§83), which had given rise to controversy when it was published as part of his will.[17] Jefferson's version may simply reflect an imperfect recollection of the original, but it seems more likely that it represents a conscious effort to adapt the epitaph to his own situation—his religious skepticism, his confidence in the integrity of his conduct and beliefs, and his stoical acceptance of fate. Strengthening this hypothesis is the fact that Jefferson, who was later to compose his own epitaph, placed his version of Buckingham's in a part of the Literary Commonplace Book that forms a series of interrelated entries on death, fate, and belief (§1-84).

A volume of Buckingham's plays or poetic works was almost certainly in Jefferson's library, but in her *Catalogue*, E. Millicent Sowerby, enacting what was reportedly one of Sheffield's great fears, attributes the volume Jefferson listed as "Buckingham" to his predecessor in the title, George Villiers (1628-1687), the second Duke of Buckingham.[18]

Samuel BUTLER (1612-1680), English satirist and poet. It is noteworthy that Samuel Butler's great burlesque of Puritanism, *Hudibras* (1662-1678), was

[15] *Lives of the English Poets*, II, 174-5.

[16] See Hazelton Spencer, *Shakespeare Improved: The Restoration Versions in Quarto and on the Stage* (Cambridge, 1927); George C. Branam, *Eighteenth-Century Adaptations of Shakespearean Tragedy* (Berkeley and Los Angeles, 1956); and John Ripley, *"Julius Caesar" on Stage in England and America, 1599-1973* (Cambridge, 1980).

[17] *The Works of John Sheffield*, 4th ed. (London, 1753), II, 265-66. See §83n for a text of Buckingham's original.

[18] Sowerby 4426. Jefferson's catalogue entry, *Buckingham. 12mo.*, almost certainly refers to *Plays. By His Grace John Sheffield, Duke of Buckingham* (Glasgow, 1751).

in all of Jefferson's libraries of which we have a record, and that it was one of the few works of English poetry to find a place in the Second Monticello Library, formed after the sale of the great library to Congress in 1815.[19] There can be little doubt that Jefferson shared the literary public's immense delight in Butler's mock-heroic narrative, written in lively tetrameter couplets and modeled after another Jefferson favorite, Cervantes' *Don Quixote*. The historian of William and Mary in the eighteenth century points out that "for almost a century [*Hudibras*] had been the best-loved poem of the Virginians who were content to transfer the butt of this mock-heroic work from England to New England and to draw from its satirizing of the Puritans . . . a comforting sense of Southern superiority."[20] Nonetheless, it should be noted that the Literary Commonplace Book extracts (§§214-17), probably entered in the 1770s or 1780s, are not representative of Butler's satire or humor, at least in the isolated form in which Jefferson quotes them, but rather focus on moralistic utterances, mostly about honor, by Hudibras and Ralpho, the characters being satirized. Moreover, *Hudibras* is classed in Jefferson's library not under "Romance—Tales—Fable," as is *Don Quixote*, but in the chapter labelled "Didactic."[21]

Gaius Valerius CATULLUS (*c.* 84-*c.* 54 B.C.), Roman poet. Jefferson seems to have owned no edition of Catullus, though as an eager young Latinist with a decided taste for poetry, he was surely familiar with his poems.[22] The sole excerpt from Catullus in the Literary Commonplace Book (§375) dates from about 1770.

Marcus Tullius CICERO (106-43 B.C.), Roman philosopher, orator, and statesman. Jefferson first encountered Cicero as a schoolboy learning Latin, and continued to read his letters and discourses as long as he lived. He admired him as a patriot, valued his opinions as a moral philosopher, and there is little doubt that he looked upon Cicero's life, with his love of study and aristocratic country life, as a model for his own. But he may have regarded him most of all as a prose stylist, calling him "the father of eloquence" and, of style, "the first master in the world."[23]

The excerpts of Cicero's writings in the Literary Commonplace Book are mainly from the *Tusculan Disputations*, a discourse in the form of a philosophical dialogue that deals with pain, grief, and the necessity of coming to terms with death. That Jefferson recorded these excerpts as a very young man not long after the death of his own father is noteworthy and affords insight into the personal resonance which these passages must have possessed for the young student. Cicero's dialogue was deeply personal, having been written

---

[19] Sowerby 4505; Poor 785; Leavitt 609. The manuscript catalogue of Second Monticello Library, on which the Poor catalogue is based, is in the Manuscript Division, DLC.

[20] J. E. Morpurgo, *Their Majesties' Royall Colledge: William and Mary in the 17th and 18th Century* (Williamsburg, 1976), p. 105.

[21] See Sowerby 4505.

[22] Jefferson did include an edition of Catullus, which may have been William Byrd's copy, in a list of books (223 volumes) he offered to buy as a lot in Philadelphia in 1791. His bid was so low that it seems not to have been accepted. See *Papers*, 20: 634-6.

[23] TJ to Amos J. Cook, 21 Jan. 1816, L & B, XIV, 404; TJ to John Adams, 5 July 1814, Cappon, p. 433.

in his mature years after the devastating loss of his daughter. Its burden was the stoical determination to accept whatever happens and bear it philosophically. This determination Jefferson adopted quite early as his own basic philosophic stance, as is evidenced by other Commonplace Book excerpts and the confidential statement to his friend John Page cited in the Introduction, and it lasted all his life. One of the few excerpts in the Literary Commonplace Book entered late in life is from Virgil, and it sounds the same theme: "whatever befall, all fortune is to be o'ercome by bearing."[24]

Jefferson's lifelong attachment to Cicero is manifest in his library, of which the 14 Cicero titles (39 bound volumes) that he sold to Congress in 1815 give only a partial account. His manuscript catalogue, in which he kept track of his constantly growing collection over a period of forty years, shows that an even larger number of Cicero titles (23) did not go to Congress but were either lost, given away, or carried over into his retirement library. And it is significant that there were eventually more books by Cicero in the library Jefferson formed after 1815 (17 titles, 46 volumes) than went to Congress with the great library, and this does not count the numerous anthologized works of Cicero in the library he maintained at Poplar Forest.[25]

Jefferson's admiration for Cicero did not extend to the celebrated orations, which he regarded as tedious. Nor did it embrace Cicero's reverence for Plato, a philosopher Jefferson came to regard as anathema. "While wading thro' the whimsies, the puerilities, and unintelligible jargon of this work [Plato's Republic]," he wrote to John Adams, "I laid it down often to ask myself how it could have been that the world should have so long consented to give reputation to such nonsense as this? How the soi-disant Christian world indeed should have done it, is a piece of historical curiosity. But how could the Roman good sense do it? And particularly how could Cicero bestow such eulogies on Plato? Altho' Cicero did not wield the dense logic of Demosthenes, yet he was able, learned, laborious, practised in the business of the world, and honest."[26] And Jefferson was also troubled by his ancient preceptor's politics. Whereas Adams lamented the loss of Cicero's discourses on government, Jefferson confessed great misgivings on the subject: "When the enthusiasm however kindled by Cicero's pen and principles, subsides into cool reflection, I ask myself What was that government which the virtues of Cicero were so zealous to restore, and the ambition of Caesar to subvert? . . . They had no ideas of government themselves but of their degenerate Senate, or the people of liberty, but of the factious opposition of their tribunes."[27]

A good indication of Jefferson's familiarity with Cicero, as well as his exacting bibliographical standards, are given in a letter written at the age of 75 to a Boston publisher, acknowledging the gift of a new edition of Cicero's works: "I happened at the time of their arrival to be reading the 5th book of Cicero's Tusculans, which I followed by that of his Offices, and concluded to

---

[24] §84. The only other work of Cicero represented in the Literary Commonplace Book is *De Fato*, from which Jefferson copied a similarly fatalistic remark. See §82. This passage also appears in the Legal Commonplace Book, without attribution, as §865.

[25] See Sowerby 1314-22, 4633-4, 4653, 4669, 4912-13; Poor 34-8, 437-43, 621-2, 815-16, 820; Leavitt 612-13, 647. The manuscript catalogue of the great library is in MHi.

[26] TJ to John Adams, 5 July 1814, Cappon, p. 432-3.

[27] John Adams to TJ, 9 July 1813; TJ to Adams, 10 Dec. 1819, Cappon, p. 351, 549.

lay aside the variorum edition, and to use yours, after which I might write more understandingly on the subject. having been extremely disgusted with the Philadelphia and New York Delphin editions, some of which I had read, and altho executed with a good type on good paper, yet so full of errors of the press as not to be worth the paper they were printed on. I wished to see the state of the classical press with you. their editions had on an average about one error for every page. I read therefore the portions of your's above mentioned with a pretty sharp eye, and in something upwards of 200. pages I found the errors noted on the paper inclosed, being an average of one for every 13. pages. this is a good advance on the presses of N. Y. and Philada., and gives hopes of rapid improvements. the errors in the Variorum editions however are fewer than these, the Elzevirs still fewer."[28]

Cicero was one of the writers from whom Jefferson believed he had learned invaluable lessons, and it was for this reason that he invoked his name, along with his trinity of great men, in a defense of formal education: "I know it is often said there have been shining examples of men of great abilities in all the businesses of life, without any other science than what they had gathered from conversations and intercourse with the world. But who can say what these men would not have been, had they started in the science on the shoulders of a Demosthenes or Cicero, of a Locke or Bacon, or a Newton?"[29] Nearly 60 years after copying Cicero's description of the qualities of the happy man from the *Tusculan Disputations* into his Literary Commonplace Book (§79), Jefferson commended this passage to the students of a schoolmaster in Maine as a summary of what study and striving were all about, "from the hand of the father of eloquence and philosophy."[30]

Robert DODSLEY (1703-1764), English poet, dramatist, and publisher. Dodsley began as a versifying footman and rose to become a respected man of letters. His greatest distinction came through his career as an enterprising publisher, who conceived or helped create such important works as *The Preceptor* (1755), an influential guide to self-education, Samuel Johnson's *Dictionary* (1755), and the *Annual Register* (1758). His *Select Collection of Old Plays* (1744) and *A Collection of Poems* (1748) were milestone literary anthologies and were both enormously popular. Most of these and many other works connected with Dodsley found a place in Jefferson's library, though not, apparently, the obscure poem extracted in the Literary Commonplace Book, "Beauty: Or, The Art of Charming" (§319), which had been pub-

[28] TJ to Wells and Lilly, 1 Apr. 1818, Worthington Chauncey Ford, ed., *Thomas Jefferson Correspondence Printed from the originals in the Collections of William K. Bixby* (Boston, 1916), p. 238.

[29] TJ to John Brazier, 24 Aug. 1819, L & B, XV, 211.

[30] TJ to Amos J. Cook, 21 Jan. 1816, L & B, XIV, 404-5. For other references to Cicero, see TJ to Peter Carr, 19 Aug. 1785, *Papers*, 8: 407; TJ to Benjamin Rush, 21 Apr. 1803, Dickinson W. Adams, ed., *Jefferson's Extracts from the Gospels: "The Philosophy of Jesus" and "The Life and Morals of Jesus,"* in Charles T. Cullen, ed., *The Papers of Thomas Jefferson: Second Series* (Princeton, 1983), p. 332; TJ to John Wayles Eppes, 17 Jan. 1810, Ford, XI, 129; TJ to George Ticknor, 14 Jan. 1816, O. W. Long, *Thomas Jefferson and George Ticknor: A Chapter in American Scholarship* (Williamstown, Mass., 1933), p. 16; TJ to William Short, 31 Oct. 1819, *Jefferson's Extracts*, p. 388; TJ to George Summers and John B. Garland, 27 Feb. 1822, L & B, XV, 353.

lished separately in 1735.[31] How and where Jefferson came across it in the late 1750s or early 1760s, when he commonplaced it, is not known.

John DRYDEN (1631-1700), English poet, dramatist, and translator. Though the Literary Commonplace Book contains only one passage that may have been taken directly from Dryden's works (§380), five others from his plays were apparently taken at second hand from *Thesaurus Dramaticus*, a collection of memorable extracts from English dramatists (§§282, 286, 287, 289, 292). Jefferson was fond of Restoration and early eighteenth-century tragedy, as evidenced by his numerous extracts from Otway and Rowe, and was probably as a young man well acquainted with Dryden's plays, an edition of which was near the top of his selected list of books recommended to Robert Skipwith in 1771. It was presumably this same six-volume edition that was in Jefferson's great library when it was sold to Congress.[32]

It is indicative of the taste of his time that Jefferson should commonplace *All for Love*, Dryden's version of the Antony and Cleopatra story, and not Shakespeare's, which was little esteemed and rarely performed. Nonetheless, Jefferson, like Dryden, thought Shakespeare the great master of the English language and may well have been prompted by Dryden's preface to *All for Love* to apply Horace's dictum about studying the examples of the Greeks to Shakespeare.[33]

EURIPIDES (*c.* 485-*c.* 406 B.C.), Greek tragedian. Jefferson copied into his Commonplace Book 70 extracts from Euripides, more extracts than from any other writer. He seems to have entered them in the 1760s, when he was studying with George Wythe, and the fact that he regarded Euripides as the easiest to read of the great Greek tragedians may indicate that these entries represent his first venture into Greek tragedy.[34] Certainly his treatment of the diacritical marks suggests an unsettled practice, but more importantly, the ordering of the plays indicates a systematic, rather than a selective, reading. As Meyer Reinhold has observed: "There is no reason for concluding that these plays were favorites of Jefferson; they were simply in the order of plays in the first volume of a text of Euripides, the traditional arrangement of Euripidean tragedies since the Middle Ages."[35]

The edition of Euripides that Jefferson used for his commonplacing was the large and lavish one of Joshua Barnes, which may have been in his first

[31] D. F. Foxon, *English Verse 1701-1750: A Catalogue of Separately Printed Poems with Notes on Contemporary Collected Editions*, 2 vols. (London, 1975), D381.

[32] TJ to Robert Skipwith, 3 Aug. 1771, *Papers*, 1: 78. Sowerby 4543. Jefferson also owned Dryden's translations of Plutarch (Sowerby 69), Juvenal (Sowerby 4487), and, most notably, his famous translation of Virgil (Sowerby 4282).

[33] Compare Dryden's preface in the California edition, Maximillian E. Novak, George R. Guffey, and Alan Roper, eds., *The Works of John Dryden* (Berkeley, 1984), XIII, 18, and the letter to Bernard Moore cited in the Shakespeake section below (note 140).

[34] Jefferson lent his grandson, whom he was tutoring in his preparation for college, a volume each of Euripides, Sophocles, and Aeschylus: "The 1st. you will find easy, the 2d. tolerable so; and the last incomprehensible in his flights among the clouds." TJ to Francis Wayles Eppes, 21 Sep. 1820, *Family Letters*, p. 433.

[35] Meyer Reinhold, "The Classics and the Quest for Virtue in Eighteenth-Century America," *Classica Americana: The Greek and Roman Heritage in the United States* (Detroit, 1984), p. 149.

library. While in Paris, directing the education of his nephew Peter Carr, he included Euripides on a reading list with very few poets, and he also took pains to acquire the final volume of a revised version of Barnes.[36] Before he sold his library to Congress in 1815, he had acquired other editions as well, including translations. His second Monticello library was well stocked with Euripides, and he retained a petit format edition for his retirement reading at Poplar Forest.[37]

There is no mistaking what attracted the young Jefferson's interest in Euripides. It is the moralizing speeches with which Euripides' plays abound, which often issue in gnomic truths. On at least one occasion he used an extract gleaned from Euripides to gloss a general proposition encountered in his legal reading.[38] It was for their memorable framing of such maxims and moral truths that Jefferson most prized the classics and why he spent so much of his retirement in re-reading them. His granddaughter, Ellen Randolph Coolidge, who was his student and amanuensis during these years, testified that she had seen her grandfather with a volume of the classics in his hand more than any other kind of book. "In his youth he had loved poetry, but by the time I was old enough to observe, he had lost his taste for it, except for Homer and the great Athenian tragics, which he continued to the last to enjoy. He went over the works of Eschylus, Sophocles and Euripides, not very long before I left him [1825]."[39] As proof of this, the edition of Euripides he owned at the time bears marginal corrections in his hand for virtually every play, both in the Greek text and in the facing Latin translation. Uncharacteristically, he wrote out his judgment of this edition on the title page: "a beautiful type, a most corrupt text and unfaithful translation."[40]

HERODOTUS (fifth century B.C.), Greek historian. Herodotus, generally regarded as the first great historian of the Western world, wrote a history of the Persian wars.

"When I was young," Jefferson wrote, "I was passionately fond of reading books of history, and travels,"[41] a fondness that demonstrably extended to the writer Cicero called "the father of history." The advice he gave his nephew Peter Carr in 1785 confirms what is clear from the many reading lists he prepared—that Jefferson regarded the works of Herodotus as a foundation for the study of history. "First read Goldsmith's history of Greece. This will give you a digested view of that field. Then take up ancient history in detail, reading the following books in the following order. Herodotus, Thucydides, Xenophontis hellenica. Xenophontis Anabasis. Quintus Curtius. Justin. This shall form the first stage of your historical reading."[42]

Judging from the handwriting of the Literary Commonplace Book entries and their immediate proximity to the readily datable Bolingbroke material,

[36] TJ to Peter Carr, 10 Aug. 1787, *Papers*, 12: 18. New edition of Barnes: same, 13: 204, 240, 300.

[37] Sowerby 4527-31; Poor 755-7; Leavitt 647.

[38] See §93n.

[39] Randall, III, 346.

[40] This is the Musgrave edition of the tragedies published in 10 volumes by Foulis in 1796 (Jefferson Supplement, Rare Book Division, DLC).

[41] TJ to Editor, *Journal of Paris*, 29 Aug. 1787, *Papers*, 12: 61-2.

[42] TJ to Peter Carr, 19 Aug. 1785, *Papers*, 8: 407.

Jefferson commonplaced Herodotus in the mid-1760s, when he was studying law with George Wythe, the leading classical scholar in Virginia, and reading other Greek works (see sections on Homer and Euripides). There are additional indications that Jefferson read Herodotus under the tutelage of George Wythe. We know that Wythe used Herodotus as a text with his students, for Peter Carr reported to his uncle, when being tutored by Wythe in 1787, that they were reading "Herodotus, Sophocles, Cicero and some parts of Horace."[43] Moreover, Wythe wrote Jefferson in 1791 about the proposed seal for the Virginia Court of Chancery in a vein that assumes Jefferson's familiarity with Book V: "Is not the skin of Sisamnes, whose story, you know, Herodotus relates, added by Mr. West to the original design, an improvement?"[44] And perhaps even more telling, E. Millicent Sowerby suggests that certain marginal notes in Jefferson's edition of Herodotus are in the hand of Wythe, who may have been the original owner.[45]

This edition is that of Jacob Gronovius, in Greek and Latin, published in nine volumes in 1763 by Foulis, the Glasgow publisher whose well-printed editions of the classics Jefferson favored. Though he usually had several versions and translations of the great classical authors, this was the only edition of Herodotus in the Monticello library. After it was sold to Congress in 1815, Jefferson acquired a later edition in six volumes and a four-volume English translation. He kept yet another edition of Herodotus in his library at his Bedford County plantation, Poplar Forest.[46]

The three excerpts in the Literary Commonplace Book may only be a sample of the passages he commonplaced from Herodotus. The interest in circumcision, the subject of the first entry, may owe something to a contemporaneous reading of *Tristram Shandy* (see §1n) and is clearly related to Bolingbroke's criticisms of the claims made for the origins of Jewish customs in the Old Testament. The subject of the other two, the nature of immortality and the soul, is also treated in the Bolingbroke entries (and in those from Cicero) and was to prove one of Jefferson's longest-standing preoccupations. That Jefferson's knowledge of Herodotus went beyond the first few books is attested not only by Wythe's reference to Book 5 but also by a marginal note in Jefferson's hand in the copy of Cheselden's *Anatomy* he sold to Congress. Alongside a discussion of bone sutures Jefferson has copied a passage from Herodotus (Book 9, Chap. 83) on the discovery at the battlefield of Plataea of a skull without sutures. There is at least a chance, made more plausible by the presence of the Herodotus quotation in a hand that resembles that of the Literary Commonplace Book entries, that this volume is the one he purchased from the office of the *Virginia Gazette* on April 20, 1764 and that it was one of the few books that subsequently survived the Shadwell fire of 1770.[47]

[43] Peter Carr to TJ, 18 Apr. 1787, *Papers*, 11: 299.
[44] George Wythe to TJ, 10 Jan. 1791, *Papers*, 18: 487.
[45] Sowerby 13. It is doubtful, however, that Jefferson could, as Sowerby suggests, have acquired this set from Wythe's estate in 1806, as the entry for this work in the 1783 manuscript catalogue of his library is clearly an original one and probably belongs to the 1770s.
[46] For the editions in the second Monticello library, see Poor 5-6; for that in the Poplar Forest Library, see Leavitt 624.
[47] See Sowerby 996.

By the time of his retirement, Jefferson had come to a decided preference for ancient over modern history, a preference he referred to often in his letters, and there is little doubt that he continued to read Herodotus. "I feel a much greater interest in knowing what has passed two or three thousand years ago, than in what is passing now. I read nothing, therefore, but of the heroes of Troy, of the wars of Lacedaemon and Athens, of Pompey and Caesar, and of Augustus too, the Bonaparte and parricide scoundrel of that day."[48]

HOMER (8th century B.C.?), Greek epic poet. In the orderly catalogue of Jefferson's principal library, the first of many chapters (or categories) on literature is "Epic," and the first poet listed is Homer. He is represented in no less than a dozen different editions, including translations in Latin, English, Italian, and French, and he was for Jefferson "the first of poets, as he must ever remain, until a language equally ductile & copious shall again be spoken."[49]

Jefferson, of course, studied Homer as a schoolboy learning Greek in the 1750s and seems to have read him in earnest in the mid-1760s, when he entered most of the extracts from Homer in the Literary Commonplace Book. Having inserted a good many passages prior to 1763 from Alexander Pope's translation of Homer (§§185-98), he seems to have returned to it while studying the Greek text in the 1760s, for additional entries from Pope's translation are in the hand of this period and correspond to passages entered in Greek (see notes to §§199-202). He used Homer for illustrative purposes in his *Notes on Virginia* (1781-1782), and a short time later chose two lines from the *Iliad* for the inscription on his wife's tombstone.[50]

Jefferson's correspondence in the 1780s shows that he continued to be concerned with Homer during his stay in Paris: collecting books for his library, directing the reading of his nephew Peter Carr, championing the ability of American farmers to read Greek, teaching Homer to a native of Greece, and working out the differences between English and Greek prosody.[51] In connection with the last project, he wrote out a document for the use of his Grecian friend that he called "A Short Greek Prosody," and about the same time composed a lengthy treatise for his friend the Marquis de Chastellux titled "Thoughts on English Prosody."[52] In attempting to answer the question, "What is Verse?" he quotes a long passage from Homer's *Iliad* and says that even if the lines were run together and it were printed as prose, "It would still be verse; it would still immortalize its author were every other syllable of his

---

[48] TJ to Nathaniel Macon, 12 Jan. 1819, Ford, XII, 110-11.
[49] Sowerby 4262-78. Sowerby is not a reliable guide to the final catalogue order of Jefferson's great library, but the same books are also listed at the head of Chapter 33, "Epic," in the Trist manuscript (Rare Book Division, DLC), which does reflect the authoritative order. TJ on Homer: TJ to John Waldo, 16 Aug. 1813, cited in Sowerby 4262.
[50] *Notes on Virginia*, p. 142, 281, 297. Tombstone verses: *Iliad*, 22. 389-90; quoted in Randall, I, 383.
[51] For references to these various activities, see entries under "Homer" in vol. 21 of *Papers*, the index to the first 20 volumes.
[52] TJ to Madame de Tott, 28 Nov. 1786, *Papers*, 10: 553-4. See the letter Jefferson wrote to accompany "Thoughts on English Prosody," TJ to Chastellux, [Oct. 1786], *Papers*, 10: 498, as well as the body of the essay, only available in a poorly transcribed and poorly edited version, L & B, XVIII, 415-51.

compositions lost."[53] Further on he confides: "When young any composition pleases which unites a little sense, some imagination, and some rhythm, in doses however small. But as we advance in life these things fall off one by one, and I suspect we are left at last with only Homer and Virgil, perhaps with Homer alone. He like 'Hope travels on nor quits us when we die.' "[54]

Quoting Pope to praise Homer probably came quite naturally to Jefferson, for as a young man he was closely familiar with both. But while his taste for Pope and most of English poetry seems to have seriously diminished with age, his enjoyment of Homer remained strong and lasted to the end of his life. He told his friend Joseph Priestley in 1800, "I enjoy Homer in his own language infinitely beyond Pope's translation of him, & both beyond the dull narrative of the same events by Dares Phrygius."[55] His retirement library, both at Monticello and Poplar Forest, was well stocked with Homer, and nearly 20 years later, at the age of 75, he could still write feelingly to John Adams of "the sublime measure of Homer."[56]

In the Autobiography he began when he was 77, he wrote of Patrick Henry, his early friend and later bitter political enemy. Passing over his misgivings about Henry's character, he paid tribute to his unique oratorical talents as fully as it was possible for him to do. "They were great indeed; such as I have never heard from any other man. He appeared to me to speak as Homer wrote."[57]

[HORACE] Quintus Horatius Flaccus (65-8 B.C.), Roman poet. The entries in the Literary Commonplace Book that are in all likelihood the earliest, inscribed in a very careful and deliberate hand, are from Horace (§§167-72). Along with the other authors represented in the earliest group of entries—Virgil and Ovid—Horace was standard reading in the Latin schools of Jefferson's day and would have been one of the first Latin poets he came to know.[58] Unlike the other two, who are present in only a few entries, Horace is relatively well represented, not only in the school period but later on as well.

The longest excerpt from Horace, which dates from about 1770, is perhaps the most indicative, being a careful condensation of the second Epode, a famous poem on country life (§378). Gilbert Chinard noted that Jefferson excised most of the strictly Roman elements so that the mode of life exemplified in his condensed version is much like that found on a Southern plantation.[59] But even more significant is his complete suppression of the ironic element, which is all-important in Horace's version and which undercuts the glorification of rural life. An even more abbreviated version of this poem is recorded in Jefferson's pocket Memorandum Book for 1771 as an inscription for a landscape design at the north spring at Monticello (see §378n).

Jefferson had multiple editions of Horace in all of his libraries, and the frequency with which he quotes him to his correspondents leaves little doubt

---

[53] L & B, XVIII, 441.
[54] Same, 448. "Hope travels on . . . ," appears in the LCB at §208.14.
[55] TJ to Joseph Priestley, 27 Jan. 1800, Ford, IX, 103.
[56] TJ to John Adams, 21 Mar. 1819, Cappon, p. 538.
[57] Ford, I, 8.
[58] See Meyer Reinhold, "The Cult of Antiquity in America," *Classica Americana: The Greek and Roman Heritage in the United States* (Detroit, 1984), p. 26.
[59] Chinard, p. 32-3.

that his familiarity with Horace continued unabated.[60] Peter Gay has pointed out that, at a time when a knowledge of the classics was a common possession of the educated, "Horace, especially Horace, the most pagan of poets, was the great favorite of the century."[61] If not his paganism, certainly the Epicurean flavor of Horace's poetry as much as his wit and poetic genius made him attractive to Jefferson, as did his avid attachment to his Sabine farm and the joys of country life.[62] What Jefferson prophetically recorded in his notebook as a schoolboy was to become a common cry in his adulthood, so much of which was spent away from Monticello: "O rural home: when shall I behold you!" (§175)

In his later years, Jefferson often expressed his preference for classical reading over the newspapers, naming Horace as an example: "I read one or two newspapers a week, but with reluctance give even that time from Tacitus and Horace, and so much other more agreeable reading."[63] In addition to reading from the many editions of Horace's works he collected for his library, there is good reason to think he still had recourse, even in his retirement, to the Literary Commonplace Book he had begun as a boy with entries from Horace. At the age of 72, in answer to a request from a Maine schoolmaster for something in his own hand for the edification of students, Jefferson copied out two entries from his school days, one from Cicero (§79) and the other from Horace (§177). The reading that launched him on his intellectual career seems to have sustained him in his closing years, for he told a correspondent late in life: "I wish at length to indulge myself in more favorite reading, in Tacitus and Horace and the writers of that philosophy which is the old man's consolation and preparation for what is to come."[64]

David HUME (1711-1776), Scottish philosopher and historian. Jefferson read and recommended Hume's literary and philosophical essays,[65] but it was his *History of England*, published between 1754 and 1762, that alarmed Jefferson and elicited a barrage of unfavorable comment. Jefferson purchased a six-volume set of Hume's history on March 2, 1764, in Williamsburg at the office of the *Virginia Gazette*,[66] and presumably had read it through by the time the single entry in the Literary Commonplace Book was made circa 1765. When in later life he wrote that Hume's *History* "is so plausible & pleasing in it's style and manner, as to instil it's errors & heresies insensibly into the minds

---

[60] Sowerby 4474-80; Poor 769-72; Leavitt 633, 647.

[61] Peter Gay, *The Enlightenment: The Rise of Modern Paganism* (New York, 1967), p. 39.

[62] Karl Lehmann, the author of the most detailed study of the subject, argues that Horace "next to Homer, remained throughout his life his most cherished poet," and that this was mainly because of Horace's "profession of Epicurean ethics." *Thomas Jefferson: American Humanist* (New York, 1947), p. 139.

[63] TJ to David Howell, 15 Dec. 1810, L & B, XII, 435-7.

[64] Quoted in Merrill D. Peterson, *Thomas Jefferson and the New Nation* (New York, 1970), p. 927.

[65] Hume's essays were in the first and second Monticello libraries, the Poplar Forest library, and in all likelihood the Shadwell library as well. (Sowerby 1261; Poor 485; Leavitt 634). They also appear on the select list of books recommended to Robert Skipwith in 1771 (*Papers*, 1: 80) and were recommend by TJ to his nephew, Peter Carr (*Papers*, 12: 19), and to his son-in-law, Thomas Mann Randolph (*Papers*, 16: 449).

[66] *Virginia Gazette Daybook* (ViU), microfilm copy.

of unwary readers,"[67] he was describing his own first experience, for a few years later he confided to William Duane: "I remember well the enthusiasm with which I devoured it when young, and the length of time, the research & reflection which were necessary to eradicate the poison it had instilled into my mind."[68]

Jefferson's subsequent campaign against Hume's *History of England*, begun in his sixties, is well known. The "poison" Jefferson refers to was Hume's persuasive rejection of certain crucial elements in the Whig version of English constitutional history to which Jefferson, along with most of his fellow revolutionaries, wholeheartedly subscribed. The most virulent of Hume's "poisons" were two: the view of the early Stuart kings, James I and Charles I, as defenders of the royal prerogative against the encroachments of Parliament, not usurpers of the people's rights; and second, a debunking of the Ancient Constitution, the supposed charter of English government, originating in Saxon times, put forward by Whig historians as the foundation of popular rights and liberties. Moreover, Jefferson charged that Hume had reinforced his "heresies" by writing his history backwards: "It was unfortunate that he first took up the history of the Stuarts, became their apologist and advocated all their enormities. To support his work, when done, he went back to the Tudors, and so selected and arranged the materials of their history as to present their arbitrary acts only, as the genuine samples of the constitutional power of the crown; and, still writing backwards, he then reverted to the early history, and wrote the Saxon & Norman periods with the same perverted view."[69]

Because even he had been taken in unawares, and because Hume's had become the standard history, Jefferson was convinced that it had "toryized" not only the British public but American readers as well. "Every one knows that judicious matter & charms of stile have rendered Hume's history the Manual of every student."[70] For one who believed that the origins of democracy and free institutions were discernible in English history, a work that obscured or denied such momentous developments was truly subversive. "It is this book," he argued, "which has undermined the free principles of the English government, has persuaded readers of all classes that these were usurpations on the legitimate and salutary rights of the crown, and has spread universal toryism over the land."[71] To counter this supposed menace to republican values, Jefferson tried in his retirement years to foster an "antidote" to Hume's *History*. Reprinting Hume's text in its entirety with corrective annotation seemed the best plan, but he feared this was impracticable.[72] Instead, he proposed that American publishers should reprint a book by the British radical John Baxter that appropriated the text of Hume in an expurgated form. "Wherever he [Baxter] has found him endeavoring to mislead, by either the suppression of a truth or by giving it a false coloring, he has changed the text to what it should be, so that we may properly call it Hume's history

[67] TJ to John Norvell, 11 June 1807, cited in Sowerby 370.
[68] TJ to William Duane, 10 Aug. 1810, cited in Sowerby 370.
[69] Same.
[70] Same.
[71] Same.
[72] TJ to Mathew Carey, 22 Nov. 1818, cited in Sowerby 405.

republicanised."[73] He later recommended that Baxter's book be employed as a primer for students of English history at the University of Virginia and that Hume's history be the last that one read.[74] It is worth noting that Jefferson makes clear in this letter that his concern is not that students might read Hume's *History*, but rather that they might read it *first*, so as to become "toryized" unknowingly. Clearly he is harking back to his own experience as an eager young reader who, much to his chagrin, had inadvertently swallowed Hume whole.

In spite of his efforts in behalf of Baxter's work, which most commentators have found regrettable, it is clear from Jefferson's correspondence and other evidence that he continued throughout his life to read Hume's *History* and, surprisingly, to hold it in very high esteem. Well after the Revolution, in 1787, he recommended part of it to his nephew, Peter Carr, just as he recommended Hume's political essays to his son-in-law in 1790. The campaign in his retirement years to reprint Baxter demonstrates among other things how closely familiar Jefferson was with Hume's text and, further, that he regretted the loss of some of the material Baxter had omitted.[75] Some of his strongest condemnations of Hume's "errors" came toward the end of his life, yet at the age of 75, he could write: "The charms of it's stile and selection of it's matter, had it but candor and freedom from political bias, would make it the most perfect sample of fine history which has ever flowed from the pen of man; not meaning to except even the most approved models of antiquity."[76] From Jefferson, this is the highest possible praise.

John LANGHORNE (1735-1779), English clergyman and poet. Jefferson copied extracts from Langhorne's popular "Hymn to Hope" into his Literary Commonplace Book (§396), but he does not seem to have owned any of the editions of Langhorne's poems in which it appears. Even though he included two of Langhorne's romantic tales in the select list of books he prepared for Robert Skipwith in 1771,[77] no book by Langhorne—who also published sermons, treatises, and translations—seems to have found a place in Jeffferson's own library.

[LIVY] Titus Livius (*c.* 59 B.C.-17 A.D.), Roman historian. Jefferson subscribed to the standard view that Livy, with Sallust and Tacitus, was one of the three greatest Roman historians, and Livy is consequently recommended on virtually every reading list Jefferson prepared that included Roman history. As the principal account of the Roman republic, whose fractious career and ultimate failure was a subject of consuming interest to the American

---

[73] TJ to John Norvell, 11 June 1807, L & B, XI, 223-4. The American publishers were William Duane and Mathew Carey (see letters cited above) and Thomas W. White (see letters cited in Sowerby 405).

[74] TJ to [George Washington Lewis], 25 Oct. 1825, L & B, XVI, 128.

[75] TJ to Mathew Carey, Sowerby 405.

[76] Same. In addition to those cited above, other notable letters on Hume are TJ to John Adams, 25 Nov. 1816, Cappon, p. 498-9, and TJ to Major John Cartwright, 5 June 1824, L & B, XVI, 42-52.

[77] *Constantia* (1763) and *Solyman and Almena* (1762); TJ to Robert Skipwith, 3 Aug. 1771, *Papers*, 1: 79.

founders, Livy's history of Rome was part of the common currency of revo-
lutionary and republican discourse.

The sole quotation from Livy in the Literary Commonplace Book is from
one of the imaginary orations by which Livy, like other classical historians,
sought to dramatize the events of his narrative. Jefferson particularly valued
this aspect of Roman historiography and on more than one occasion called
attention to these speeches as proper models (unlike the Ciceronian) for political oratory. "The models for that oratory which is to produce the greatest
effect by securing the attention of hearers and readers," he told his son-in-
law, "are to be found in Livy, Tacitus, Sallust, and most assuredly not in
Cicero."[78]

Numerous incidents illustrate that, for Jefferson, reading Livy was a basic
and important part of acquiring an education. For example, when his daughter, Martha, wanted to get back at her father for going off alone to the south
of France and not writing her, she taunted him from her convent school: "Titus Livius puts me out of my wits." He promptly obliged her with an extended remonstrance.[79] In advising his young nephew, Peter Carr, on the
proper way to consider the claims of Christianity, he repeated what he had
learned from Bolingbroke: "Read the bible then, as you would read Livy or
Tacitus."[80]

As one might expect, Livy occupies an important niche in all of Jefferson's
libraries, and his letters amply demonstrate his close familiarity with Livy's
text. "I am glad to find you are thinking of printing Livy," he wrote to a
Boston publisher in 1818, for "there is not, nor ever has been an edition mer-
iting the name of an editio optima. The Delphin edition might have been, but
for it's numerous errors of the press, and unmanageable size in 4to. It's notes
are valuable, and it has the whole of Freinsheim's supplement with the marginal references to his authorities. Clerk's edition is of a handy size, has the
whole of Freinsheim, but without the references, which we often wish to turn
to, and it is without notes. The late Paris edition of La Malle has only the
supplement of the 2d decad and no notes. I possess these two last mentioned
editions, but would gladly become a subscriber to such a one as I describe,

[78] TJ to John Wayles Eppes, 17 Jan. 1810, Ford, xi, 129.
[79] Martha Jefferson to TJ, 25 Mar. 1787, Papers, 11: 238. This amusing episode actually begins in Martha's letter of 8 Mar. 1787, in which she complains that her Livy is
"in such ancient italian that I can not read with out my master and very little with him
even." Papers, 11: 203 This has caused many observers to assume that she was reading
Livy in an Italian translation, but this seems not to have been the case. Jefferson says in
his reply: "I do not like your saying that you are unable to read the antient print of your
Livy," which clearly implies that the difficulty, which he was presumably able to judge,
had to do with the printing and not the language of Martha's edition. TJ to Martha
Jefferson, 28 Mar. 1787, Papers, 11: 251. Many years later TJ confessed "I may sometimes be disappointed in the choice [of edition] I have hazarded, in the Greek classics
particularly by the obsolete type of that which I have selected, in the Latin by the Italian
letter which is disagreeable to the eye." TJ to George Ticknor, 4 July 1815, in Sigmund
Diamond, ed., "Some Jefferson Letters," Mississippi Valley Historical Review, 28 (1941),
235.
[80] TJ to Peter Carr, 10 Aug. 1787, Papers, 12: 15. For Bolingbroke's comparable use
of Livy, see entry §58.

that is to say, an 8vo edition with the Delphin notes and all Freinsheim's supplements and references."[81]

Especially in his retirement years, when much of his reading was concentrated in the classics, Jefferson praised the moralistic and patriotic point of view with which Livy and other historians approached their subjects. "It is true that I am tired of practical politics," he wrote William Duane in 1813, "and happier while reading the history of ancient than of modern times. . . . I turn from the contemplation [of the immorality of modern politicians] with loathing, and take refuge in the histories of other times, where, if they also furnish their tarquins, their Catilines and Caligulas, their stories are handed to us under the brand of a Livy, a Sallust and a Tacitus, and we are comforted with the reflection that the condemnation of all succeeding generations has confirmed the censures of the historian, and consigned their memories to everlasting infamy, a solace we cannot have with the Georges and Napoleons but by anticipation."[82]

James MACPHERSON (1736-1796), Scottish poet and writer. Macpherson was a versatile writer, a number of whose works on politics and British history and whose translation of the *Iliad* were in Jefferson's library.[83] But he is best remembered for his supposed translations of the poems of Ossian, whom he represented as a third-century Celtic bard. Having published some specimens of this material with great success as *Fragments of Ancient Poetry Collected in the Highlands of Scotland and Translated From Gaelic or Erse Language* (1760), he was encouraged and financially supported by influential Scots to search out and recover remnants of the bardic tradition from oral and manuscript sources in the Scottish highlands. This effort resulted in the publication of *Fingal, An Ancient Epic Poem* (1762), which also contained, in addition to the epic of the title, a number of shorter poems attributed to the same author, Ossian. A year later, he published a supposed translation of another epic, *Temora*. Subsequent investigations have shown that most of this material bears only a tangential relation to Gaelic originals, and that more important sources seem to have been the Bible and Macpherson's own imagination.[84]

Although some, like Dr. Samuel Johnson, rejected the Ossian poems as fraudulent, and some, like Thomas Gray and David Hume, were intrigued but skeptical, the general reception was strongly positive, not only in Scotland, where the national pride was involved, but in England and eventually

---

[81] TJ to Wells and Lilly, 1 Apr. 1818, Worthington Chauncey Ford, ed., *Thomas Jefferson Correspondence Printed from the original in the Collections of William K. Bixby* (Boston, 1916), p. 238-9.

[82] TJ to William Duane, 4 Apr. 1813, L & B, XIII, 230. For other references to Livy, see TJ to the Rev. James Madison, 19 July 1788, *Papers*, 13: 381-3; TJ to Nicolas Dufief, 9 Jan. 1813, Sowerby, I: 27; TJ to William Short, 4 Aug. 1820, L & B, XV, 257-8; TJ to David Harding, 20 Apr. 1824, L & B, XVI, 30; TJ to Joseph Coolidge, Jr., 12 Apr. 1825, L & B, XVIII, 337.

[83] See Sowerby 333, 3107, 3137, 4278.

[84] See Derick S. Thomson, *The Gaelic Sources of Macpherson's Ossian* (Edinburgh and London, 1952), and the same author's article on Macpherson in the *Encyclopdia Britannica* (Chicago, 1973), XIV, 545.

in Europe as well. Thomas Jefferson was just one of a host of eighteenth-century luminaries, which included Goethe and Napoleon, who were smitten by Ossian. In 1773, very close to the time he recorded the 14 entries from Ossian in the Literary Commonplace Book, Jefferson took the extraordinary step of writing to Macpherson's brother Charles, with whom he was acquainted, and asking his assistance in procuring copies of the Gaelic originals. In describing his admiration for Ossian, he pulls out all the stops: "These peices have been, and will I think during my life continue to be to me, the source of daily and exalted pleasure. The tender, and the sublime emotions of the mind were never before so finely wrought up by human hand. I am not ashamed to own that I think this rude bard of the North the greatest Poet that has ever existed. Merely for the pleasure of reading his works I am become desirous of learning the language in which he sung and of possessing his songs in their original form." He asked his correspondent to guide him in the acquisition of books in Gaelic, including a grammar and a dictionary, and to pay no regard to the expense involved. "The glow of one warm thought," he declared, "is to me worth more than money."[85]

Given this sort of enthusiasm, it is hardly surprising that when his brother-in-law and dearest friend, Dabney Carr, died a few months later at the age of 29, Jefferson considered some lines from Ossian for a proposed tombstone inscription: "This stone shall rise with all it's moss and speak to other years 'here lies gentle Carr within the dark and narrow house where no morning comes with her halfopening pages.' When thou, O stone, shalt fail and the mountain stream roll quite away! Then shall the traveller come, and bend here perhaps in rest. When the darkened moon is rolled over his head, the shadowy form may come, and, mixing with his dreams, remind him who is here."[86]

As he grew older and became more engrossed in politics, Jefferson's interest in poetry began to wane, but his enthusiasm for Ossian continued. When he was visited at Monticello by the Marquis de Chastellux in 1782, their friendship was apparently galvanized by a mutual admiration for the Celtic bard. "I recall with pleasure," the Marquis wrote in his *Travels*, "that as we were conversing one evening over a 'bowl of punch,' after Mrs. Jefferson had retired, we happened to speak of the poetry of Ossian. It was a spark of electricity which passed rapidly from one to the other; we recalled the passages of those sublime poems which had particularly struck us, and we recited them for the benefit of my traveling companions, who fortunately knew English well and could appreciate them, even though they had never read the poems. Soon the book was called for, to share in our 'toasts'; it was brought forth and

[85] TJ to Charles McPherson, 25 Feb. 1773, *Papers*, 1: 96-7.
[86] The source for this passage is *The Works of Ossian, the Son of Fingal*, 2 vols. (London, 1765), II, 53. TJ has adapted the passage to his purposes and, in the line "within the dark and narrow house where no morning comes with her halfopening pages," has incorporated some phrases from other parts of Ossian. The manuscript from which this is taken appears to have been part of a notebook that was a forerunner to the Garden Book. It is in the Manuscript Department, ViU, whose curators provided invaluable assistance in the transcription of the almost microscopic handwriting. They also supplied the inscription that actually appeared on Carr's tombstone, which concludes: "To his virtue, good sense, learning and friendship / this stone is dedicated by / Thomas Jefferson / who, of all men loved him most" (*Record of Cemeteries in Albemarle County*, III, 159).

placed beside the bowl of punch. And, before we realized it, book and bowl had carried us far into the night."[87]

Signs of Jefferson's continued interest in Ossian abound. He copied a passage from Ossian into a volume of Gibbon's *Decline and Fall of the Roman Empire*.[88] Along with Milton, Pope, and Swift, he recommended the reading of Ossian to his nephew Peter Carr to improve his English writing style. (Peter complied, but confessed that he would "be more pleased with them if there were more variety."[89]) He told his youngest daughter in 1799 that a letter from her had been "as Ossian says, or would say, like the bright beams of the moon on the desolate heath."[90] He acquired additional copies of the work at various times, and as President, he was still purchasing Ossian's poems to give away.[91] It seems clear that Ossian appealed to something not merely adolescent or transient in his nature but rather to something deep and permanent. Even in old age, when their pretensions to be ancient had been thoroughly exposed, Jefferson clung to his high estimate of the poems. He wrote his friend Lafayette that Frances Wright's *A Few Days in Athens* is better than "anything in that line left us by the ancients; and like Ossian, if not ancient, it is equal to the best morsels of antiquity."[92] From Jefferson, this was the ultimate compliment.

David MALLET (1705?-1765), Scottish poet and author. Though little known to twentieth-century readers, Mallet was a popular and successful writer in his own day. Born David Molloch in rural Scotland, he shed his Scottish name along with his accent, and rose to fame in London as a poet, playwright, biographer, and political pamphleteer. A friend and collaborator of James Thomson, he is still remembered as co-author with Thomson of "Rule Britannia."

Mallet's name is connected with two books of great importance to Thomas Jefferson. The first is a four-volume folio edition of the works of Sir Francis Bacon, published in 1740 with a life of the author by Mallet, a work that occupied a prominent place in Jefferson's library.[93] Along with Newton and Locke, Jefferson considered Bacon one of the "three greatest men that have ever lived, without any exception."[94] Mallet was also, as literary executor to Lord Bolingbroke, the editor and publisher of Bolingbroke's posthumous *Philosophical Works* (1754),[95] which are commonplaced at such length in the Literary Commonplace Book (§§4-34, 36-58) and which seem to have had such a profound impact on the development of Jefferson's rationalistic religious views.

---

[87] Marquis De Chastellux, *Travels in North America in the Years 1780, 1781, and 1782*, trans. Howard C. Rice, Jr. (Chapel Hill, 1963), p. 392.

[88] Sowerby 101.

[89] TJ to Peter Carr, 19 Aug. 1785, *Papers*, 8: 407; Peter Carr to TJ, 30 Dec. 1786, *Papers*, 10: 648.

[90] TJ to Mary Jefferson Eppes, 7 Feb. 1799, *Family Letters*, p. 173.

[91] See Sowerby 4377. TJ almost certainly had a copy of Ossian in his first library, and he retained a copy in his retirement library at Poplar Forest. See Leavitt 646.

[92] TJ to Lafayette, 4 Nov. 1823, L & B, xv, 493.

[93] Sowerby 4915.

[94] TJ to John Trumbull, 15 Feb. 1789, *Papers*, 14: 561.

[95] Sowerby 1265.

That Jefferson was fond of Mallet's poetry is evident from the fact he entered his verses in his Commonplace Book both as a boy in his teens (§§316-18) and as a successful young lawyer about 10 years later (§§350-1, 353-5). A few years later, in 1771, he placed Mallet's poetic works on his select list of books recommended to Robert Skipwith.[96] This partiality was solidly confirmed in 1773 when he adapted one of the passages he had recorded in his Commonplace Book as a possible inscription for the tomb of his dearest friend, Dabney Carr.[97]

Marcus MANILIUS (1st century A.D.), Roman poet. Nothing is known of Manilius except that he was the author of the *Astronomica*, a long didactic poem on astrology. A copy of this work was in the great library Jefferson sold to Congress.

John MILTON (1608-1674), English poet. Like most educated, English-speaking people of his time, Jefferson regarded Milton as one of the greatest poets in the language. In his *Notes on Virginia* and elsewhere, he linked Milton's name with that of Shakespeare to indicate the height of achievement in English poetry.[98]

The entries from Milton's *Paradise Lost* and *Samson Agonistes* are among the earliest in the Literary Commonplace Book and may well date from Jefferson's school days, before he entered college in 1760. They reflect an attraction for strong expressions of rebellion and defiance of authority that is characteristic of his commonplacing in this period, and from both works he copied out passages of prototypical Miltonian misogyny.[99] Jefferson's misogyny seems to have been strictly an adolescent phenomenon, but his affinity for rebellion, which did much to make him famous later on, lasted as long as he lived. In the last year of his life, writing with fervor on a topic that still aroused his combative instincts, he invoked some lines from a speech by Satan in *Paradise Lost* that he had set down in his Commonplace Book more than 60 years earlier: "The battle of Hastings, indeed, was lost, but the natural rights of the nation were not staked on the event of a single battle. Their will to recover the Saxon constitution continued unabated, and was at bottom of all the unsuccessful insurrections which succeeded in subsequent times. The victors and vanquished continued in a state of living hostility, and the nation may say, after losing the battle of Hastings,

> 'What though the field is lost?
> All is not lost; the unconquerable will
> And study of revenge, immortal hate,
> And courage never to submit or yield.' "[100]

Jefferson was familiar with the works of Milton, the political and religious reformer, as well as those of the poet. As reformers, in fact, the two men had much in common. In drawing up legislation for the disestablishment of the

[96] TJ to Robert Skipwith, 3 Aug. 1771, *Papers*, 1: 78.
[97] Manuscript at ViU. See §354n.
[98] *Notes on Virginia*, Query VI; "Essay on Anglo-Saxon," L & B, XVIII, 390.
[99] For *Paradise Lost*, see especially §236, 237, 239, 242; for *Samson Agonistes*, see especially §341.
[100] TJ to [George W. Lewis], 25 Oct. 1825, L & B, XVI, 127.

Church in the new commonwealth of Virginia, he studied two of Milton's tracts on religious freedom, *The Reason of Church-Government urged against Prelaty* and *Of Reformation in England*, and there are interesting similarities in their reformist views on education.[101] But it was as a poet that Milton made the greatest impression on Jefferson. Milton is given a prominent position and a relatively full representation in the Literary Commonplace Book, a notebook that reflects in its entries not only youthful enthusiasms but, in its ultimate contents and arrangement, which were fixed upon in the 1780s, the judgments of maturity. Another telling document that dates from the 1780s is the essay "Thoughts on English Prosody," in which Milton's poetry is prominently represented, most of the passages being taken from the entries in the Literary Commonplace Book. One that was not is the famous opening of *Paradise Lost*, offered as an instance of the grandeur of blank verse, "the most precious part of our poetry." Another passage from Milton's epic is cited to show the way in which a great poet can transcend the rules of prosody: "There are but two regular pauses in this whole passage of seven verses. They are constantly drowned by the majesty and rhythm and sense. But nothing less than this can authorize such a license."[102]

Jefferson included Milton's works on reading lists for students, and he recommended the study of Milton to his nephew Peter Carr for the improvement of his writing style.[103] "Milton's works" was one of the earliest purchases for his personal library that we have record of, and, when he sold his great library to Congress in 1815, he retained one of its many editions of Milton for his retirement library.[104] There is little doubt that he continued to read Milton, for near the end of his life he could still write of him in terms of familiarity. "I learn from you with great pleasure," he wrote a correspondent in 1825, "that a taste is reviving in England for the recovery of the Anglo-Saxon dialect of our language; for a mere dialect it is, as much as those of Piers Plowman, Gower, Douglas, Chaucer, Spenser, Shakespeare, Milton, for even much of Milton is already antiquated."[105]

Edward MOORE (1712-1757), English writer and dramatist. Moore was a minor literary figure in the mid-eighteenth century who authored fables, poems, and plays and who edited a literary journal, *The World*. Only the latter seems to have found a place in Jefferson's library. The text of the song by Moore he records in the Literary Commonplace Book (§352) is noticeably different from the published version, indicating that Jefferson may have heard it sung and set it down from memory.

---

[101] See "Notes on Episcopacy," *Papers*, 1: 552-3, and Irby Cauthen, "Jefferson and Milton," *Virginia Quarterly Review*, LV (1979), 222-33.

[102] L & B, XVIII, 447.

[103] Reading lists: TJ to Robert Skipwith, 3 Aug. 1771, *Papers*, 1: 78; TJ to Peter Carr, 10 Aug. 1787, same, 12: 18. Style: TJ to Peter Carr, 19 Aug. 1785, same, 8: 407.

[104] The Virginia Gazette Daybook reveals that Jefferson bought a copy of "Milton's Works" on 10 Feb. 1764. The two-volume edition of Milton (1784) that he purchased in Paris was withheld from the sale to Congress and appears in the manuscript catalogue of the second Monticello library and the 1829 auction catalogue of Nathaniel Poor. See Poor 741.

[105] TJ to the Hon. J. Evelyn Denison, M.P., 9 Nov. 1825, L & B, XVI, 130.

Thomas MOSS (d. 1808), English clergyman and poet. Moss took holy orders after receiving a B.A. at Cambridge in 1761. His *Poems on Several Occasions* was published anonymously at Wolverhampton in 1769, though most of the poems, according to an advertisement, were written when the author was about 20.[106] The first poem in the book is "The Beggar," which was apparently very popular in its day. Where and when Jefferson became familiar with it is not known, but its pathetic appeal to family misfortunes clearly touched a responsive chord.

Six quatrains of this poem are cited in Jefferson's "Thoughts on English Prosody" as a "Specimen of Parisyllabic verse."[107]

Thomas OTWAY (1652-1685), English Restoration dramatist. The name Thomas Otway is not a familiar one to modern readers, but for eighteenth-century audiences, according to Samuel Johnson, it was "one of the first names in the English drama."[108] During a ten-year career (1675-1685) in which he produced as many plays, Otway established himself as the leading tragedian of the age, though he apparently died in straitened circumstances at the height of his fame. Two of his tragedies were not only hugely successful in his day but became part of the standard repertory of the English stage: *The Orphan: Or, The Unhappy Marriage* (1680) and *Venice Preserved* (1682), considered his masterpiece.

Otway was not only immensely popular with British theater audiences, but he was applauded by literary critics as well. Praised by his more illustrious contemporary, John Dryden, Otway's plays fared well with succeeding generations, earning the approval of Addison, Gay, Thomson, and others.[109] In the eighteenth century, Otway's name was often linked to that of Shakespeare, whose Romeo and Juliet he imitated, and until 1768, editions of Otway's works "kept pace with the editions of Shakespeare."[110] No less a figure than Alexander Pope wrote of his country's dramatic achievements:

> Not but the tragic spirit was our own,
> And full in Shakespeare, fair in Otway shone.[111]

In 1759, about the time Jefferson was commonplacing *The Orphan* and *Venice Preserved*, Oliver Goldsmith spoke for his time, calling Otway "next to Shakespeare, the greatest genius England has produced in tragedy."[112]

Despite his present obscurity, Otway's popularity is notable in the history of the English stage. Playing Otway's heroes, for example, was an important ingredient in David Garrick's career as England's leading actor. Writing about a hundred years after its appearance, Dr. Johnson remarked that *The Orphan* "is one of the few plays that keep possession of the stage, and has pleased for almost a century through all the vicissitudes of dramatick fash-

---

[106] *Dictionary of National Biography*, XIII, 1081.
[107] L & B, XVIII, 426-7.
[108] *Lives of the English Poets*, I, 241.
[109] Same, p. 248n.
[110] Aline Mackenzie Taylor, *Next to Shakespeare: Otway's "Venice Preserved" and "The Orphan" and Their History on the London Stage* (Durham, N.C., 1950), p. 3.
[111] Same, p. 262.
[112] Same, p. 3.

ion," and that *Venice Preserved* "continues to be one of the favourites of the publick."[113] In fact, Otway's popularity continued far into the nineteenth century, attracting the talents of all the great actors and actresses of the British and American stage. In Jefferson's time, *The Orphan* and *Venice Preserved* were played in Williamsburg, and it is a virtual certainty that Jefferson, who was fond of the theater as a young man, saw at least one of them performed.[114]

Otway's plots seem implausible and his speeches bombastic and overwrought by twentieth-century standards, but his emotionalism had great appeal for nearly two hundred years, and it is clear that the young Jefferson found much to admire in the language of these plays, particularly in speeches that exemplified boldness or defiance.

[OVID] Publius Ovidius Naso (43 B.C.-17 A.D.), Roman poet. One of the greatest and most gifted of all Roman poets, Ovid was a member of the generation that came after Horace and Virgil, and was the most celebrated poet of Augustan Rome when he was summarily banished by Augustus in A.D. 8. He was a favorite of the Renaissance, whose works became standard reading in schools, and it is a virtual certainty that Jefferson encountered him as a boy learning Latin in the school of the Rev. William Douglas (1752-1757). While the Ovid entries in the Literary Commonplace Book are quite early, they probably do not date this far back and are more likely to have been made— along with those of Virgil, Horace, and Cicero—when Jefferson was a student of the Rev. James Maury (1758-1760). The presence of the heading "Ovid: Met:" in the earliest pagination series indicates that Jefferson had at some point anticipated commonplacing Ovid's *Metamorphoses*, though no entries from that work survive.

If Jefferson's acquaintance with Ovid was early, the evidence of his libraries suggests that it continued throughout his life. His great library that he sold to Congress was well stocked with Ovid in many editions, and his carefully-selected retirement library held no less than five titles at Monticello, one of which was an edition of the *Opera*, and a petit format edition at Poplar Forest.[115] The *Heroides*, from which the Literary Commonplace Book entries are drawn, is particularly well represented, as is the *Metamorphoses*, from which Jefferson could still quote late in life.[116]

Alexander POPE (1688-1744), English poet. Pope, who died the year after Jefferson was born, was already considered one of the greatest of English poets, and it is clear that Jefferson so regarded him. Extracts from "An Essay on Man" seem to be the earliest entries of English poetry in the Literary Commonplace Book, and these were eventually placed in the section given

---

[113] *Lives of the English Poets*, I, 245-6.

[114] *Venice Preserved* was performed in Williamsburg on 8 Apr., and *The Orphan* on 15 Apr. 1768. *Virginia Gazette* (Purdie & Dixon), 7, 14 Apr. 1768. TJ seems to have been in Gloucester County on 8 Apr., but his pocket Memorandum Book shows that he was back in Williamsburg on 11 Apr. and bought play tickets, presumably for the performance on 15 Apr. (1768 Memorandum Book, ViU).

[115] Sowerby 4339-41, 4387-90; Poor 777-9, 784, 797; Leavitt 647.

[116] TJ to Francis Van der Kemp, 9 Feb. 1818, in Frank H. Severance, ed., "A Bundle of Thomas Jefferson's Letters Now First Published," *Publications of the Buffalo Historical Society*, VII (1904), 1-32.

over to the English poets that Jefferson, as a young man, seems to have esteemed the most—Pope, Milton, Young, Shakespeare, and Thomson. Pope's translations of Homer's *Iliad* are also well represented in the Literary Commonplace Book and seem to have been important in the development of the budding young classicist.

The entries from "An Essay on Man" (§§203-13) belong to the period prior to 1763, and may date from Jefferson's school days in the 1750s. The poem was criticized for its deistic tendencies, said to have been prompted by conversations with Lord Bolingbroke, but Jefferson's attention at this stage does not seem to have been drawn to this aspect of the poem. Though he was apparently strongly influenced several years later by the rationalistic deism of the essays that Bolingbroke addressed to Pope (see §§4-34, 36-58), Jefferson's youthful reading of "An Essay on Man" was probably akin to the early reception of the poem described by Dr. Johnson: "So little was any evil tendency discovered that, as innocence is unsuspicious, many read it for a manual of piety."[117] One of the interesting things shown by Jefferson's commonplacing of this poem is the thoroughness and care with which he read it, several times copying out variant lines from the footnotes in William Warburton's edition.

In poring over Warburton's edition, Jefferson seems also to have taken notice of Pope's gardening activities at Twickenham, and he contemplated at one time incorporating some lines of Pope's verse into a landscape design.[118] There is little doubt that he studied him carefully, for years later he told John Bernard that, along with Shakespeare, Pope "gave him the perfection of imagination and judgment, both displaying more knowledge of the human heart—the true province of poetry—than he could elsewhere find."[119] In view of this, it is scarcely surprising that Pope is one of the authors frequently cited in his "Thoughts on English Prosody" or that he urged students to read Pope to form their style.[120]

The order in which the extracts are entered and the variations in the handwriting make it likely that the Literary Commonplace Book contains gleanings of two separate encounters with Pope's translations of the *Iliad*, the second coming at about the same time he was studying Greek and making entries from the same passages in Homer.[121] Pope's translation had enormous standing in the eighteenth century, Dr. Johnson declaring it "the noblest version [translation] of poetry which the world has ever seen" and calling its publication "one of the great events in the annals of learning."[122] This must be understood in order to properly weigh the import of Jefferson's famous remark to Joseph Priestley: "I enjoy Homer in his own language infinitely beyond Pope's translation of him. . . ."[123] In fact, the passages copied into the

[117] *Lives of the English Poets*, III, 164.
[118] See William Beiswanger, "Jefferson's Designs for Garden Structures at Monticello," *Journal of the Society of Architectural Historians*, XXXV (1976), 310-12. The verses are in the 1771 Memorandum Book (MHi).
[119] John Bernard, *Retrospections of America*, p. 238.
[120] TJ to Peter Carr, 19 Aug. 1785, *Papers*, 8: 407; TJ to Nathaniel Burwell, 14 Mar. 1818, L & B, XV, 166.
[121] §§185-98 and 199-202. The second grouping is in the distinctive handwriting of 1762-1764.
[122] *Lives of the English Poets*, p. 119.
[123] TJ to Joseph Priestley, 27 Jan. 1800, Ford, IX, 103.

Literary Commonplace Book from Pope's *Iliad*, far from being blotted out by his mastery of the Greek, were sufficiently alive to him that he could quote from one of them in a letter to John Adams some 50 years later.[124]

QUINTUS SMYRNAEUS (4th century A.D.), Greek epic poet. All that is known of Quintus is that he was a native of Smyrna and that he produced a long epic in Greek hexameters, sometimes referred to as the *Posthomerica* because it takes up the story of Troy where the *Iliad* leaves off. The manuscript for this poem was discovered in Calabria, which is why Jefferson knew the poet as Quintus Calaber. Editions of this epic were in the great library Jefferson sold to Congress and in his retirement library (Sowerby 4298, Poor 738). The presence of Quintus' epic in the latter carefully selected collection makes it a virtual certainty that the poem formed part of the program of extensive classical reading that Jefferson carried on in his retirement. The fatalistic passage from the poem, which concludes, "No man may live for ever: each man's fate is foreordained," was probably entered at this time and stands at the end of the Literary Commonplace Book as the final statement of a theme that had found expression in its pages early and often.

Jean RACINE (1639-1699), French poet and dramatist. French was the first modern foreign language Thomas Jefferson learned and the first he urged upon others. He called the study of French "an indispensable part of education,"[125] and there can be little doubt that this was true in his own case. A substantial portion of the books in his great library were in French, which makes it all the more surprising that the four extracts from Racine (§§392-5) should stand as the only entries in that language in the whole of the Literary Commonplace Book.

An interest in the plays of Racine, the preëminent seventeenth-century French tragedian, is readily understandable in an admirer of Euripides, Racine's great master, and Otway, his English contemporary and imitator. What is remarkable is that Racine should not earn a place in any of Jefferson's libraries of which we have a record. If his works were included, alongside those of Molière and Corneille, in the Petit Format Library that ended up at Poplar Forest, they were removed before the catalogue of that library was made in 1873.[126] Nonetheless, Jefferson continued after his youth, when the Literary Commonplace Book entries were made, to think well of Racine, recommending him to his nephew, Peter Carr, and as reading for the education of young women: "Pope, Dryden, Thompson, Shakespeare, and of the French, Molière, Racine, the Corneilles, may be read with pleasure and improvement."[127]

Nicholas ROWE (1674-1718), English poet and dramatist. Remembered now only as the editor of the first critical edition of Shakespeare (1709), Nicholas Rowe was a notable man of letters in the early eighteenth century, ending his career as Poet Laureate (1715-1718). In Jefferson's youth, his reputation as a playwright was still very much alive, particularly as the author of so-called

[124] TJ to John Adams, 1 Aug. 1816, Cappon, p. 83. Cf. §202.
[125] TJ to Nathaniel Burwell, 14 Mar. 1818, L & B, xv, 167.
[126] Leavitt 622.
[127] TJ to Nathaniel Burwell, 14 Mar. 1818, L & B, xv, 166.

"she-tragedies" in which the protagonist is a woman. The most successful of these was *The Fair Penitent* (1703), one of the most popular and frequently performed plays of the century.

In addition to extracts made from two other plays by Rowe, *Tamerlane* (1702) and *Lady Jane Gray* (1715), Jefferson entered passages from *The Fair Penitent* in his Literary Commonplace Book on three separate occasions.[128] This preferred treatment simply confirmed the decided partiality of his age. A measure of the esteem in which this play was held more than 75 years after it first appeared is the fulsome praise accorded it by the crusty Samuel Johnson. *The Fair Penitent*, he wrote, "is one of the most pleasing tragedies on the stage, where it still keeps its turns of appearing; and probably will long keep them, for there is scarcely any work of any poet at once so interesting by the fable and so delightful by the language."[129]

Like the works of Thomas Otway, which they in some ways resembled, Rowe's works were in Jefferson's library and appeared on the list of recommended books he sent to Robert Skipwith in 1771. In that year, sketching a description for a family burying ground at Monticello, Jefferson tried to invoke the mood by quoting some lines from *The Fair Penitent* that he had copied into his Commonplace Book and may well have memorized.[130] Hannah More reported that Dr. Johnson himself once took her by the hand in the middle of dinner and repeated "with no small enthusiasm, many passages from *The Fair Penitent*."[131]

Lucius Annaeus SENECA, the Younger (*c.* 4 B.C.-A.D. 65), Spanish-born philosopher and tragedian. Jefferson regarded Seneca as a preëminent moralist, and he had copies of his works in all of his libraries. In working out his famous "Syllabus of an estimate of the merit of the doctrines of Jesus, compared with those of others," he cited Seneca, along with Cicero, to confirm his characterizations of the heathen moralists.[132] His assessment of Seneca is probably summed up in a passage from a letter to his friend William Short: "Seneca is indeed a fine moralist, disfiguring his work at times with some Stoicisms and affecting too much of antithesis and point, yet giving us on the whole a great deal of sound and practical morality."[133]

The only two excerpts from Seneca in the Literary Commonplace Book (§§373-4) are from his tragedy, *Medea*, which may have been modeled after the version by Euripides that Jefferson had commonplaced at length (§§126-38) some years earlier.

William SHAKESPEARE (1564-1616), English poet and dramatist. Jefferson's views of Shakespeare seem to have been those of his century and were thus rather conventional. He regarded Shakespeare, along with Milton, as the greatest of English poets.[134] He followed the efforts of successive eigh-

---

[128] *Tamerlane*, §§312-15; *Lady Jane Gray*, §§320-3; *The Fair Penitent*, §§296, 307-8, 379.
[129] *Lives of the English Poets*, p. 67.
[130] See §379n.
[131] *Lives of the English Poets*, p. 67n.
[132] TJ to Benjamin Rush, 21 Apr. 1803, Ford, IX, 460n.
[133] TJ to William Short, 31 Oct. 1819, Sowerby 1324.
[134] See, for example, *Notes on Virginia*, p. 64.

teenth-century editors to improve the reliability of Shakespeare's text. He was interested in the Restoration and early eighteenth-century attempts to "improve" Shakespeare's plays, as evidenced by the inclusion of certain excerpts in the Literary Commonplace Book (§§297-300). And he believed that a close familiarity with Shakespeare could improve the writing style of the diligent student.[135]

The library that Jefferson sold to Congress in 1815 contained the four-volume selection of 20 plays edited by George Steevens and the 12-volume edition of the complete works edited by Steevens and Samuel Johnson, with the supplement by Edmund Malone.[136] But he also owned at one time or another the famous editions of Lewis Theobald and Edward Capell, Stockdale's edition in one volume and Bell's in several dozen, the latter edition being the one he used in his retirement at Poplar Forest.[137] Though he kept up with the controversies of the warring scholars, he complained of "the volumes of idle commentaries and conjectures with which that divine poet has been masked and metamorphosed."[138]

The edition from which he copied most of the Shakespeare entries into the Literary Commonplace Book was that of Sir Thomas Hanmer, which may have been in his first library.[139] The extracts from Shakespeare (§§268-80) are among the earliest in the Commonplace Book and may even antedate his entry into the College of William and Mary in 1760. Most were taken from Hanmer, but a few were gleaned from *Thesaurus Dramaticus*, a collection of memorable lines from the British dramatists (§§281-2, 291, 294). It seems likely that he studied Shakespeare intensively in his youth, as he often advised young students to read him, and while still a young man himself, he counselled Bernard Moore: "Read the best of the poets, epic, didactic, dramatic, pastoral, lyric &c. But among these Shakespeare must be singled out by one who wishes to learn the full powers of the English language. Of him we must advise as Horace did of the Grecian models, 'vos exemplaria Graeca Nocturna versate manu, versate diurna.' [For yourselves, handle Greek models by night, handle them by day.]"[140]

That Jefferson's Commonplace Book should contain excerpts from rewritings of Shakespeare's plays by Dryden and the Duke of Buckingham is not surprising, given the belief of the age, from which not even Samuel Johnson was immune, that the plays could be "improved." Jefferson labels one of his entries (§294) as coming from the *Jew of Venice*, apparently because this is the title of the version of *The Merchant of Venice* by Lord Landsdowne that

[135] TJ to Nathaniel Burwell, 14 Mar. 1818, L & B, XV, 166.

[136] Sowerby 4538-9.

[137] Theobald: 1783 manuscript catalogue of TJ's Library, MHi; erased but clearly visible. Capell: selections from TJ's manuscript catalogue by William Short, c. 1788-1789, Short Papers, DLC. Stockdale: undated manuscript catalogue of books acquired 1784-1789, MHi. Bell: Paris correspondence 1786-1788, Leavitt 658.

[138] TJ to John Evelyn Denison, 9 Nov. 1825, L & B, XVI, 133-4.

[139] See §§268-80n.

[140] TJ to John Minor, 30 Aug. 1814, Ford, XI, 424-5. The letter to Minor contains a copy of the letter to Bernard Moore, probably written in the early 1770s. The phrase "versate diurna" was mistakenly transcribed "diversate diurna" in Ford's edition and has been corrected from a photocopy of the manuscript and the polygraph copy retained by Jefferson.

was more popular with eighteenth-century audiences than Shakespeare's original. In fact, when this play was performed in Williamsburg, it was advertised as "A Play call'd The Merchant of Venice (written by Shakespeare)."[141]

Like many people who are familiar with Shakespeare, Jefferson quoted and alluded to the plays in his correspondence and other writings. He referred more than once, for example, to the passage in *The Tempest* that speaks of "the baseless fabric of a vision," and in an unexpected quarter—his legal brief in the Batture case—he humorously compared his adversary's claims to Falstaff's escalating estimates of the number of his assailants.[142] In arguing for the moral efficacy of literature, he urged that the fictitious murder of Duncan by Macbeth produced "as great horror of villainy" as an actual one and that "a lively and lasting sense of filial duty is more effectually impressed on the mind of a son or daughter by reading King Lear, than by all the dry volumes of ethics and divinity that ever were written."[143] Though his taste for English poetry declined with age, he seems to have never lost the high regard for Shakespeare he formed in his youth. When he was President, he told the actor John Bernard, that Shakespeare "gave him the perfection of imagination and judgment" and a sure knowledge of the human heart, "the true province of poetry."[144]

Laurence STERNE (1713-1768), English novelist. For readers of Jefferson's generation, the writings of Sterne were a common possession to which they alluded freely in their conversations and correspondence. Sterne's meteoric literary career was launched with the publication of the first two volumes of *The Life and Opinions of Tristram Shandy* in 1760, the year Jefferson left the piedmont for Williamsburg and enrolled at the College of William and Mary. The enormous vogue enjoyed by Sterne's novels and sermons in the 1760s— in America, as well as in England and Europe—coincided with Jefferson's intellectual coming of age and thus formed a significant part of his literary education.

It is not known when he began to read *Tristram Shandy*, but it is reasonably certain Jefferson was familiar with it when he purchased Sterne's sermons from the office of the *Virginia Gazette* on 8 Aug. 1765.[145] A letter dated a year later yields the first of many echoes and allusions in his correspondence to the writings of Sterne.[146] In 1771, responding to a friend's request for a list of books to constitute a small library, Jefferson offers a much-quoted defense of fiction, invoking the example of Sterne's *A Sentimental Journey*: "We neither know nor care whether Lawrence Sterne really went to France, whether he

---

[141] Quoted in Kimball, p. 59.

[142] *The Tempest*: TJ to John Page, 21 Feb. 1770, *Papers*, 1: 35; TJ to John W. Eppes, 6 Nov. 1813, Ford, xi, 331. Falstaff: L & B, xviii, 2.

[143] TJ to Robert Skipwith, 3 Aug. 1771, *Papers*, 1: 77.

[144] John Bernard, *Retrospections of America*, p. 238.

[145] *Virginia Gazette Daybooks* (ViU), microfilm copy.

[146] TJ to John Page, 25 May 1766: "Surely never did small hero experience greater misadventures than I did on the first two or three days of my travelling." *Papers*, 1: 18-9. Near the beginning of *Tristram Shandy*, the author complains of Fortune that this "ungracious Duchess has pelted me with a set of as pitiful misadventures and cross accidents as ever small Hero sustained." (Book 1, Chap. 5)

was there accosted by the poor Franciscan, at first rebuked him unkindly, and then gave him a peace offering; or whether the whole be not a fiction."[147] When he himself had occasion to pass through Calais in 1786, he recorded in his Memorandum Book: "gave the successor of Sterne's monk at Calais, 1 f, 4."[148]

Judging from references in his correspondence while living in Paris in the 1780s and from purchases of Sterne's works he made at the time, it seems likely that Jefferson was re-reading the novels and sermons that he had enjoyed in his youth.[149] Returning to Paris from a trip in 1788, he wrote to Maria Cosway: "At Strasbourg I sat down to write to you. But for my soul I could think of nothing at Strasbourg but the promontory of noses, of Diego, of Slawkenburgius his historian, and the procession of the Strasburgers to meet the man with the nose. Had I written you from thence it would have been a continuation of Sterne upon noses, and I knew that nature had not formed me for a Continuator of Sterne."[150] Though this suggestive reference to the story of Diego from *Tristram Shandy* probably constitutes an expressive gesture in the fading love affair of Jefferson and Maria Cosway, it is difficult to discern whether it was intended as anything more than light-hearted banter.

Because of his own experience, Jefferson recognized the attraction of Sterne's uninhibited style for the young and recommended his writings accordingly. He could offer Sterne as a model of English eloquence to college students, and he once told his young nephew Peter Carr that "the writings of Sterne particularly form the best course of morality that ever was written."[151] That Jefferson sincerely admired Sterne as a writer and moralist is beyond question, but these superlatives must be taken in context. Jefferson was trying to steer younger readers to something that they would relish and remember as he did.

The passage from *Tristram Shandy* inscribed in the Literary Commonplace Book (§81) has strong associations with Jefferson's marriage and his wife, Martha Wayles Jefferson. They were married in 1772, which, if the handwriting is indicative, was close to the time the passage was entered.[152] Their

[147] TJ to Robert Skipwith, 3 Aug. 1771, *Papers*, 1: 77.

[148] Cited in Kimball, p. 156.

[149] In addition to other Paris letters cited herein, see TJ to Angelica Church, 17 Aug. 1788, *Papers*, 13: 521. A famous passage in *Tristram Shandy* is my Uncle Toby's solution to my Father's quandary on noses: "There is no cause but one . . . why one man's nose is longer than another, but because that God pleases to have it so" (Book 3, Chap. 41). For an interesting echo, compare Jefferson's explanation, in his essay on prosody written in Paris, of why only certain musical tones gives pleasure: "The reason is that it has pleased God to make us so." "Thoughts on English Prosody," L & B, XVIII, 419. For the purchase of the works of Sterne in Paris, see Sowerby 4335.

[150] TJ to Maria Cosway, 24 Apr. 1788, *Papers*, 13: 104. Julian P. Boyd notes: "But the association of noses and Strasbourg is another indication of the thoroughness with which he knew his Sterne. 'Slawkenbergius's Tale' of the man who arrived in Strasbourg from the Promontory of Noses and precipitated a revolution in the affairs of the city because of the curiosity of the inhabitants about the size of his nose is to be found in *Tristram Shandy*, Book 3, ch. 31-42." *Papers*, 13: 104n.

[151] See TJ to George W. Summers and John B. Garland, 27 Feb. 1822, L & B, XV, 353; TJ to Peter Carr, 10 Aug. 1787, *Papers*, 12: 15.

[152] For a discussion of the dating of the LCB passage (§81), see Appendix A.

happy marriage was punctuated, because of Jefferson's political commitments, by a number of painful partings and separations in the years following, perhaps none more difficult than Jefferson's extended stay in Philadelphia from May to September of 1776. At some point, possibly on her deathbed in 1782, Martha Jefferson copied onto a slip of paper the first part of this passage: "Time wastes too fast: every letter I trace tells me with what rapidity life follows my pen. The days and hours of it are flying over our heads like clouds of windy day never to return more[.] every thing presses on———" Jefferson then completed it in his own hand: "and every time I kiss thy hand to bid adieu, every absence which follows it, are preludes to that eternal separation which we are shortly to make!"[153]

This "affecting exchange of sentiment," as Julian Boyd has aptly called it, was almost certainly copied or memorized from the Literary Commonplace Book.[154] The omissions of words and phrases from Sterne's text are the same in both documents, and Jefferson's portion includes an exclamation mark that occurs in the Literary Commonplace Book but not in the text of *Tristram Shandy* itself (see §81n). Contrasting sharply with the comic narrative in which it is imbedded, the passage appears in the ninth and final book as a lyrical cry of the heart addressed to the author's beloved Jenny. Sterne was a doomed man, writing about his own forthcoming demise, something that Jefferson and his wife would have known; this lends poignancy both to the passage itself and to the Jeffersons' exchange.

[TERENCE] Publius Terentius Afer (*c.* 190-*c.*159 B.C.), Roman playwright. Jefferson probably first encountered Terence, the great writer of Latin comedies, as a schoolboy,[155] though the four extracts in the Literary Commonplace Book (§§179-80, 390-1) seem to have been entered in the late 1760s and 1770s. Editions of Terence appear in all of the Jefferson libraries of which we have a record, and the presence of three different editions in the carefully selected second Monticello library is a clear indication that Terence formed part of Jefferson's retirement reading.[156]

James THOMSON (1700-1748), Scottish poet. Though he had a successful career as a writer of plays, masques, and patriotic poems, Thomson was best known as the author of a four-part cycle of poems, *The Seasons* (1726-1730). The reception and subsequent reputation of this work were extraordinary,

---

[153] This badly faded scrap of paper, in which a lock of Martha Jefferson's hair was originally wrapped, was undoubtedly one of the private mementos described by Randall: "On Mr. Jefferson's own decease, forty-four years after that of his wife, in the most secret drawer of a private cabinet which he constantly resorted to, were found locks of hair, and various other little souvenirs of his wife, and of each of his living and lost children. . . ." Randall, I, 384. It is now in the James Monroe Law Office, Fredericksburg, Virginia, and has been published in *Papers*, 6: 196.

[154] Same.

[155] TJ to Peter Carr, 19 Aug. 1785, *Papers*, 8: 407: "In Latin and Greek poetry, you have read or will read at school Virgil, Terence, Horace, Anacreon, Theocritus, Homer." For an authoritative list of classical authors read in eighteenth-century American schools, see Meyer Reinhold, "The Cult of Antiquity in America," *Classica Americana: The Greek and Roman Heritage in the United States* (Detroit, 1984), p. 26.

[156] Sowerby 4576-7; Poor 765-7; Leavitt 647.

prompting a modern scholar to remark that "it is impossible to exaggerate the popularity of *The Seasons*."[157] Writing in blank verse, a mode that had had little currency since Milton, Thomson created an original kind of nature poetry that not only had enormous popular appeal but would prove an important innovation for succeeding generations of English poets.

Celebrating agriculture and rural life in the manner of Virgil's *Georgics*, Thomson's *Seasons* was particularly important for those, like Jefferson and his fellow Virginians, with ties to the soil, for it painted an enobling picture of the life around them. "The sacred plow," Thomson reminded them,

> Employ'd the kings and fathers of mankind,
> In antient times. And some . . .
> Have held the scale of justice, shook the lance
> Of mighty war, then with descending hand,
> Unus'd to little delicacies, seiz'd
> The plow, and greatly independent lived.[158]

The aptness of this heroic image of Cincinnatus was not lost on Americans, nor were the vivid scenes glorifying nature that may have seemed more appropriate to their own countryside than to England's. "The reader of *The Seasons*," wrote Samuel Johnson, "wonders that he never saw before what Thomson shews him, and that he never yet has felt what Thomson impresses."[159]

Thomson states in the Argument to "Spring" that his poem is intended to treat "its [i.e., Spring's] influence on inanimate Matter, on Vegetables, on brute Animals, and last on Man; concluding with a Dissuasive from the wild and irregular passion of love, opposed to that of a purer and more reasonable kind."[160] The longest single passage of verse in the Literary Commonplace Book (§285) is from Thomson's "Spring," which, having been entered in the distinctive handwriting of Jefferson's earliest letters, can be assigned to the period 1762-1764. That this corresponds to the period in which Jefferson was enamored of Rebecca Burwell would seem to be no coincidence, for the wretchedness he professes in his letters to his college friend John Page appears perfectly represented in Thomson's "dissuasive" description of the "charming agonies" of love.[161]

In the selection and arrangement of the material from his notebooks to be included in the Literary Commonplace Book, Jefferson positioned these early extracts from Thomson in the section occupied by what were for him the major English poets—Pope, Milton, Young, and Shakespeare. That Thomson continued to rank high in Jefferson's estimation, even after he had ceased to read much English poetry, is suggested by his reply to Nathaniel Burwell, who had written for recommendations on educational reading matter for

---

[157] Douglas Grant, *James Thomson: Poet of "The Seasons"* (London, 1951), p. 98.

[158] *The Seasons* (London, 1730), ll. 57-9, 61-4. For a discussion of how Thomson and the English georgic is reflected in TJ's ideas, see Douglas L. Wilson, "The American *agricola*: Jefferson's Agrarianism and the Classical Tradition," *South Atlantic Quarterly*, LXXX (1981), 339-54.

[159] *Lives of the English Poets*, p. 299.

[160] 1730 edition.

[161] See TJ to John Page, 25 Dec. 1762; 20 Jan. 1763; 15 July 1763; 7 Oct. 1763; 19 Jan. 1764; 23 Jan. 1764; *Papers*, 1: 3-15.

young women. Jefferson warned against too much fiction but advised that some poetry was useful "for forming style and taste. Pope, Dryden, Thompson, Shakespeare . . . may be read with pleasure and improvement."[162]

[VIRGIL] Publius Virgilius Maro (70-19 B.C.), Roman epic poet. Fond as he was of Horace and other Latin poets, Jefferson seems to have regarded Virgil as his favorite among the Romans and, with Homer, one of the greatest poets of all time. In his *Notes on Virginia*, he pubicly affirmed the supremacy traditionally accorded Virgil as representing the apex of poetic achievement in Latin, and in his several libraries he privately paid tribute to Vigil by acquiring editions of his works in Latin, English, Italian, and French.[163]

Jefferson's strong partiality for Virgil, however, is not discernible in the Literary Commonplace Book, where the poet is represented by only five brief excerpts. Marie Kimball suggests that Virgil and Ovid are sparsely represented because Jefferson had already "assimilated what they had to say to him before he started his commonplace book," a suggestion that gains force when one considers the heavy exposure to these writers his Latin schooling probably entailed.[164] In fact, in recalling those days in a letter to a schoolmate, he refers to the "time that has passed since you and I were scanning Virgil together."[165] At least two of the excerpts, and possibly four, date from the earliest stage of the Commonplace Book and probably belong to Jefferson's school days in the 1750s. The last belongs to a much later period, perhaps to his retirement years when he was systematically re-reading the works of antiquity with great relish and attention.[166] During these years, he could quote Virgil's *Aeneid* to his purpose, apparently spontaneously and from memory, in his celebrated correspondence with John Adams.[167]

It is in the essay written for his friend, the Marquis de Chastellux, "Thoughts on English Prosody," that Jefferson's personal estimate of Virgil first emerges. He had written of his own experience with poetry: "When young any composition pleases which unites a little sense, some imagination, and some rhythm, in doses however small. But as we advance in life these things fall off one by one, and I suspect we are left at last with only Homer and Virgil, perhaps with Homer alone."[168] In the first year of his presidency, apropos of the same tendency, he lamented: "So much has my relish for poetry deserted me that at present I cannot read even Virgil with pleasure."[169] Though negatively phrased, these pronouncements are clear indications of Jefferson's high regard for Virgil and his particular affinity for his poetry as a young man. Other, less direct, evidence can be adduced to support the conclusion that Jefferson was especially responsive to the work of Virgil's that

[162] TJ to Nathaniel Burwell, 14 Mar. 1818, L & B, XV, 166.

[163] *Notes on Virginia*, p. 64. For Virgil in TJ's libraries, see Sowerby 4279-85, 4383, 4464-5; Poor 739-40; Leavitt 647.

[164] Kimball, p. 113.

[165] TJ to James Maury, 15 June 1815, L & B, XIV, 312.

[166] The two earliest excerpts, §§163-4; the two that may be later, §§165-6; the last, §84. This reckoning does not include the passage from the *Aeneid* that appears as a footnote to §382.

[167] TJ to John Adams, 5 July 1814, Cappon, p. 432.

[168] "Thoughts on English Prosody," L & B, XVIII, 448.

[169] TJ to John D. Burke, 21 June 1801, Ford, IX, 267.

does *not* appear in the Literary Commonplace Book, his *Georgics*. From this long poem in praise of agriculture and the joys of country life, and from the poetic tradition it engendered in the eighteenth century, came part of the inspiration for Jefferson's much-discussed agrarianism, his vision of America as a nation of self-sufficient farmers.[170]

Edward YOUNG (1683-1765), English poet. When Jefferson was a young man studying English poetry in the 1750s and 1760s, the poetry of Edward Young was enjoying a great vogue, both in England and on the continent. His long, meditative poem in blank verse, *The Complaint; or Night-Thoughts on Life, Death, and Immortality* (1742-1746), attracted widespread attention and quickly became a favorite, especially with serious-minded and impressionable young readers, such as Thomas Jefferson. When, in his twenties, he selected and arranged the contents of his literary notebooks, he classed Young as a major poet, along with Pope, Milton, and Shakespeare. Though Young's appeal and his reputation eventually faded, his stature in the eighteenth century was considerable, and even Samuel Johnson was moved to pay the grudging tribute, "But, with all his defects, he was a man of genius and a poet."[171]

The evidence of the handwriting in the Literary Commonplace Book indicates that the earliest entries from Young's *Night-Thoughts* (§§258-61) belong to the period prior to 1763, perhaps dating from Jefferson's school days in the 1750s. A four-volume edition of Young's *Works* bought by Jefferson in Williamsburg in 1764 is one of the first of his library purchases of which a record remains.[172] Additional entries from Young (§§247-57, 262-7) in the distinctive handwriting of the late 1760s signify Jefferson's continued interest, and references in his correspondence and his "Thoughts on English Prosody" show that he was still on familiar terms with Young during his stay in Paris in the 1780s.[173] In fact, a cryptic remark in a letter from Maria Cosway suggests that they had been reading or discussing *Night-Thoughts* during the brief but intense courtship they carried on in Paris in 1786.[174]

Though Jefferson's interest in English poetry seriously declined with age, he was still quoting passages from Young recorded in the Literary Commonplace Book in letters to Abigail and John Adams long after he had left the presidency and retired to Monticello.[175]

[170] Wilson, "The American *agricola*, p. 339-54.

[171] *Lives of the English Poets*, III, 399.

[172] Virginia Gazette Daybooks, 13 July 1764 (ViU).

[173] TJ to James Currie, 20 Dec. 1788, *Papers*, 14: 365: " 'Procrastination is the thief of time.' So sais Young, and so I find it." Cf. §266. "Thoughts on English Prosody," *passim*, L & B, XVIII, 416-51.

[174] See Maria Cosway to TJ, [17 Nov. 1786], *Papers*, 10: 539-40n. Unfortunately, this letter is damaged so that the surviving text lacks a crucial part of the reference to *Night-Thoughts*, but what remains is quite provocative and seems to contain allusions to previous discussions.

[175] TJ to Abigail Adams, 11 Jan. 1817, Cappon, p. 504; TJ to John Adams, 1 June 1822, Cappon, p. 577. In these letters TJ adapts §254 in two different ways.

APPENDICES

THE HANDWRITING OF THE LITERARY COMMONPLACE BOOK

The Early Handwriting—1762-1773

The manuscript of Thomas Jefferson's Literary Commonplace Book presents a bewildering variety of handwriting styles. Some are readily recognizable as Jefferson's, but some appear cruder and less polished than one would expect, while others, paradoxically, are more polished and "prettier." The family tradition on this point is recorded by Jefferson's great-granddaughter, Martha Jefferson Trist Burke, who inherited the manuscript and wrote on its flyleaf: "This book I always understood to have been a scrap book used by Thomas Jefferson before his hand was fully formed and up to late in life. . . ."[1] Mrs. Burke identifies an entry at the end of the manuscript as being in the hand of Jefferson's daughter, Martha Randolph, but she says nothing of the fact that some of the other entries, as Marie Kimball observed, "do not appear to be in [Jefferson's] writing at all."[2] The handwriting of the Literary Commonplace Book thus runs the gamut from the unmistakable to the dubious.

In order to establish the authenticity of the handwriting and assign reliable dates to the entries, a survey of Jefferson's handwriting as exhibited in the earliest surviving documents is necessary. Though he ranks as one of the most prolific letter writers in history, only 13 of Jefferson's letters written in the 1760s (when he was between the ages of 17 and 27) survive in manuscript.[3] In terms of handwriting characteristics, the first three surviving letters, written in 1762 and 1763, may be said to form a group.[4] These letters show a clear and carefully executed hand that slants noticeably to the right, begins sentences with capital letters, capitalizes "God," capitalizes other nouns freely for emphasis, makes frequent use of the long s, and exhibits a terminal d that often hooks back over the word with a decided flair (see Fig. 1). The next four surviving

Figure 1. December 25, 1762. Library of Congress

[1] *Thomas Jefferson Papers, Series 5: Commonplace Books*, Manuscript Division, DLC. The Library acquired the manuscript from Mrs. Burke's heirs in 1918. A much abbreviated version of this account appears in the editor's article, "Thomas Jefferson's Early Notebooks," *William and Mary Quarterly*, XLII (1985), 433-52.

[2] Kimball, p. 115.

[3] The texts of two others have come down to us in printed form.

[4] The location of the first letter, 25 Dec. 1762 to John Page, remains unknown, though reasonably clear photostats of it exist in various libraries. I have examined copies at DLC

letters—those of October 1763 and 19 January, 20 March, and 9 April 1764—form a second group, in which one sees the inception of Jefferson's practice of beginning sentences without capitalizing the initial letter of the first word, spelling "God" with a lowercase *g*, and not capitalizing nouns for emphasis. The hooked terminal *d* is also much more subdued, and the slant to the right is less pronounced (see Fig. 2).

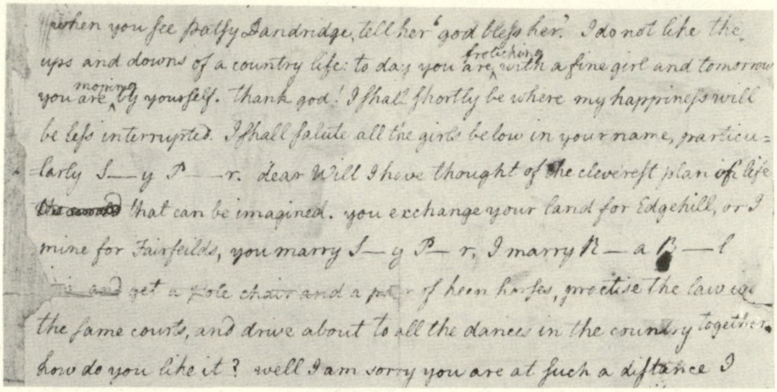
when you see Patsy Dandridge, tell her 'god bless her.' I do not like the ups and downs of a country life: to day you are frolicking with a fine girl and tomorrow you are moping by yourself. thank god! I shall shortly be where my happiness will be less interrupted. I shall salute all the girls below in your name, particu-larly S—y P—r. dear Will I have thought of the cleverest plan of life that can be imagined. you exchange your land for Edgehill, or I mine for Fairfields, you marry S—y P—r, I marry R—a B—l, join and get a pole chair and a pair of keen horses, practise the law in the same courts, and drive about to all the dances in the country together. how do you like it? well I am sorry you are at such a distance I

Figure 2. C. October 1763. Rosenbach Museum

The next extant letter is dated 25 May 1766, and it reveals a distinctly different handwriting style, one that is much more clearly the recognizable antecedent to the familiar handwriting of the draft of the Declaration of Independence, written a decade later. The slant to the right is now much less pronounced, the characters are noticeably smaller, and the writing, while clear, does not have the deliberateness and precision that obtained in previous letters. Another distinct change is in the writing of the small *t*, which in previous letters had been crossed with a separate stroke of the pen but is now written without lifting the pen from the paper (see Fig. 3). Another letter written two months later confirms the

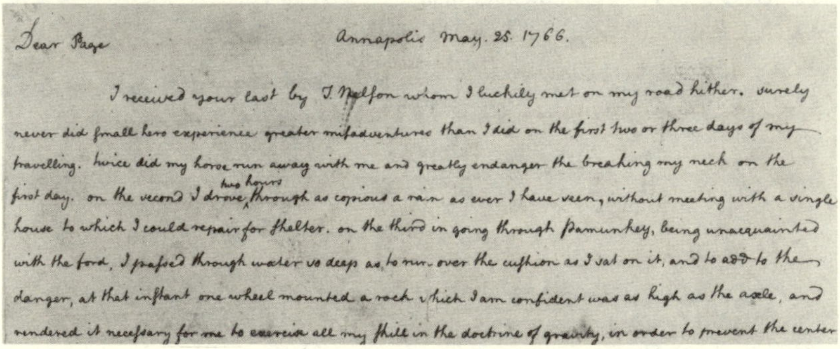
Dear Page Annapolis May. 25. 1766.

I received your last by T. Nelson whom I luckily met on my road hither. surely never did small hero experience greater misadventures than I did on the first two or three days of my travelling. twice did my horse run away with me and greatly endanger the breaking my neck on the first day. on the second I drove two hours through as copious a rain as ever I have seen, without meeting with a single house to which I could repair for shelter. on the third in going through Pamunkey, being unacquainted with the ford, I passed through water so deep as to run over the cushion as I sat on it, and to add to the danger, at that instant one wheel mounted a rock which I am confident was as high as the axle, and rendered it necessary for me to exercise all my skill in the doctrine of gravity, in order to prevent the center

Figure 3. May 25, 1766. New York Public Library

and at ViU. The locations of the other letters referred to in this discussion are listed in *Papers*, vol. 1, except that the third, TJ to John Page, 15 July 1763, is now at Colonial Williamsburg.

change in handwriting style from what the copybooks of the time called the "italic" to the "round" hand—a less pretentious, more vertical hand and one that was coming to dominate English and American handwriting in the latter half of the eighteenth century. For the rest of his life, Jefferson would continue to write in the "round" hand.[5]

No letters survive from 1767, but in this year, in conjunction with the beginning of his law practice, Jefferson began to keep pocket-sized Memorandum Books, which do survive.[6] Though the writing in the Memorandum Books is typically less careful and deliberate than that of the letters, certain entries in each—such as the annual reckoning of cases and fees—show sufficiently well his current handwriting style. This is confirmed in the present case by the only surviving letter of 1768, written just a year after the first surviving entries of the first Memorandum Book.[7] The most conspicuous feature of Jefferson's handwriting in this period is the rigorous suppression of the long *s* and the regular substitution of an open or serpentine character. This open *s* seems to have emerged late in 1766 or early in 1767 and is the hallmark of Jefferson's hand for the period 1767-1772 (see Fig. 4). In the beginning, Jefferson seems to have employed it as a means of ridding his hand of the long *s*, for the arrival of the one coincides with the departure of the other. For the first two or three

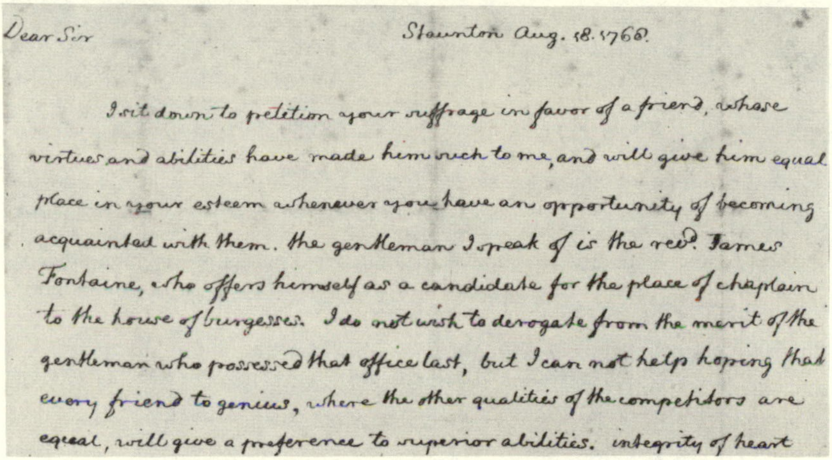

Dear Sir Staunton Aug. 18. 1768.

I sit down to petition your suffrage in favor of a friend, whose virtues and abilities have made him such to me, and will give him equal place in your esteem whenever you have an opportunity of becoming acquainted with them. the gentleman I speak of is the revd. James Fontaine, who offers himself as a candidate for the place of chaplain to the house of burgesses. I do not wish to derogate from the merit of the gentleman who possessed that office last, but I can not help hoping that every friend to genius, where the other qualities of the competitors are equal, will give a preference to superior abilities. integrity of heart

Figure 4. August 18, 1768. New York Public Library

[5] See Laetitia Yeandle, "The Evolution of Handwriting in the English-Speaking Colonies of America," *The American Archivist*, 43 (1980), 294-311, and Ray Nash, *American Writing Masters and Copybooks: History and Bibliography through Colonial Times* (Boston, 1959). Jefferson had at least two copybooks in his library that illustrated the "italic" and "round" hands: George Fisher, *The American Instructor; or Young Man's Best Companion*, the first American edition of which was printed by Benjamin Franklin in 1748, and Thomas Wise, accountant, *The Newest Young Man's Companion*, many editions 1755-1782. Sowerby 1117-18.

[6] The Memorandum Book for 1767, formerly on deposit at DLC, is now at ViU. TJ used the term "memorandum book," and his use is followed here.

[7] The first Memorandum Book, which is in imperfect condition, may well have originally had entries earlier than August 1767.

years of this period, the open *s* predominates overwhelmingly in his writing, in spite of the obvious difficulty of forming it, and the conventional cursive or short *s* appears only occasionally.[8] Gradually, the conventional cursive *s* returned to Jefferson's handwriting, beginning about 1770, first in the terminal position of a word but eventually in the initial and medial positions as well, so that by late 1772 the conventional cursive *s* begins to predominate and the open *s* appears less and less frequently. The Memorandum Book for 1772 (MHi) illustrates this development very well. The open *s* never entirely disappears from Jefferson's writing, as is also true of the long *s* that he went to such lengths to suppress. The draft of the Declaration of Independence contains examples of each. Another distinctive feature of the writing of the period 1767-1772 is the frequent occurrence of the ligature connecting the letters *c* and *t* when they appear in a word such as "respect" or "act" (see Fig. 5).

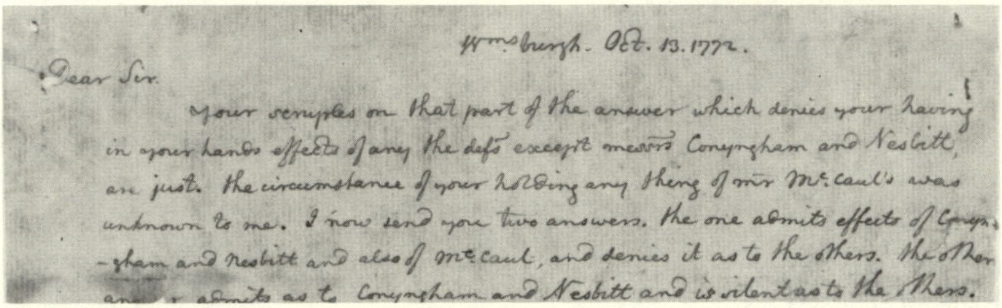
Wmsburgh. Oct. 13. 1772.
Dear Sir
your scruples on that part of the answer which denies your having in your hands effects of any the defts except messrs Conyngham and Nesbitt, are just. the circumstance of your holding any thing of mr Mccaul's was unknown to me. I now send you two answers. the one admits effects of Conyngham and Nesbitt and also of Mccaul, and denies it as to the others. the other admits as to Conyngham and Nesbitt and is silent as to the others.

Figure 5. October 13, 1772. Yale University

A distinguishing characteristic of the period 1770-1772, at least in documents that are carefully written, is in the treatment of certain ascenders, such as the letters *l*, *b*, and *t*. These are frequently open or spread where one would expect to find them crossed or closed (see Fig. 6). This is not Jefferson's invariable practice, but it is quite distinctive where it occurs and, as a common phenomenon, is more or less peculiar to this period.

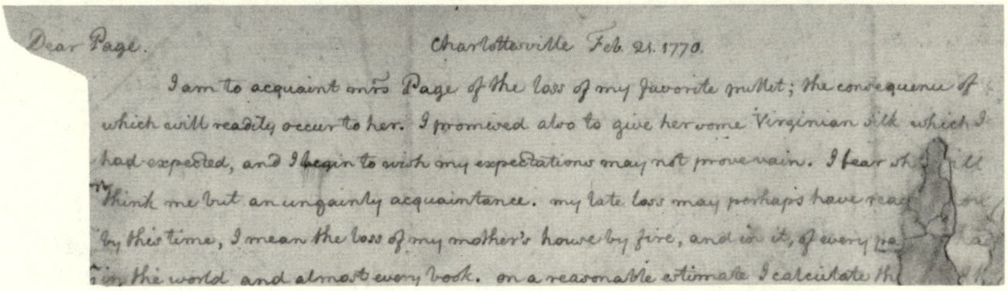
Dear Page. Charlottesville Feb. 21. 1770.
I am to acquaint mrs Page of the loss of my favorite mullet; the consequence of which will readily occur to her. I promised also to give her some Virginian silk which I had expected, and I begin to wish my expectations may not prove vain. I fear
think me but an ungainly acquaintance. my late loss may perhaps have
by this time, I mean the loss of my mother's house by fire, and in it, of every
in the world and almost every book. on a reasonable estimate I calculate

Figure 6. February 21, 1770. Yale University

[8] Besides the letters, the best examples of the handwriting of this period are the Memorandum Books. The temptation to treat the pre-1770 entries in the Case Book (Huntington Library), the Fee Book (Huntington Library), and the 1767-1770 Account Book (ViU) as contemporaneous should be resisted, as these all seem to have been started after the 1770 fire and the data filled in retrospectively from the Memorandum Books and other notes. The same is true of the Garden Book (MHi), which seems to have been

By the end of 1773, Jefferson's hand is mature, and he ceases to experiment or consciously seek to modify his handwriting style. The familiar hand of the 1770s blends seamlessly with that of the 1780s, so that dating documents by the handwriting in this period becomes very problematical. But this state of affairs does not pose serious problems in the Literary Commonplace Book, as more than 97 percent of the material was entered by 1773, when Jefferson was just 30 years old.

Dating the LCB Handwriting

The first editor of the Literary Commonplace Book, Gilbert Chinard, paid scant attention to the variety of handwriting styles and had very little to say on the subject. In editing the Legal Commonplace Book a few years earlier, he had expressed a decided disinclination to use handwriting as a means of dating the entries: "To be more definite and to attempt to date more exactly [than by reliance on actual dates cited] the different parts of the manuscript would be dangerous and misleading. The evidence given by the handwriting and the color of the ink is very dubious. A certain progress could perhaps be noted in the first third of the manuscript. The other differences are too slight to be relied on. . . ."[9] But close attention to the "progress" Chinard refers to enables the student of Jefferson's early handwriting to date many of the entries in a way that, while by no means infallible, is neither dangerous nor misleading.

The only serious and sustained attempt to date the entries of the commonplace books was not by an editor but by a biographer, Marie Kimball. For her section on Jefferson's formative years in *Jefferson: The Road to Glory 1743-1776*, Kimball made a study of the handwriting in the three commonplace books that have come down to us from this period—the Literary Commonplace Book, the Legal Commonplace Book, and the Equity Commonplace Book.[10] Kimball proceeds on the basis that "no study of the commonplace books, which have so much to tell, can be undertaken without a careful analysis of Jefferson's handwriting."[11] What Chinard had noted grudgingly as "a certain progress" in Jefferson's early handwriting, Kimball sees more discerningly as a series of changes in handwriting styles, each having "definite characteristics." The present discussion of Jefferson's early handwriting is much indebted to Kimball's pioneering study, though a number of the conclusions offered here are at variance with hers.

---

started early in 1774 at the same time as the Farm Book (MHi). I have detailed the reasons for this conclusion in the case of the Garden Book in "Thomas Jefferson's Early Notebooks," p. 436-8. Jefferson's entries in the notebook containing summaries of cases in the Virginia courts for 1768 and 1769 (DLC) are probably contemporaneous or nearly so, though one passage seems to have been interpolated in the 1770s.

[9] Gilbert Chinard, ed., *The Commonplace Book of Thomas Jefferson: A Repository of his Ideas on Government* (Baltimore, 1926), p. 12.

[10] Kimball, p. 85-9. The Literary and Legal Commonplace Books are in the Manuscript Division, DLC; the Equity Commonplace Book is in the Huntington Library. The first two have been edited by Gilbert Chinard, as noted above; the Equity remains unpublished. These commonplace books and their relationships to one another are discussed in my article "Thomas Jefferson's Early Notebooks," cited above.

[11] Kimball, p. 85.

APPENDIX A

The LCB Hands—Post-1762

At least nine discernibly different handwriting styles are present in the Literary Commonplace Book. (For a listing of the different hands and the entries they comprehend, see Table 1 in Appendix D.) Disregarding the extracts in Greek, more than two-thirds of the roman-alphabet entries fit readily into the pattern of development, outlined above, that is evident in the surviving dated documents in Jefferson's hand from late 1762 onward. Extracts from Thomson, Pope, and Livy are in a hand quite similar to that of the earliest letters, 1762-1764, supporting Kimball's belief that these extracts, as the earlier annotations in Mercer's *Abridgement*, belong to the same period (see Fig. 7).[12] The next

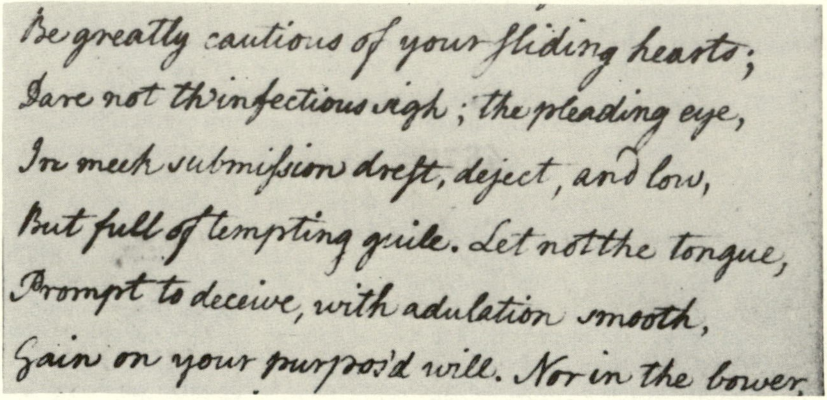
Be greatly cautious of your sliding hearts;
Dare not th'infectious sigh; the pleading eye,
In meek submission drest, deject, and low,
But full of tempting guile. Let not the tongue,
Prompt to deceive, with adulation smooth,
Gain on your purpos'd will. Nor in the bower

Figure 7. Literary Commonplace Book. Library of Congress

stage in the development of Jefferson's handwriting—the shift in the mid-1760s to a smaller, more vertical hand that is less "italic" and more "round"—is evident in the extracts from Bolingbroke, which, at 10,200 words, constitute far and away the largest selection from a single author. In a section of this length, there is bound to be some variation in the handwriting, as no writer can be expected to enter 10,000 words over a period of time with the same degree of concentration, at the same speed, in the same light, using the same nib and ink, all of which affect the appearance of the writing. But as the variations do not seem to reflect any basic changes in handwriting style, one may assume that the entries were made in a reasonably short period of time—perhaps as brief as a few weeks and probably not longer than a few months. Though most extracts

[12] There is some confusion in Kimball's account, with the result that she seems at one point (p. 114) to place the Thomson passages prior to 1762 and later (p. 115) to suggest that they belong to 1764. But she is surely wrong to group the Thomson passages with those of Pope's *Essay on Man*, as the hands are distinctly different. (Compare Fig. 7 with Figs. 16-1 and 16-2.) Kimball's error no doubt comes from calculating on too narrow a base, as she does on a number of occasions, particularly where the long *s* is concerned. Part of the reason for this is that her examination of the manuscripts themselves was seriously hampered by a lack of access to them during World War II. The copy of John Mercer, *An Exact Abridgement of all the Public Acts of Assembly of Virginia* (1759), referred to is in ViU. It was apparently used by Jefferson when he was a student of the law and contains marginal annotations in two different handwriting styles. The earlier appear to date from 1762-1764 and the later, 1766-1767.

in the Literary Commonplace Book seem to have been entered fair at a later time, the character of the notation, in running together passages that occur separately in the text, suggests that these extracts may have been entered at the time of reading. As the work being commonplaced runs to five volumes, some little time would have been required simply to read it through, and as Jefferson probably portioned readings of this kind to a few hours per day at this time of his life, the reading of this five-volume edition of Bolingbroke's *Philosophical Works* may have required several weeks.[13]

It seems clear that the hand of the Bolingbroke extracts represents a direct development from the hand of the earliest letters. The hand is clear and precise; capitalization is kept to a bare minimum; the long *s* is used, though not as frequently or as consistently as had been the case in the letters. One significant change is evident in the course of the Bolingbroke passages, and the foreshadowing of another is also present. The change is in the treatment of the small *t*, which is carefully crossed with a separate stroke of the pen in the first 33 manuscript pages of extracts, but in the final 21 pages it is not (see Fig. 8). This is

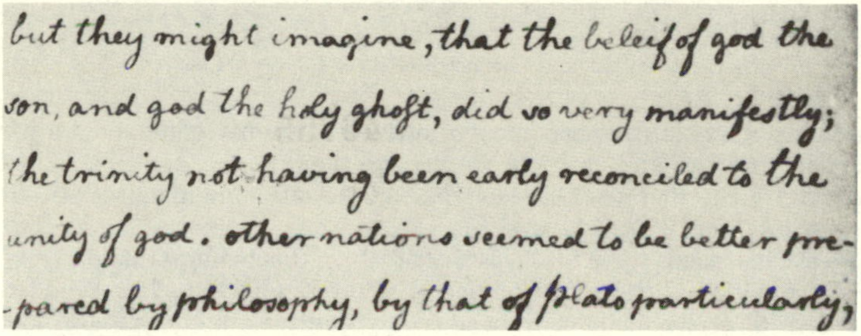
but they might imagine, that the beleif of god the
son, and god the holy ghost, did so very manifestly;
the trinity not having been early reconciled to the
unity of god. other nations seemed to be better pre-
-pared by philosophy, by that of Plato particularly,

Figure 8-1. Literary Commonplace Book. Library of Congress

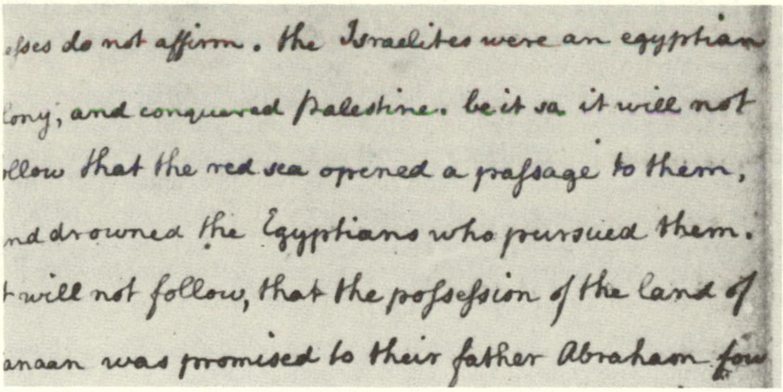
oses do not affirm. the Israelites were an egyptian
lony; and conquered Palestine. be it so. it will not
llow that the red sea opened a passage to them,
nd drowned the Egyptians who pursued them.
t will not follow, that the possession of the land of
anaan was promised to their father Abraham fou

Figure 8-2. Literary Commonplace Book. Library of Congress

[13] Jefferson was studying law when he made these entries, *circa* 1765. Some time later, probably in the early 1770s, he prescribed a daily regimen of reading for a student of the law that included reading in various fields for specified periods of the day. If he was there describing his own practice in the mid-1760s, he would have been reading Bolingbroke from early in the morning until 8 a.m. See his letter to Bernard Moore, recopied many years later in a letter to John Minor, 30 Aug. 1814, in Ford, XI, 420-6.

precisely what happens, as we have seen above, between the letter of 9 April 1764 and the next surviving letter of 25 May 1766. While Jefferson used both kinds of t's quite early and went back and forth between them, the sustained and consistent use of first the one and then the other seems to indicate a deliberate, self-conscious shift. The foreshadowed change is in the appearance about halfway through the Bolingbroke section of a handful of serpentine versions of the small *s* in the words "breast," "restrain," "just," and "establish" (see Fig. 9).

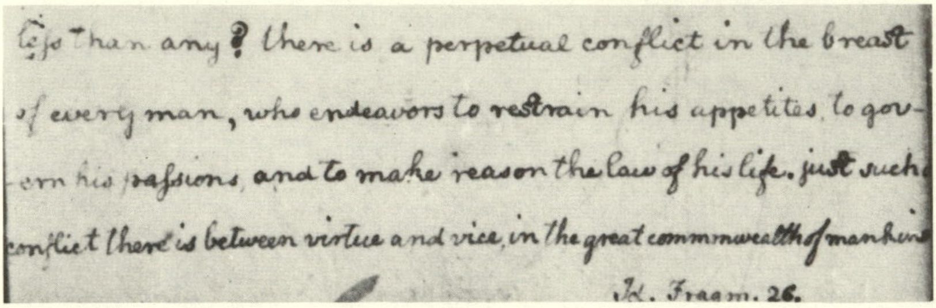
less than any? there is a perpetual conflict in the breast
of every man, who endeavors to restrain his appetites, to govern his passions, and to make reason the law of his life. just such
conflict there is between virtue and vice, in the great commonwealth of mankind
Id. Fragm. 26.

Figure 9. Literary Commonplace Book. Library of Congress

Together with a similar phenomenon in the Thomson section about a year or so earlier, these experiments look forward to the dramatic arrival a short time later of the open *s* that would predominate in the surviving manuscripts written between 1767 and 1772.

Given what seems to be the clear anteriority of this hand to that of the letters of 1766, together with its developmental affinities with the 1762-1764 letters, a date of 1765 seems likely. This hand is very similar to that seen in the opening pages of the simultaneously kept Legal and Equity Commonplace Books, a hand which, before many entries, comes to resemble almost precisely the hand of the 1766 letters. This would place the beginning of the Legal and Equity Commonplace Books late in 1765 or 1766, a period which makes eminently good sense in terms of Jefferson's preparation for the bar.[14]

The next hand evident in the Literary Commonplace Book that fits the chronological framework described earlier is the open *s* hand, which is readily dated from 1767 to 1772. Slightly more than 20 percent of the material in the Literary Commonplace Book is in this hand and was thus entered after his student years and during an extraordinarily active period of his life. The defining characteristic of this hand is, of course, the predominance of the open or serpentine *s*. Its emergence as part of Jefferson's regular handwriting practice is dramatically evident in the Legal and Equity Commonplace Books, which appar-

[14] Kimball has a different theory regarding the handwriting of 1765, which is based on three documents. Two of these, a document on marriage and a copy of a 1727 law, are difficult to accept as being in Jefferson's hand. I have been unable to locate them in the Jefferson Papers at the Library of Congress, but the photographic representations she prints in her biography appear very dubious. Her third example, the Akenside material from the Literary Commonplace Book, is unmistakably an open *s* hand, corresponds to the single surviving letter and the Memorandum Book belonging to 1768, and is quite unlike anything in Jefferson's hand prior to 1767. We are roughly agreed that the inception of the Legal and Equity Commonplace Books belongs to the period of 1765-1766, though Kimball mistakenly concludes that the Equity was begun first, whereas the order

ently were added to most assiduously in the months preceding Jefferson admission to the bar in February 1767. A comparison of entries makes it clear that Jefferson first began the Legal Commonplace Book and then, while commonplacing his second law reporter, Salkeld's *Reports of Cases*, began a separate commonplace book for cases in the law of equity. The numbering of the entries and the sequence of case numbers in Salkeld and succeeding law reporters make it quite clear that he alternated notebooks according to the nature of the cases being reported.

Only 15 entries from the beginning of the Equity Commonplace Book, the open *s* appears and thereafter is used almost exclusively in a notebook that contains over 2,000 entries and runs to some 80,000 words. This corresponds to a similar development in the Legal Commonplace Book at §181, where the open *s*, after making fitful appearances, establishes its predominance through §696 (see Fig. 10). Thus, nearly all of the Equity Commonplace Book and a substan-

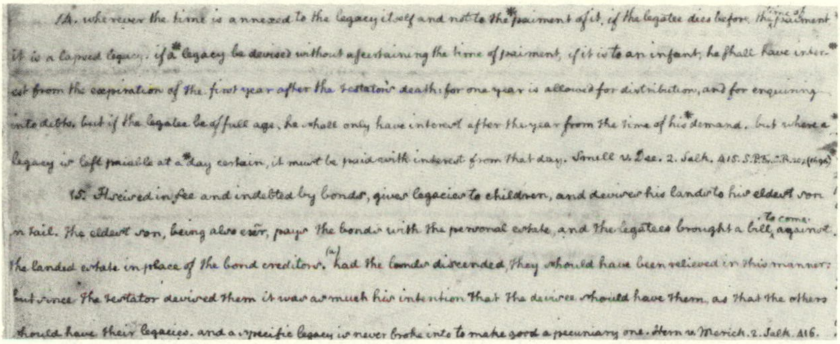
14. wherever the time is annexed to the legacy itself and not to the paiment of it, if the legatee dies before the time of paiment it is a lapsed legacy. if a legacy be devised without ascertaining the time of paiment, if it is to an infant, he shall have interest from the expiration of the first year after the testator's death: for one year is allowed for distribution, and for enquiring into debts. but if the legatee be of full age, he shall only have interest after the year from the time of his demand. but where a legacy is left paiable at a day certain, it must be paid with interest from that day. Sonell v. Dee. 2. Salk. 415.

15. A seised in fee and indebted by bonds, gives legacies to children, and devises his lands to his eldest son in tail. the eldest son, being also exr, pays the bonds with the personal estate, and the legatees brought a bill, to come against the landed estate in place of the bond creditors. (a) had the lands descended, they should have been relieved in this manner; but since the testator devised them it was as much his intention that the devisee should have them, as that the others should have their legacies. and a specific legacy is never broke into to make good a pecuniary one. Hern v. Merick. 2. Salk. 416.

Figure 10-1. Equity Commonplace Book. Huntingdon Library

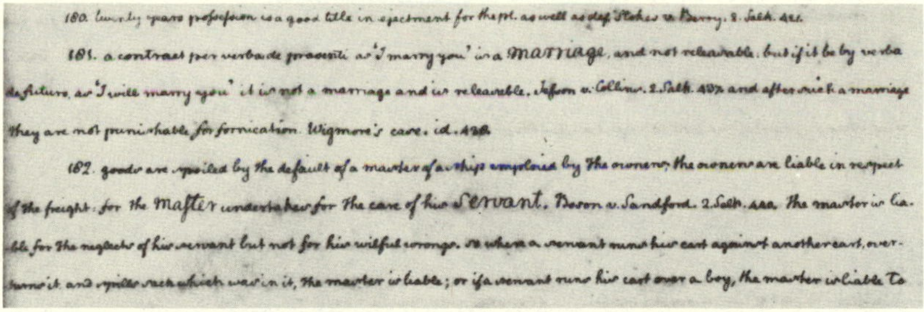
180. twenty years possession is a good title in ejectment for the plt. as well as deft. Stokes v. Berry. 2. Salk. 421.

181. a contract per verba de praesenti as 'I marry you' is a marriage, and not releasable. but if it be by verba de futuro, as 'I will marry you' it is not a marriage and is releaseable. Jesson v. Collins. 2. Salk. 437. and after such a marriage they are not punishable for fornication. Wigmore's case. id. 438.

182. goods are spoiled by the default of a master of a ship employed by the owners; the owners are liable in respect of the freight: for the master undertakes for the care of his servant. Boson v. Sandford. 2. Salk. 440. the master is liable for the neglects of his servant but not for his wilful wrongs. so where a servant runs his cart against another cart, overturns it and spills sack which was in it, the master is liable; or if a servant runs his cart over a boy, the master is liable to

Figure 10-2. Legal Commonplace Book. Library of Congress

tial portion of the Legal appear in the open *s* hand. If these afford an ideal look at the inception and early development of this hand, the Literary Commonplace Book gives a better picture of its three discernible phases. The early phase, 1767-1769, reveals a small upright hand with little slant and letters that are

of the entries from Salkeld's *Reports* in each book, as I have argued in my article on Jefferson's early notebooks, shows that Jefferson began the Equity after he had already made 113 entries in the Legal. See below.

somewhat squat and rounded, as in the selections from Akenside (see Fig. 11). In the second phase, 1770-1771, the ascenders frequently show the character-

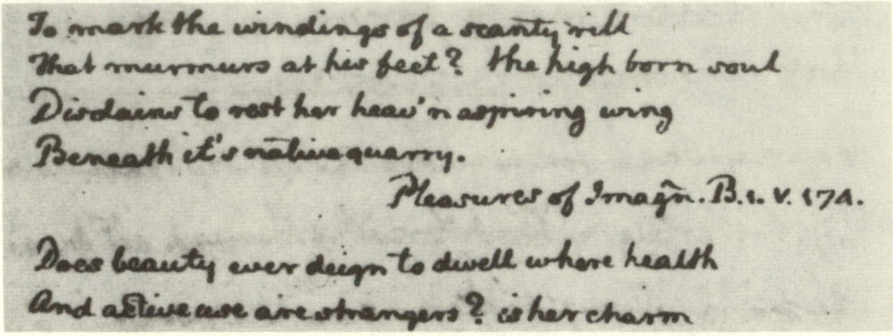
To mark the windings of a scanty rill
That murmurs at his feet? the high born soul
Disdains to rest her heav'n aspiring wing
Beneath it's native quarry.
Pleasures of Imagn. B. 1. v. 174.

Does beauty ever deign to dwell where health
And active use are strangers? is her charm

Figure 11. Literary Commonplace Book. Library of Congress

istic treatment of certain ascenders described earlier in connection with the dated material, as in the passages from Horace's second epode (see Fig. 12).

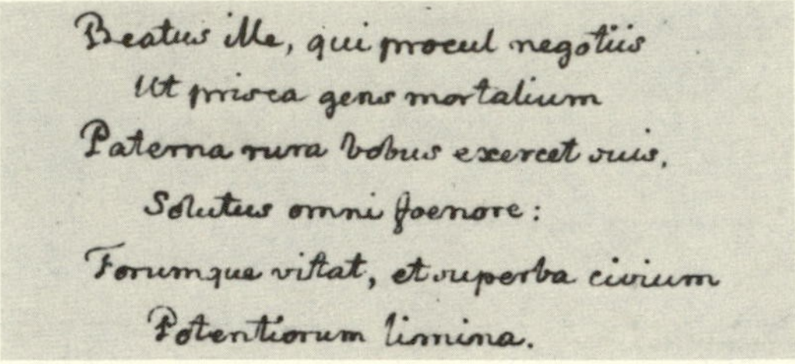
Beatus ille, qui procul negotiis
Ut prisca gens mortalium
Paterna rura bobus exercet suis,
Solutus omni foenore:
Forumque vitat, et superba civium
Potentiorum limina.

Figure 12. Literary Commonplace Book. Library of Congress

The final phase, which seems to belong to 1772-1773, features a hand that is less constricted and more fluent than the others. All the excerpts from Ossian, about whom he corresponded so exuberantly in early 1773, are in this hand (see Fig. 13).[15]

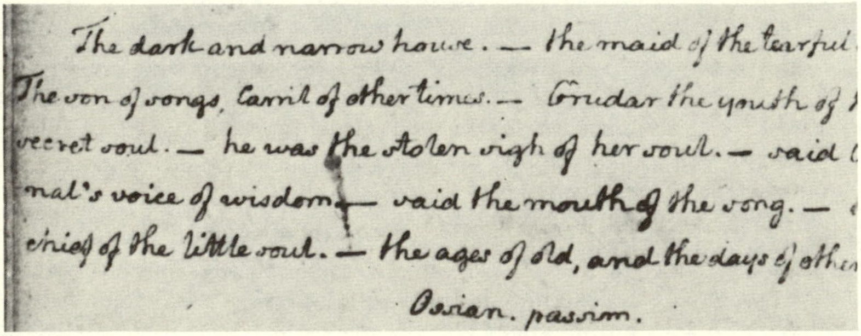
The dark and narrow house. — the maid of the tearful
The son of songs, Carril of other times. — Crudar the youth of
secret soul. — he was the stolen sigh of her soul. — said
nal's voice of wisdom. — said the mouth of the song. —
chief of the little soul. — the ages of old, and the days of other
Ossian. passim.

Figure 13. Literary Commonplace Book. Library of Congress

[15] TJ to Charles Macpherson, 25 Feb. 1773, in *Papers*, 1: 96.

As can be seen from Table 1 in Appendix D, a small number of entries appear to have been written later than 1773, and most of these probably belong to the 1770s or early 1780s. Some are written with a bolder, more flowing line (presumably formed by a broader nib) and somewhat larger letters, but more often they exhibit a smaller, more streamlined hand, perhaps the most straightforward and businesslike in the entire manuscript (see the Sterne and Cicero extracts in Fig. 14).[16] While it is difficult to judge where Jefferson's mature hand is concerned, very few entries appear to have been made after the 1770s, which underscores the degree to which Jefferson regarded this commonplace book and preserved it as a product of his youth and early manhood.

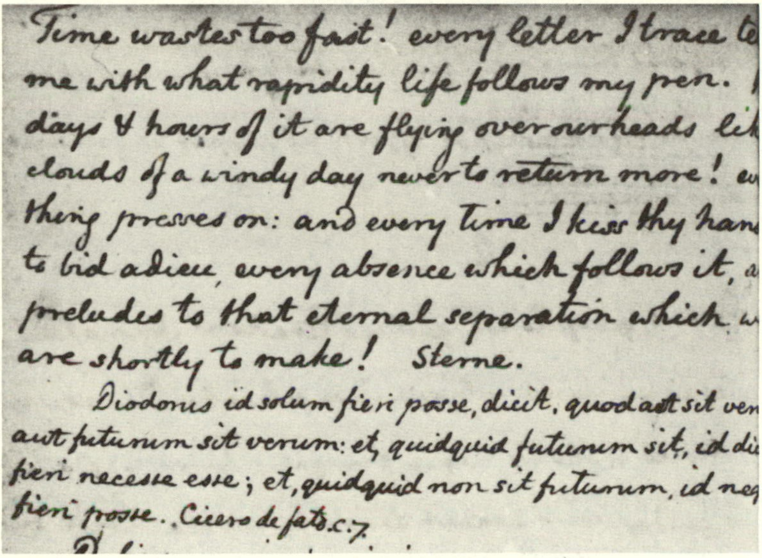
Time wastes too fast! every letter I trace te
me with what rapidity life follows my pen.
days & hours of it are flying over our heads lik
clouds of a windy day never to return more! ev
thing presses on: and every time I kiss thy han
to bid adieu, every absence which follows it, a
preludes to that eternal separation which w
are shortly to make! Sterne.

Diodorus id solum fieri posse, dicit, quod aut sit ver
aut futurum sit verum: et, quidquid futurum sit, id di
fieri necesse esse; et, quidquid non sit futurum, id neg
fieri posse. Cicero de fato. c. 7.

Figure 14. Literary Commonplace Book. Library of Congress

The Pre-1763 Entries

But there is a substantial amount of material in the Literary Commonplace Book—about one-fourth of the total—written in handwriting that does not fit the chronological pattern found in the letters and other datable documents, and some of these entries are of the greatest importance and interest. They include selections from Shakespeare, Milton, Pope (both as poet and translator), and the British dramatists, as well as Horace, Virgil, and Cicero. Since these entries do not appear to be contemporary with or later than the other hands in the Literary Commonplace Book, they must be regarded as earlier. As such, they must belong to the period of Jefferson's formal education, most likely the time

[16] This distinctive style is in evidence as early as 1772 and is well established by 1773 (see the letter to William Fleming, 19 May 1773, DLC); while it is frequently employed in the 1770s, it never actually predominates and seems to have been frequently employed as a copying hand.

spent at the Rev. James Maury's school (1758-1760) and at the College of William and Mary (1760-1762).[17]

It is possible that what appears to be the earliest hand even antedates this period and dates from the time, before the death of Jefferson's father in August 1757, when Jefferson was learning the rudiments of Latin at the school of the Rev. William Douglas. This is the "Horace" hand, which is seen in only six entries, all from Horace, and in two headings for Ovid. It is an extremely deliberate hand, the most precise and carefully drawn in the entire manuscript. The letters are large and graceful, the long *s* is in evidence, and the hand bears a striking resemblance to certain examples of the model handwriting of Peter Jefferson, from whom Jefferson is reported to have learned penmanship (see Figs. 15-1, 15-2).[18] If not actually inscribed by Peter Jefferson himself, these entries

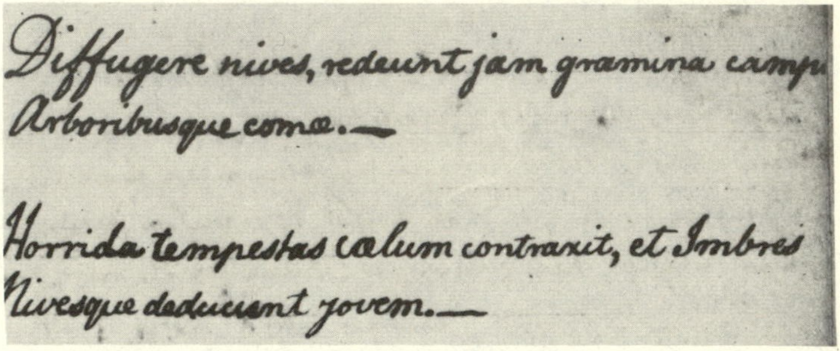
Diffugere nives, redeunt jam gramina camp
Arboribusque comæ.—
Horrida tempestas cœlum contraxit, et Imbres
Nivesque deducunt Jovem.—

Figure 15-1. Literary Commonplace Book. Library of Congress

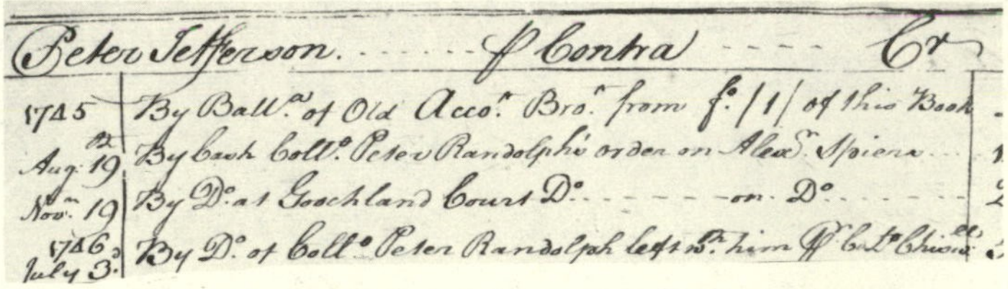
Peter Jefferson ...... ℘ Contra --- Cr
1745 By Ball.a of Old Acco.t Bro.t from f.o 1 of this Book
Aug. 19 By Cash Coll.o Peter Randolph's order on Alex.r Spiers
Nov.r 19 By D.o at Goochland Court D.o ------ on D.o
1746 July 3 By D.o of Coll.o Peter Randolph

Figure 15-2. Peter Jefferson's Account Book. Huntington Library

were probably written in imitation of his attractive hand. Another reason for thinking that the origins of the Literary Commonplace Book may reach back this far is that its paper bears the same watermark as that of the Account Book that Peter Jefferson kept in the 1750s, and one of the LCB leaves bears the names of two of his contemporaries.[19]

[17] There is a small slip of paper in Jefferson's mature hand in the Coolidge Collection, MHi, that reads in part: 1758 Jan. 17 I went to Mr Maury
1760 Jan. ended
went to College.
1762 quitted college & began study of law.

[18] Henry S. Randall, the source of this information, refers to the "marked resemblance in the handwriting of the father and the son." *The Life of Thomas Jefferson* (New York, 1858), 1: 15.

[19] Peter Jefferson's Account Book is in the Huntington Library. The paper for both books is the type of Dutch-made foolscap known as "Vryheyt." See William A. Churchill,

The next three hands are closely related and may well have been co-existent. That is to say, they may not represent definite stages of development but rather different handwriting styles that Jefferson was employing at about the same time. There is little doubt that one hand sometimes appears to metamorphose into another in the course of a long series of entries from a single work.[20] This is hardly surprising in light of the dramatic changes that occurred in the young Jefferson's handwriting in the period immediately after the present one. The earliest of these three seems to be the "Pope" hand, which is larger than the post-1762 hands and more boldly drawn (see Fig. 16-1). This may at first ap-

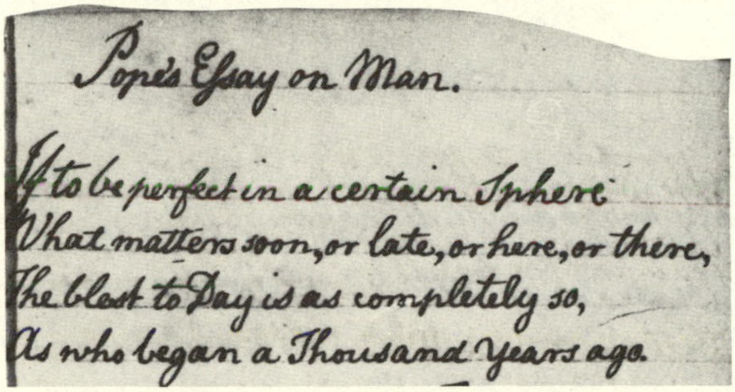
Pope's Essay on Man.
f to be perfect in a certain Sphere
hat matters soon, or late, or here, or there,
he blest to Day is as completely so,
s who began a Thousand Years ago.

Figure 16-1. Literary Commonplace Book. Library of Congress

pear to be a stylistic regression from the attractive and fluent hand of the first Horace entries, but if the "Horace" hand was an imitation of his father's hand, the "Pope" hand may well represent the early stages of Jefferson's attempt to find a style of his own. At any rate, the hand is obviously very early, exhibiting a liberal sprinkling of capitalized nouns (even more, typically, than the copy-text contained), and it shows great deliberation. This can be seen clearly in the treatment of the descenders, which are rather tightly reined in. This is even clearer when one compares the passages from Pope's *Essay on Man* with the slightly later excerpts in the same basic hand from Milton's *Paradise Lost*.[21] Here the descenders are given freer play, and the hand has a slightly less deliberate, more fluent look (see Fig. 16-2).

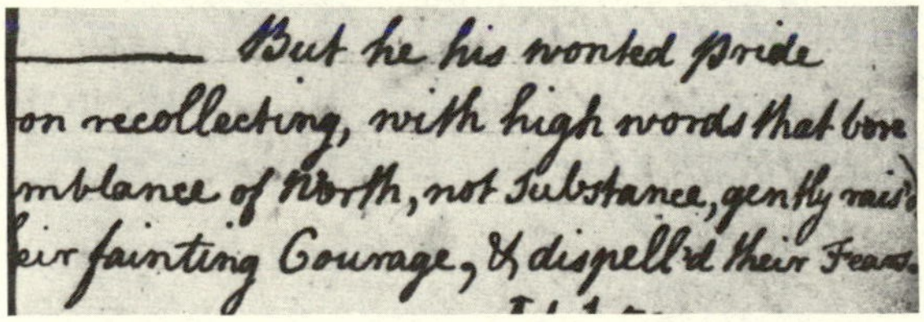
But he his wonted Pride
on recollecting, with high words that bore
mblance of Worth, not Substance, gently rais'd
eir fainting Courage, & dispell'd their Fears.

Figure 16-2. Literary Commonplace Book. Library of Congress

Watermarks in Paper in Holland, England, France, etc. (Amsterdam, 1967), XLIX ff. I am grateful to Thomas Gravell for examining the paper of the Literary Commonplace Book and confirming his identification. The contemporaries of Peter Jefferson are James Wheery and Christopher Lawson.

[20] The most clear-cut example is the section Milton's *Paradise Lost*, which begins in the "Pope" hand and moves toward the "Shakespeare" hand.

[21] I say "later" on the basis of the pagination. Though not conclusive, the appearance

The hand of the Cicero section, which is also the hand of many of the later Horace entries, is not nearly so careful and deliberate as the "Horace" or the "Pope" hands, and the characters are somewhat smaller. It is near the end of the Cicero section that we first encounter the terminal *d* that is hooked back over the word (see Fig. 17). And this feature, noted in the earliest surviving letters, is one of the hallmarks of the hand in which the remainder of the *Paradise Lost* entries appear, the "Shakespeare" hand.

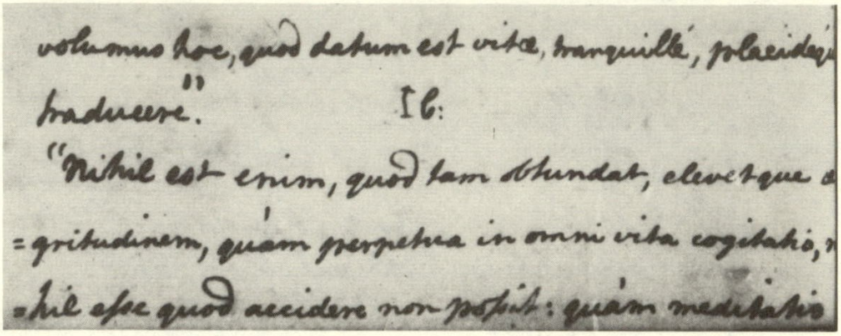
volumus hoc, quod datum est vitae, tranquillè, placideq
traducere." Ib:
"Nihil est enim, quod tam obtundat, elevetque a
=gritudinem, quam perpetua in omni vita cogitatio, n
=hil esse quod accidere non possit: quam meditatio

Figure 17. Literary Commonplace Book. Library of Congress

The "Shakespeare" hand is the most energetic and flamboyant of all Jeffersonian hands, as outgoing and dramatic as the "Pope" hand is reserved and self-contained. Like the "Cicero" hand, its letters are less rounded, narrower, and closer together than those of the "Pope" hand. One might almost say that the "Shakespeare" hand is an animated version of the "Cicero" (see Fig. 18). What

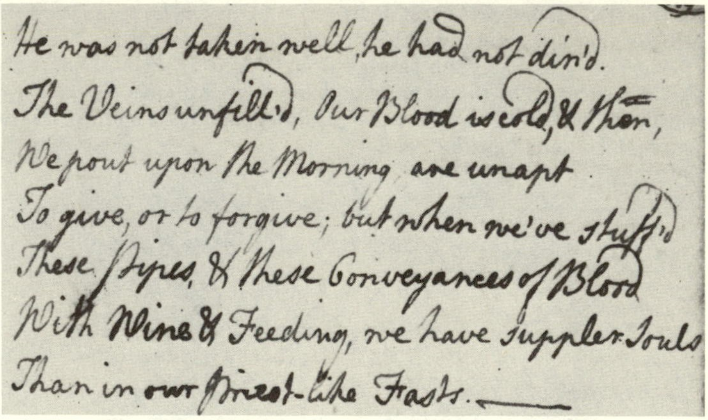
He was not taken well, he had not din'd.
The Veins unfill'd, our Blood is cold, & then,
We pout upon the Morning, are unapt
To give, or to forgive; but when we've stuff'd
These Pipes, & these Conveyances of Blood
With Wine & Feeding, we have suppler Souls
Than in our Priest-like Fasts.

Figure 18. Literary Commonplace Book. Library of Congress

of these passages very close together in the reconstituted notebook and in the same pagination series lends weight to the notion that the *Paradise Lost* extracts (beginning on p. 48) were entered after Pope's *Essay on Man* (begining on p. 39).

seems likely in this merging of characteristics and hands is that, as previously noted, these passages were all entered in a period when Jefferson was varying his writing style and experimenting—now with larger, now smaller letters, now writing with tight control, now with a flourish. Whether he went from the "Pope" hand to the "Cicero" hand to the "Shakespeare" hand in that order and without returning to a previous style is, of course, impossible to determine. One could even argue that the "Shakespeare" hand precedes the others, and that the "Pope" and "Cicero" hands represent different attempts to moderate and control it. What seems certain is that these hands represent commonplacing activity considerably prior to December 1762, the date of the earliest surviving letter.

The Greek Entries

The Greek entries present an additional problem insofar as the dating of the handwriting is concerned, for, as Marie Kimball has noted, "we have no extensive basis for comparison of the Greek characters Jefferson inscribed at varying periods of his life, as we have of his English."[22] Indeed, what Greek we have in his hand tends to be surprisingly uniform in appearance, regardless of date. There are some clues, however, that seem to indicate that most of the Greek passages in the Literary Commonplace Book were entered in the first half of the 1760s. That was the period when Jefferson was studying law with George Wythe, who was renowned in Virginia as a classical scholar. The English headings of the longest Greek excerpts, particularly those for Homer's *Iliad* and *Odyssey*, exhibit a marked "italic" appearance and seem to be of a piece with other specimens of Jefferson's writing during these years. The heading of the Euripides section is not so clearly "italic" (it may have been entered later), but the line citations after each passage carry the same distinctive crossed *v* as seen in the Homer. Perhaps even stronger evidence is the fact that five of the six Greek passages from the *Iliad* in this part of the book also appear in the excerpts from Pope's translation, and four of the five are in the distinctive "italic" hand of the early 1760s. This suggests that, while he had read Pope's translation and recorded some extracts in an earlier hand, Jefferson was re-reading it in the 1760s at the same time that he was studying the Greek text. The practice of comparing originals and translations he would follow all his life, as can readily be seen in his library, where he had editions of originals and translations taken apart and conflated by the binder.[23] While one may doubt Kimball's suggestion that the disparaging passages about women from Euripides may reflect "the unhappy ending of his love affair with Rebecca Burwell,"[24] her dating of these passages in the 1760s is confirmed by the evidence given above.

The Herodotus extracts are inscribed on the reverse side of the same leaf that begins the Bolingbroke section, and the roman-alphabet citations appear to be in the Bolingbroke hand, which is readily datable *circa* 1765. The few remaining entries in Greek are much more difficult to date. Though the passages from the *Iliad* that appear in the Ossian section can be dated about 1772-1773, they are not really separate entries reflecting Jefferson's reading in Greek, but rather are footnotes copied from the Ossian text. The two passages from the *Iliad*

22 Kimball, p. 111.
23 See, for example, his editions of Plutarch in DLC. (Sowerby 68-9.)
24 Kimball, p. 111.

that appear near the end of the book were probably entered sometime early in the 1770s, to judge from the neighboring entries. Finally, the placement of the lines from Quintus Smyrnaeus at the very end of the book, together with their valedictory character, suggests a date in Jefferson's retirement years, when on a number of occasions in his letters he wrote about his readiness for death.

Caveats

The conclusions about the dating of the entries in the Literary Commonplace Book offered here are not all equally firm, and it is not claimed that they all rest on an equal footing. Though it has occasionally been possible to date specific entries confidently within a year or so, in most cases the question of dating must be treated with somewhat more latitude. Nonetheless, the editor believes the classification of entries in four general periods, shown in Table 1, to be well founded and essentially reliable. A few exceptions are discussed below.

1. Assigning as specific a date as 1772-1773 to three excerpts—Sterne (§81), Langhorne (§395), and "Sweet are the jasmine" (§404)—presents problems. The position of the Langhorne excerpt in the manuscript among passages from the early 1770s and the appearance of the writing present the strongest evidence for this dating, and the Sterne excerpt closely resembles the Langhorne. The "Sweet are the jasmine" verses are included on the basis of the mix of the open and conventional *s*. Even though this is the period of transition at which one would expect to find such a mix, it must be acknowledged that Jefferson was capable of using this combination of *s*'s for many years following 1772, and any of these entries could conceivably belong to a somewhat later period.

2. Two more entries that are especially problematical are the two from the *Aeneid* in the Virgil section (§§165-6). These entries are distinguishable from those of the *Eclogues* (§§163-4) and must have been entered later, but they yield very few clues as to date. In some respects they appear to belong to a very early period, a conjecture which is confirmed by the romantic and mildly misogynistic content. But the writing most nearly resembles the nearby Terence entries, whose citations are given in a form characteristic of many later entries, and both have been classified accordingly. Nevertheless, the issue remains clouded.

3. The entry from Cicero's *De Fato* (§82) is assigned to the period after 1773, largely on the basis that it had to be entered after the Sterne entry (§81) which precedes it, and that a certain amount of time seems to have passed between the two entries. On the basis of the mix of open and conventional *s*'s, one might assign it to an earlier period, a hypothesis that would be strengthened by the fact that this passage appears on a document from Jefferson's law practice dated 1772.[25] The same passage, however, also appears in the Legal Commonplace Book at §865,[26] where it was

[25] This is a large legal notebook in the Coolidge Collection, MHi.
[26] Legal Commonplace Book, p. 345. This passage is also written by Jefferson in the margin of a volume of Helvétius, *Le Vrai sens du Système du Nautre*, at ViU. Another volume of Helvétius is commonplaced slightly earlier in the Legal Commonplace Book at §§849-50.

entered sometime in the mid- to late 1770s. While it thus seems certain that Jefferson remarked this passage in the early 1770s and entered it in his Legal Commmonplace Book a number of years later, it is not entirely clear when the entry in the Literary Commonplace Book was made, though the first half of the 1770s seems likely.

A DESCRIPTIVE ANALYSIS OF THE MANUSCRIPT

Paper

The Literary Commonplace Book consists almost exclusively of laid paper of Dutch or French manufacture, a foolscap bearing the "Vryheyt" watermark—a crowned double circle containing the motto "Pro Patria Eiusque Libertate" and a lion rampant within, and a countermark consisting of the initials GR crowned over laurel leaves within a circle.[1] It is very difficult to say how many lots of paper are represented, but as there appear to be at least four distinguishable "Vryheyt" watermarks, no less than two lots of this paper must be present.[2] There is also a single leaf bearing a "Britannia" watermark and a flyleaf, undoubtedly supplied much later by the binder, bearing an "FB" watermark.

Paper of this sort was common in the mid-eighteenth century, but it has not been possible to date the paper used in the Literary Commonplace Book more precisely. However, the Account Book that Peter Jefferson kept in the 1750s was fashioned from paper that bears the same watermark, an indication that such paper was available to Jefferson in that period.[3] Moreover, certain non-Jeffersonian writing and the date "Jouly 1757" on one of the leaves suggest that the paper may have been used by someone else prior to its being used by the young Jefferson as a literary notebook (see p. 219).

The foolscap sheets from which the commonplace book was made measured approximately 13 x 16 inches. Each sheet was folded three times to form a fascicle, or gathering, of eight leaves, the basic unit of the notebook, which could be cut at the edges and laced at the folds with string or thread. The extent to which these fascicles were kept individually or were bound together into larger units cannot be ascertained precisely, but such groupings as can be discerned are described below. The cropping of the leaves by the binder has resulted in the present page size of 3 3/4 x 6 inches.

Binding

The manuscript was originally bound in leather. Willman Spawn of the American Philosophical Society Library has indentifed the tooling on the original sheepskin binding as having been done in the Philadelphia bindery of Ben-

---

[1] For representations of this watermark, see Edward Heawood, *Watermarks Mainly of the 17th and 18th Centuries* (Hilversum, 1950), no. 3148; and W. A. Churchill, *Watermarks in Paper In Holland, England, France, Etc. in the* XVII *and* XVIII *Centuries and Their Interconnection* (Amsterdam, 1935), no. 95.

[2] Lots of paper were produced in pairs of trays, each having a hand-sewn and distinguishable watermark. For this and other invaluable information and counsel concerning the paper of the Commonplace Book, the editor is greatly indebted to Thomas L. Gravell of Wilmington, Delaware.

[3] HM 911, Huntington Library.

jamin January in the 1780s.[4] The most likely time for this to have occurred would have been in 1783 or 1784, prior to Jefferson's departure for France.

At some point the volume was unbound so that the paper could be laminated by the Barrow process, after which it was rebound. No records could be found in the Manuscript Division relating to this procedure, but it was apparently performed by the Government Printing Office in the 1940s or 1950s. The object of this procedure was the protection and preservation of the paper, but an unfortunate result was that when the laminated contents were rebound, they proved too bulky for the original binding, making the volume quite difficult to open and causing some of the leaves to come loose from the sewing. This was the state the manuscript was in when the present editor first examined it in 1979.

In 1985, the Preservation Office of the Library of Congress undertook the restoration of the manuscript, a process that involved unbinding the volume, removing the lamination, washing and de-acidifying the paper, reinforcing and resewing the leaves, and rebinding the restored leaves in new leather covers. The restored manuscript will now lie open and can be examined without straining the leaves and binding. The original leather binding is preserved in the same protective box as the manuscript. This work was completed in November 1985 by David Brock under the supervision of Tom Albro. The last leaf of the manuscript now bears the inscription: "This book received full restoration treatment. For further information refer to number 6-85-926 in the Rare Book Section file of the Restoration Office."

Contents

The manuscript of the Literary Commonplace Book contains 123 leaves, not counting the flyleaves that were inserted by the binder. In the discussion that follows, leaves are referred to by foliation number; the side of the leaf referred to is indicated by r (recto) and v (verso). It should be noted that while Jefferson paginated much of the material that eventually went into the final version of the notebook, many of these page numbers, having been placed at the corners of the page, have chipped away because of age and use, and are now wholly or partially illegible.

That the manuscript as it is now constituted had previously existed in a variety of different forms is indicated in several ways. For example, there is clearly more than one pagination sequence in evidence. In what seems to be the earliest, the numbers are larger in size, and there is at least one point at which the sequences overlap, so that pages numbered 35 and 36 occur twice, once in the larger numerals and once in the smaller. There seem to be only two pagination sequences present now, but there may well have been more originally, for many of the smaller page numbers have been erased and changed. And it should be noted that the three largest sections of the manuscript—Bolingbroke, Cicero, and Euripides—show no page numbers at all. In addition to the evidence of the pagination, there are two marginal notes that refer to another volume. At the bottom of f. 66v, a note that has been almost completely cut off by the binder may read: "For a Continuation page 37." At the bottom of f. 71r a note reads:

[4] Spawn identified the tool marks from rubbings in 1982 and confirmed his identification upon inspecting the binding at the Manuscript Division, DLC, on 3 Feb. 1983.

"For a Continuation Vol. 2. page 27." Both of these notes seem clearly to have been inserted as guides to additional material commonplaced from the same work in another location, and in both instances additional material from the work (Pope's translation of Homer and Milton's *Paradise Lost*) has been inserted.

Even though the foregoing makes it evident that the Literary Commonplace Book existed in earlier states, it is difficult to specify in anything but a fragmentary way what these states might have been. The obvious rearrangement of some of the leaves, the evident absence of some of the original material, the illegibility of many of the page numbers, and the changes made in the pagination all present serious obstacles to reconstruction. Nonetheless, what follows are descriptive reconstructions, in chronological order, of what appear to have been portions of original commonplace book units. The reconstruction of fragmented units has been done largely on the evidence of the pagination and the paper. The chronological ordering is mainly on the basis of the handwriting, and the dates given are intended to suggest a no-earlier-than / no-later-than framework.

Where the pagination is illegible, the conjectural number is shown in brackets; where partially legible, the number is shown in italics. The foliation indicates the present location of each leaf in the bound manuscript.

A.   This, the earliest section of the Literary Commonplace Book, which features distinctively large page numbers, may well have been related to or even part of Jefferson's schoolwork, inasmuch as it seems to have been devised to accommodate excerpts from the Latin poets most frequently studied in eighteenth-century schools. The notebook apparenty had at least four headings spaced at three- to six-page intervals: *Virgil* (now missing), *Horat:*, *Ovid: Met.*, and *Ovid: Epist:*. The surviving headings and the earliest entries are all written on pre-drawn lines, a distinctive feature of the earliest pages. The first two pages of the Virgil have been lost, and no entries were made for Ovid's *Metamorphoses*. Most of these entries are in the same hand as the Cicero section (see C below), but the first six entries of the Horace section are in a much more elegant and polished hand and either were entered earlier by someone else or were written in a hand that Jefferson soon abandoned. When the original notebook is reconstructed, it becomes evident that Jefferson's rearrangement was aimed at moving blank leaves forward, presumably to make them available to accomodate Greek entries. This would perhaps suggest that this rearrangement was done by Jefferson in the 1760s, when most of the Greek entries seem to have been made, and he may have anticipated including even more.

Jefferson's insertion of two passages from Terence in this section at a much later time may indicate that his first acquaintance with Terence belonged to the period when this notebook was started.
Date: 1756-1760

Page No.	Content	Foliation
[3]	Virgil	61r
4	Blank	61v
5	Blank	43r
6	Blank	43v
7	Horace	62r
[8]	Horace	62v

Page No.	Content	Foliation
9	Horace	63r
10	Terence [1770s]	63v
11	Ovid: Met:	44r
12	Blank	44v
13	Blank	64r
14	Ovid: Epist:	64v
[15-16]	Missing	
17	Blank	45r
18	Blank	45v
19	Blank	46r
20	Blank	46v
21	Blank	47r
22	Blank	47v

B.   This section may well have been part of the previous section, as its pagination consists of the same large numerals. If the previous section presents a
picture of the first 22 pages of the original notebook, this section may depict the
last 15.[5] What, if anything, occupied the intervening 13 pages is not clear, but
similarites of handwriting and content, as well as partially legible pagination,
suggest that some of the leaves containing Pope's translations from Homer (ff.
65-6) originally preceded the material in this section. Like the headings and
earliest entries in the previous section, almost everything in this section (and ff.
65-6) is written on pre-drawn lines.

If the previous section was part of a notebook created in connection with
Jefferson's school reading, as seems evident, and this section was indeed a part
of the same notebook, then together they form the earliest surviving remnant of
Jefferson's literary education.

Date: 1756-1760

Page No.	Content	Foliation
35	Milton's P. L. [later]	72r
36	Blank	72v
[37-8]	Missing	
39	Pope's Essay on Man	68r
40	Pope's Essay on Man	68v
41	Pope's Essay on Man	69r
42	Pope's Essay on Man	69v
[43-6]	Missing	
47	Hudibras [later]	70r
48	Milton's Paradise Lost	70v
49	Milton's Paradise Lost	71r
[50]	Lawson and Wheery	71v

[5] There are two strong indications that page 49 was the last page of text in the notebook
of which this was a part: first, page 49 contains the note referred to above that reads "For
a Continuation Vol. 2. page 27"; and second, this leaf, the verso of which contains the
date "Jouly 1757" and addresses for Cristfer Lawson and James Wheery in non-Jeffersonian writing, would seem to be an end leaf. (For more on Lawson and Wheery, see
Appendix C.) No leaves are found containing pagination in the large numerals beyond
49.

C. The handwriting indicates that this, the Cicero section, is early, and be-cause it is the hand of the Virgil, Ovid, and later Horace entries, it would seem to represent a stage somewhat later than the very earliest entries. Though read-ily distinguishable from the Pope and Shakespeare hands, the Cicero hand has much in common with them and would seem to be closely contemporaneous (see p. 204). That the Cicero entries, together with the other Latin entries in the same hand, belong to Jefferson's years at Maury's school is a virtual certainty.

Date: 1758-1760

Page No.	Content	Foliation
None	Cicero	32-4r/v
None	Cicero	35r
None	Sterne, etc. [later]	35v

D. This section represents the first of the pagination sequence exhibiting smaller numbers. The lowest number of this sequence is 31, none of the earlier pages being in evidence. If this pagination is that of the "Vol. 2" mentioned in the marginal note referred to above, then we may presume that pages 27-30 were given over to Milton's *Paradise Lost* and that the transitional entries in a later hand (§§225-9) were part of the substance of that material. Another pas-sage that may also have been present is the one from Book 3 cited by Jefferson as a footnote to §557 of his Legal Commonplace Book.[6]

The handwriting of the first entries in this section seems to be somewhat later than that of the Milton material of the previous section (to which it was spliced in the final version of the commonplace book) and to exhibit the same charac-teristics of the Young and Shakespeare entries that follow. In fact, since the numbering on the pages containing the Young and Shakespeare entries has been changed, it seems quite possible that these pages originally preceded those containing the Milton and were repositioned and renumbered when the leaves with the Milton entries, with their higher page numbers, were joined to those of the earlier volume.

Asterisks indicate page numbers that appear to have been changed.

Date: 1758-1762

Page No.	Content	Foliation
31-6	Milton's Paradise Lost	73-5r/v
37	Milton's Paradise Lost	76r
38	Young [added later]	76v
39*-40*	Young [added later]	77r/v
41*	Young	78r
42	Young [partially later]	78v
43*-4*	Young [added later]	79r/v
45*	Shakespeare	80r
46	Shakespeare	80v
47*	Shakespeare	81r
48	Shakespeare	81v
49*	Shakespeare	82r
50	Shakespeare	82v

[6] Legal Commonplace Book, p. 98.

Page No.	Content	Foliation
51	Shakespeare	83r
52	Blank	83v

E.   This section was probably copied somewhat later than the previous section, but it is in the same hand. Whether it belongs to the same pagination sequence is not clear but appears likely, though what may have occupied the intervening pages (53-78) is not evident. The section seems to have been copied out in a short period of time and to have served as a repository for a wide variety of dramatic verse, beginning with 11 excerpts copied from *Thesaurus Dramaticus* (see §§286-96) and concluding with 18 extracts from Milton's *Samson Agonistes*.

Date: 1758-1762

Page No.	Content	Foliation
79-80	Thesaurus Dramaticus	87r/v
81	Thesaurus Dramaticus	88r
82	Thesaurus and Buckingham	88v
83	Buckingham	89r
84	Otway	89v
85-6	Otway	90r/v
87	Rowe and Otway	91r
88	Otway	91v
89	Rowe	92r
90	Rowe and Mallet	92v
91	Mallet and Dodsley	93r
92	Rowe	93v
93	Rowe and Milton's Samson	94r
94-9	Milton's Samson	94v-97r
100	Milton's Samson and Akenside [later]	97v

F.   Since the Euripides section records extracts from the plays in the order in which they were traditionally printed, its entries were probably the outgrowth of a systematic reading of the works. And since Jefferson regarded Euripides as the easiest to read of the Greek tragedians, these extracts may represent a certain milestone in his Greek studies. For a discussion of the dating of this section, see p. 205.

Date: 1762-1765

Page No.	Content	Foliation
None	Euripides	48r/v
None	Blank	49-51r/v
None	Euripides	52-8r/v

G.   This is the longest section of the commonplace book, and it is clear from the number of incomplete entries that it was once much longer. Without pagination or other indicators, there is little basis for estimating its original length. It is equally difficult to determine whether the Herodotus section was originally more extensive than the three entries on the reverse side of the leaf on which the Bolingbroke section begins.

Date: 1765-1766

Page No.	Content	Foliation
None	Herodotus	3r
None	Bolingbroke	3v
None	Bolingbroke	4-14r/v
None	Bolingbroke and Hume	15r
None	Hume	15v
None	Hume and Bolingbroke	16r
None	Bolingbroke	16v-31v

H.   The final section of the manuscript presents few difficulties. The numbering of the pages is regular and uniform, and there is every indication that, with a few exceptions, the extracts were entered chronologically, one after another. Since Jefferson seems to have made a selection and arrangement of previous material prior to making any entries in this section, he may have attached these leaves to the others at that time to accommodate subsequent entries. Since the 1768 material (Akenside) begins on the same page as the last of the extracts from Milton's *Samson*, entered several years earlier, it seems that the rearrangement provided for this kind of continuity.

The Terence and Racine entries on f. 105v appear to be in the same hand as other dramatic material entered in 1768-1769—Young, Buchanan, and Seneca—and probably were entered at about the same time, though at some remove in the manuscript. A possible explanation of the present order is that subsequent entries filled the resulting hiatus, making it necessary to complete the commonplacing from Ossian beyond the Terence and Racine entries. In the meantime, the Langhorne material had been added, beginning on the same page as the Terence and Racine, and had to be bypassed as well, resulting in an Ossian section that was probably entered all at once but is interrupted in the manuscript by the Terence, Racine, and Langhorne material.

The numbering continues for 25 pages beyond what is shown here, but no Jeffersonian material occurs; clippings and other entries by Jefferson's family cover much of this space (see Appendix C).

Date: 1768-1772-3

Page No.	Content	Foliation
101	Akenside	98r
102	Akenside and Horace	98v
103	Anacreon, etc.	99r
104	Mallet, Moore	99v
105	Mallet, Young	100r
106	Young	100v
107	Young	101r
108	Buchanan	101v
109	Buchanan, Seneca	102r
110	Catullus, Pope	102v
111	Pope, Horace	103r
112	Horace, Rowe, Dryden	103v
113-14	Ossian	104r/v
115	Ossian	105r

Arrangement

The foregoing descriptive analysis of the recognizable fragments of the Literary Commonplace Book affords a clearer picture of how the manuscript that has come down to us evolved and what it represents. It began as a commonplace book for the standard Latin school poets—Virgil, Horace, and Ovid—and was perhaps extended to include some standard English poets—Pope and Milton—with Pope's translations of Homer serving as a bridge between the two. During the same period, Jefferson copied out separately on the same kind of folded paper 21 extracts from Cicero's *Tusculan Disputations*. Beginning another poetry volume with numbered pages, Jefferson entered extracts from Young and Shakespeare, and returned as well to Milton's *Paradise Lost*, of which only two books had been commonplaced in the first volume. He also continued his commonplacing of English poets during this period, concentrating in at least one section on dramatic verse. In the 1760s, he made lengthy extracts on the same kind of folded paper from two works—the plays of Euripides and the *Philosophical Works* of Bolingbroke.

Soon after completing the Bolingbroke section, Jefferson began the intensive program of preparation for his legal career that is recorded in his Legal and Equity Commonplace Books and presumably gave less attention to literary matters. There is reason to think that about this time he made a selection and arrangement of the literary and philosophical material he had been commonplacing, ordering it into four categories: prose; Latin and Greek poets; the most notable English poets; and dramatic verse. In addition to the material described above, Jefferson included several pages of verse from Thomson and Homer (in Greek) that he had copied out early in the 1760s.

About a year after taking up the practice of law, Jefferson began commonplacing poetry again. Although he returned to an earlier section on Young's *Night-Thoughts* to make numerous additions, for the most part he simply entered passages from poems and plays seriatim at the end of the notebook, thereby leaving a chronological tracing of his poetic interests from 1768 to about 1773. To the Cicero section, which had a special significance for him, he would afterward append a few thematically related entries. Some entries of a transitional sort (between the two Milton sections) seem to have been made at the time the manuscript was sent to the binder in 1783 or 1784, and the *Hudibras* section may have been added at the same time. Except for a small handful of entries added later, the Literary Commonplace Book was now virtually complete.

The manuscript thus represents a combination of several commonplacing efforts, as widely different in their apparent purpose as in the time of execution. The final result, it must be emphasized, represents a process not only of accumulation but of winnowing.

NON-JEFFERSON ENTRIES

The following items of text are either inscribed in the Literary Commonplace Book by someone other than Thomas Jefferson or are newspaper clippings inserted in its pages. Of the latter, it is the Editor's judgment that only one might have been included by Jefferson himself and that the others, because of their sentiments, apparent dates, and position in the back pages, were added by his daughter Martha or other members of the family. The kind of entry (clipping or inscription) and its location by foliation is indicated in brackets for each item.

1. [Clipping: front pastedown]

A small volume of manuscript poetry, the production of a friend who has found an "early grave," has recently come into our possession,—some extracts from which have already enriched our columns. The annexed sonnets are from this volume. We shall occasionally present to our readers a gem from this literary casket, under the head of

ORIGINAL POETRY
BY T.
SONNET TO MR. JEFFERSON.

"Clarum, et venerabile nomen,
"Gentibus, et multum nostræ quod proderat urbi."

Immortal man! not only of thine own
   The best and greatest, but of ev'ry age;
   Thou,—whose meridian strength was prompt to wage
For Liberty, the war against a throne;
When thy gigantic mind had plac'd thee lone
   And high, thou didst controul the wildest rage
   Of rival factions,—scorning to assuage:
To thee all Nature's mysteries are known.
   Oh! how shall we of less etherial mould
Address our souls to thine: thy GREATNESS weigh'd,
   Our love were too familiar and too bold;
Thy GOODNESS, admiration were too cold;
   But both, united, in men's hearts have made
A monument, whose glory shall not fade.

———

"I stood among them, but not of them."

Far from the haunts of man and his abode,
   I find 'midst Nature and her works a home
   More fitted to my spirit, when I roam
Or by the silent shore or shady wood,
Where, though alone, 'tis not in solitude;
   For I can read or in the starry dome

Above, or in the things around, as in a tome,
With none to check my thoughts, or to intrude
On meditations, which can wo beguile
Of half its bitterness—and dreams, which sleep
Hath not engender'd: but, alas! the while
Where youth and wit and wealth and beauty keep
Their midnight revels, must I stand and smile,
As one who smiles because he would not weep.

Note: This clipping has been taken from a Virginia newspaper, judging from the references on the reverse side to the Albemarle Auxillary Colonization Society. "Dabney Terril" has been written above the line "ORIGINAL POETRY," apparently in the hand of Martha Jefferson Randolph, whose handwriting is evident elsewhere in the manuscript. In all likelihood, she is responsible for attaching this clipping to the pastedown sheet on the inside cover. Jefferson once advised Dabney Terrell on a course of reading for the law (TJ to Dabney Terrell, 26 Feb. 1821, L & B, 15: 318-22.)

2. [Inscription: f. 1r]

Heu! quanto minus est cum reliqui[s] versari quam tui memmenisse.

Note: This Latin motto, inscribed on the first page of the manuscript by Martha Jefferson Randolph, was engraved on an urn as part of a memorial to William Shenstone's niece, Maria Dolman. The urn was displayed at Shenstone's ornamented farm, The Leasowes, along with a Latin epitaph that Jefferson imitated to honor his sister Jane, and is reproduced in Robert Dodsley's "Description of The Leasowes" (see p. 9n). Someone, presumably Martha Jefferson Randolph, pinned a copy of this motto clipped from a newspaper to the "deathbed adieu" that Jefferson had left for her at his death. Photostats of this family document (48628) and another on which someone has copied the verses of the "adieu," the Latin motto, and an English translation (44203) are on file at the Jefferson Office in the Princeton University Library. Also on file is a photostat of another scrap of paper (44205) on which Martha Jefferson Randolph has written Shenstone's motto. The translation, which possibly derives from Jefferson himself, reads: "To live with them is far less sweet / Than to remember thee!"

3. [Inscription: f. 2r]

This book I always understood to have been a scrap book used by Thomas Jefferson before his hand was fully formed and up to late in life, in the end is some printed matter and a poem of Mrs Barbuld's in Mrs Randolph's hand writing, she always kept this book of her father's among her treasures —
M.J.T. Burke

Alexandria V*a*
Jan 29*th* 1898.

Note: The Literary Commonplace Book passed from Jefferson to his daughter, Martha Jefferson Randolph, and from her to her daughter and son-in-law, Virginia and Nicholas P. Trist. It then passed to their daughter, Martha Jefferson Trist Burke, the writer of this inscription, who was still in possession of it at her death in 1915. As explained in the introduction, Mrs. Burke's testimony about the early date of some of the handwriting coincides with that of her father, who had acted as Jefferson's private secretary (see p. 6n).

4. [Inscription: f. 71v]

[a] Jouly 1757
     11 Doumfres

[b] [mark] so Mr Cristfer Lawson
     Att the Bell and Casters
     In fallr Lan Howborn
     London

[c]   To the Care of Mr
     James Wheery att the Black
     Layon king Streat
          Whithaven

Note: This page, as explained in Appendix B, seems to have been the back page of the first volume of Jefferson's original notebook. It appears to bear a date (July 1757), a place (Dumfries), the names of two Virginians who were contemporaries of Peter Jefferson, and the addresses of inns in London and Whithaven. (For listings for Lawson and Wheery, see the *Virginia Historical Index*.) The first two notations (a and b) are in the same handwriting, but neither this nor the hand of c is remotely like Jefferson's. It seems altogether likely that these notations were made prior to Jefferson's taking possession of the paper, which may have belonged to his father, his guardians, or his teacher, the Rev. James Maury. Nevertheless, the writing seems to have been done after the paper had been folded three times to achieve notebook size.

At the bottom of this page is §225, a passage from Milton's *Paradise Lost* that was apparently entered at the time the two Milton sections were bridged (see p. 211).

a. This notation is at the extreme top of the page so that the top of the second "7" is cut off. Though it is possible this was written as the numeral "1", it lacks any vestige of the upstroke that is clearly evident in the other "1s" and therefore seems most likely to have been written as a "7."

b. The mark at the beginning of this notation resembles the square root sign. The word *Casters* may not be correct; it is difficult to read, having been written up against the edge of the page and continued above the first part of the word. The street in the address may be Fuller's Rents.

c. Before the word "Whithaven" is written "Thos.," an abbreviation for Thomas that may be in Jefferson's hand. Jefferson may have simply tried it out on what was then, in effect, a waste page.

5. [Clipping: f. 107r]

ELEGY.

Sigh not ye winds, as passing o'er,
The chambers of the dead ye fly!
Weep not, ye dew, for these no more
shall ever weep, shall ever sigh!

Why mourn? the throbbing heart's at rest,
How still it lies within the breast!
Why mourn? since death presents us peace,
And in the grave our sorrows cease.

The shatter'd bark, from adverse winds,
Rest in this peaceful haven finds,
And when the storms of life are past
Hope drops her anchor here at last.

Note: It is possible that this newspaper clipping may have been placed in the commonplace book by Jefferson himself. The long *s* is used in the typography, possibly indicating an eighteenth-century date, and the theme of hope is consonant with that of the entry from Langhorne, which ends at the top of the same page. It is, however, in the same elegaic vein as the other clippings, which do not seem to have been inserted by Jefferson. This clipping follows §398. The author of the poem is unidentified.

6. [Clipping: f. 110v-111r]

MESSAGE TO THE DEAD*
By Mrs. Hemans.

Thou'rt passing hence, my brother!
Oh! my earliest friend farewell!
Thou'rt leaving me without thy voice,
In a lonely home to dwell,
And from the hills, and from the hearth,
And from the household tree,
With thee departs the lingering mirth,
The brightness goes with thee.

But thou, my friend brother!
Thou'rt speeding to the shore
Where the dirge-like tone of parting words
Shall smite the soul no more!
And thou wilt see our holy dead,
The lot of earth and main;
Into the sheaf of kindred hearts
Thou wilt be bound again!

Tell thou our friend of boyhood,
That yet his name is heard
On the blue mountains, whence his youth
Pass'd like a swift bright bird:
The light of his exulting brow,
The vision of his glee,
Are on me still—oh! still I trust
That smile again to see.

And tell our fair young sister,
The rose cut down in spring,
That yet my gushing soul is fill'd
With lays she lov'd to sing:

Her soft deep eyes look through my dreams
   Tender and sadly sweet:
Tell her my heart within me burns
   Once more that gaze to meet!

And tell our white hair'd father,
   That in the paths he trod,
The child he loved, the last on earth,
   Yet walks and worships God;
Say, that his last fond blessing yet
   Rests on my soul like dew,
And by its hallowing might I trust
   Once more his face to view.

And tell our gentle mother,
   That o'er her grave I pour
The sorrows of my spirit forth,
   As on her breast of yore!
Happy thou art that soon, how soon!
   Our good and bright will see;
Oh! brother, brother! may I dwell
   Ere long with them and thee!

*Messages from the living to the dead are not uncommon in the highlands. The Gael have such a ceaseless consciousness of immortality, that their departed friends are considered as merely absent for a time; and permitted to relieve the hours of separation by occasional intercourse with the objects of their earliest affection.

Note: This newspaper clipping was almost certainly pasted into the commonplace book by Jefferson's daughter, Martha Jefferson Randolph. At line 17, she has crossed out the "boy" in "boyhood" and written next to it "childhood." The clipping of the verses is attached to the verso of the leaf bearing Jefferson's final entry, §407; that of the footnote has been attached to the next page (f. 111r). The author is the popular English poet, Felicia Dorthea (Browne) Hemans (1793-1835); the poem appeared in her collection of poems *Songs of Affection* (1830).

7. [Clipping: f. 111v-112r]

THE DESERTED HOUSE.
By Mrs. Hemans.

Gloom is upon thy lonely hearth,
O silent House! once filled with mirth;
Sorrow is in the breezy sound
Of thy tall poplars whispering round.

The shadow of departed hours
Hangs dim upon thine early flowers;
Even in thy sunshine seems to brood
Something more deep than solitude.

Fair art thou, fair to stranger's gaze,
Mine own sweet Home of other days!
My children's birth-place!—yet for me
It is too much to look on thee!

Too much! for all about thee spread,
I feel the memory of the dead,
And almost linger for the feet
That never more my step shall meet.

The looks, the smiles,—all vanished now,
Follow me where thy roses blow;
The echoes of kind household words
Are with me midst thy singing-birds.

Till my heart dies, it dies away
In yearnings for what might not stay;
For love which ne'er deceived my trust,
For all which went with "dust to dust!"

What now is left me, but to raise
From thee, lorn spot! my spirit's gaze,
To lift through tears my straining eye
Up to my Fathers's House on high?

Oh! many are the mansions there,*
But not in one hath grief a share!
No haunting shades from things gone by
May there o'ersweep the unchanging sky.

And they are there, whose long-loved mien
In earthly home no more is seen;
Whose places, where they smiling sate,
Are left unto us desolate.

We miss them when the board is spread,
We miss them when the prayer is said;
Upon our dreams their dying eyes
In still and mournful fondness rise.

But they are where these longings vain
Trouble no more the heart and brain;
The sadness of this aching love
Dims not our Father's House above.

Ye are at rest, and I in tears,†
Ye dwellers of immortal spheres!
Under the poplar boughs I stand,
And mourn the broken household band.

But by your life of lowly faith,
And by your joyful hope in death,
Guide me, till on some brighter shore,
The severed wreath is bound once more.

Holy ye were, and good, and true!
No change can cloud my thoughts of you,
Guide me like you to live and die,
And reach my Father's House on high!

*"In my Father's house are many mansions." St. John, chap. xiv.
†From an ancient Hebrew dirge—"Mourn for the mourner, and not for the dead; for he is at rest, and we in tears."

Note: This newspaper clipping was probably inserted by Martha Jefferson Randolph. The last four stanzas and the footnotes are on f. 112r. The author is Felicia Dorothea (Browne) Hemans (1793-1835); the poem appeared in her collection of poems *Songs of Affection* (1830).

8. [Clipping: f. 112r]

THE DAYS THAT ARE GONE.

No more shall the spring my lost pleasure restore,
    Uncheered, I still wander alone,
And, sunk in dejection, for ever deplore
    The sweets of the days that are gone.
While the sun, as it rises, to others shines bright,
    I think how it formerly shone;
While others cull blossoms, I find but a blight,
    And sigh for the days that are gone.

I stray where the dew falls, through moonlighted groves,
    And list to the nightingale's song;
Her plaints still remind me of long-banished joys,
    And the sweets of the days that are gone.
Each dew-drop that steals from the dark eye of night,
    Is a tear for the bliss that is flown;
While others cull blossoms, I find but a blight,
    And sigh for the days that are gone.

Note: This newspaper clipping may have been inserted by Martha Jefferson Randolph. It follows the conclusion of the previous clipping on the same page.

9. [Clipping: f. 113r]

THE INVOCATION.—*By Mrs. Hemans.*

Answer me burning stars of night!
    Where is the spirit gone,
That, past the reach of human sight,
    Even as a breeze hath flown?
—And the stars answered me—"We roll
    In light and power on high,
But of the never dying soul,
    Ask things that cannot die.

O many toned chainless wind!
    Thou art a wanderer free;

Tell me if *thou* its place can find,
    Far over mount and sea?
—And the wind murmured in reply,—
    "The blue deep have I cross'd
And met its barks and billows high
    But not what thou hast lost."

Ye clouds that gorgeously repose
    Around the setting sun,
Answer, have ye a home for those
    Whose earthly race has run?
—The bright clouds answer'd—"We depart,
    We vanish from the sky,
Ask what is deathless in thy heart,
    For that which cannot die."

Speak then, thou Voice of God within,
    Thou of the deep low tone?
Answer me thou life's restless din,
    Where is the Spirit flown?
—And the Voice answer'd—"Be thou still!
    Enough to know is given:
Clouds, Winds, and Stars *their* task fulfill,
    Thine is to trust in Heaven!"

Note: This newspaper clipping was probably inserted by Martha Jefferson Randolph. The author is Felicia Dorothea (Browne) Hemans; the poem appeared in her collection *Records of Woman* (1828).

10. [Inscription: f. 120r]

"Beautiful country! whether clad in the delicate garb of spring, or in thy summer glory; or crowned with snow and sparkling in frost work—what is so grand, so lovely as thou! My native land! my beautiful my own! there are many who will call thy mountains mole hills, and thy streams rivulets, but I, who have crossed the Alps, and ascended with daring foot the Mount Chimborazo—I will still think of thee, as in times gone by, when I looked from the terraces of *Monti*cello and thought "all the kingdoms of the world and the glory thereof" lay spread before. —
    Every feature of that landscape has it's own spell upon my heart; — can bring back the living breathing presence of those long mingled with the clods of the valley, — can renew for a moment youth itself. youth, with its equiste enjoyments, it's ardent friendships, and Oh! dearer than all, it's first, purest, truest love!" Harriet Randolph

Note: This inscription seems to be in the hand of Martha Jefferson Randolph. Harriet Randolph was the sister of Martha's husband, Thomas Mann Randolph. A word prior to "clods" has been crossed out.

11. [Inscription: f. 122r & v]

    Pure spirit! O where art thou now!
    Oh whisper to my soul!

O let some soothing thought of thee,
This bitter grief control

'Tis not for thee these tears I shed
Thy sufferings now are o'er;
The sea is calm, the tempest past,
On that eternal shore.

No more the storms that wreck thy peace,
shall tear that manly breast;
Nor summer's rage, nor Winter's cold,
Thine aged frame molest.

Thy peace is sealed, thy rest is sure
My sorrows are to come;
A while I weep and linger here,
Then follow to the tomb,

And is the awful veil with drawn,
That shrouds from mortal eyes,
In deep impenetrable gloom,
The secrets of the skies?

O, in some dream of visioned bliss,
Some trance of rapture, shew
Where on the bosom of thy God
Thou rest'st from human woe!

Thence may thy pure devotion's flame
On my forlorn, descend;
To me thy strong aspiring hopes
Thy faith thy fervors lend.

Let these my lonely path illume,
And teach my weakened mind
To welcome all that's left of good,
To all that's lost resigned.

Farewell! with honour, peace, and love
Be thy dear memory blest!
Thou hast no tears for me to shed,
When I too am at rest

————————

Mrs Barbauld

Note: These verses are inscribed in Martha Jefferson Randolph's hand on the penultimate leaf in the Commonplace Book, seemingly as her valedictory to her father. The poem begins on the recto, and the last two stanzas are on the verso. The author is Anna Laetitia (Aiken) Barbauld (1743-1825).

12. [Inscription: rear pastedown]

Go seek the turf where worth, where wisdom lies
Wisdom and worth, ah, never to return

> There, kneeling, weep my tears, and breathe my sighs
> A daughters sorrows o'er her father's urn!

Note: This inscription is in the hand of Martha Jefferson Randolph. The author is unidentified.

13. [Inscription: rear pastedown]

> Death-sever'd love the grave embalms
> And passion sears strife-broken ties
> But there is nought that blunts or calms
> When friendship *slowly*, *coldly* dies.

Note: Written just below the previous item, this may be in the handwriting of Martha Jefferson Trist Burke. See no. 3 above.

TABLES

Table 1.
LCB Authors, Entries, and Words
by Period and Hand

Hand	Author	Entries	Words	%
1. Pre-1763				
Horace	Horace §§167-72	6	45	
Pope	Pope's *Trans.* §§185-98	14	500	
	Pope's *Essay* §§203-13	11	545	
	Milton §§218-24	7	236	
Cicero	Cicero §§59-72	14	465	
	Cicero §§73-9	7	281	
	Virgil §§103-4	2	13	
	Horace §§173-8	6	171	
	Ovid §§181-4	4	40	
Shakespeare	Milton §§230-46	17	852	
	Young §§258-61	4	199	
	Shakespeare §§268-82	15	829	
	Thesaurus Dramaticus:			
	Dryden §§286-7	2	65	
	Jonson §288	1	37	
	Dryden §289	1	27	
	Southerne §290	1	14	
	Shakespeare §291	1	31	
	Dryden §292	1	30	
	Otway §293	1	32	
	Shakespeare §294	1	63	
	Congreve §295	1	37	
	Rowe §296	1	65	
	Buckingham §§297-300	4	247	
	Otway §§301-6	6	414	
	Rowe §§307-8	2	79	
	Otway §§309-11	3	167	
	Rowe §§312-15	4	197	
	Mallet §§316-18	3	125	
	Dodsley §319	1	62	
	Rowe §§320-3	4	250	
	Milton §§324-41	18	761	
TOTAL (Pre-1763)		163	6,889	26.0

Hand	Author	Entries	Words	%
2. 1762-1766				
Italic (1762-1764)	Livy §80	1	37	
	Pope's *Iliad* §§199-202	4	222	
	Thompson §§283-5	3	721	
Greek (1762-1765)	Herodotus §§1-3	3	145	
	Euripides §§85-154	70	1,388	
	Homer's *Iliad* §§155-60	6	191	
	Homer's *Odyssey* §§161-2	2	100	
Bolingbroke (1765-1966)	Bolingbroke §§4-34, 36-58	54	10,200	
	Hume §35	1	452	
Total (1762-1766)		144	13,456	50.8
3. 1768–1772/3				
Open *S* (1768–1772/3)	Young §§247-57, 262–7	17	1,032	
	Akenside §§342–5	4	558	
	Horace §346	1	22	
	Thomson §349	1	88	
	Mallet §§350–1	2	94	
	Moore §352	1	48	
	Mallet §§353–5	3	261	
	Young §§356–66	11	481	
	Buchanan §§367–72	6	218	
	Seneca §§373–4	2	17	
	Catullus §375	1	59	
	Pope §§376–7	2	128	
	Horace §378	1	144	
	Rowe §379	1	70	
	Dryden §380	1	30	
	Virgil* §382n	1	6	
	Statius* §382n	1	14	
	Ossian §381–9	9	736	
	Terence §390–1	2	52	
	Racine §392–5	4	110	
	Ossian §§399–403	5	604	
Sterne (1772–1773)	Sterne §81	1	68	
	Langhorne §396	1	434	
	"Sweet are . . ." §405	1	51	
Greek	Anacreon §§347–8	2	27	
	Homer* §382n	3	71	
	Homer §§397–8	2	58	
Total (1768–1772/3)		86	5,481	20.7
4. Post–1773				
	Cicero §82	1	32	
	Buckingham §83	1	17	

Hand	Author	Entries	Words	%
	Virgil §84	1	12	
	Virgil §165–6	2	16	
	Terrence §§179–80	2	18	
	Butler §§214–17	4	82	
	Milton §§225–9	5	112	
	Moss §404	1	287	
	Manilius §406	1	15	
Greek	Quintus Smyrnaeus §§407	1	25	
TOTALS (Post–1773)		19	616	2.3
GRAND TOTAL		412	26,442	

Note: The entry and word totals include the Greek and Latin footnotes to Ossian (§382). Thus, the total of 412 entries represents 407 numbered entries and five footnote entries indicated above by asterisks.

Table 2.
LCB Entries by Period and Language

	Entries	Words	% of Total	Cumulative %
1. Pre-1763				
English	124	5,874		
Latin	39	1,015		
TOTAL	163	6,889	26.0	26.0
2. 1762-1766				
English	62	11,595		
Latin	1	37		
Greek	81	1,824		
TOTAL	144	13,456	50.8	76.9
3. 1768-1772/3				
English	60	4,683		
Latin	15	532		
Greek	7	156		
French	4	110		
TOTAL	86	5,481	20.7	97.6
4. Post-1773				
English	10	481		
Latin	8	110		
Greek	1	25		
TOTAL	19	616	2.3	99.9
5. Summary				
Total English	256	22,633	85.5	
Total Latin	63	1,694	6.4	
Total Greek	89	2,005	7.5	
Total French	4	110	.4	
GRAND TOTAL	412	26,442	99.9	

Table 3.
LCB Entries by Category and Author
in Manuscript Order

1. Works in Prose
Herodotus
Bolingbroke
Hume
Bolingbroke
Cicero
Livy
Sterne
Cicero
Buckingham
Virgil

2. Classical Poetry
Euripides
Homer
Virgil
Virgil
Horace
Terence
Ovid
Pope's Homer

3. English Poetry
Pope
Butler
Milton
Milton
Milton
Young
Young
Young
Shakespeare
Thomson

4. Dramatic Poetry
Thesaurus Dramaticus
Dryden
Jonson
Dryden
Southerne
Shakespeare

Dryden
Otway
Shakespeare
Congreve
Rowe
Buckingham
Otway
Rowe
Otway
Rowe
Mallet
Dodsley
Rowe
Milton

5. Poetic Miscellany
Akenside
Horace
Anacreon
Thomson
Mallet
Moore
Mallet
Young
Buchanan
Seneca
Catullus
Pope
Horace
Rowe
Dryden
Ossian
Terence ⎫
Racine ⎭ 1768-1769
Langhorne
Homer
Ossian
Moss
Unidentified
Manilius
Quintus Smyrnaeus

Note: Sections 1-4 seem to have been compiled and arranged before 1768, with the italicized entries added later, most likely in the 1770s or early 1780s. Section 5 was begun about 1768 and was virtually complete by the mid-1770s, with very few entries being added after 1773. Note that the Terence and Racine entries were entered prior to the Ossian entries, which precede and follow them.

Table 4. Summary of Greek Entries by Author and Period

Period	Author	Entries	Words
1762-1766	Herodotus §§1-3	3	145
	Euripides §§85-154	70	1,388
	Homer's *Iliad* §§155-60	6	191
	Homer's *Odyssey* §§161-2	2	100
1768-1773	Anacreon §§347-8	2	27
	Homer* §382n	3	71
	Homer §§397-8	2	58
Post-1773	Quintus Smyrnaeus §407	1	25
GREEK TOTAL		89	2,005

Note: The three entries from Homer marked by an asterisk are not treated as numbered entries in the text but as parts of a footnote to §382, some of which was copied from an edition of Ossian. Greek word count comprises 7.5 percent of the total for the LCB.

INDEX

Abraham, 30, 54
"Account Book, 1767-1770" (TJ), 194n
Adam, 20, 37, 42, 53
Adams, Abigail: letters to, 10, 102n
Adams, Henry, 14
Adams, John: letters to, 10, 102n, 157n, 160, 186; admires Bolingbroke, 156
Addison, Joseph, 176
Aeneid. See Virgil
Aeschylus, 162n
"Air." *See* Moore, Edward
Akenside, Mark, 8, 155, 198n, 200, 214; Extracts from *Pleasures of the Imagination*, 127-9 (§§342-5)
Albro, Tom, 209
Alexandre Le Grand. See Racine, Jean
Anacreon: read in schools, 184n; referred to, 8, 9, 14, 129-30n, 155. *See also* *Anacreontea*
Anacreontea: Extracts from, 129-30 (§§347-8); referred to, 130-1n
Anatomy. See Cheselden, William
Andria. See Terence
Annual Register, 161
Apocalypse of Peter, 37
Arrianus, Flavius, 33
Art of Charming, The. See Dodsley, Robert
Asgill, John, 25
Astronomica. See Manilius
Augustine, St., of Canterbury, 34
Augustus, 165
Aurengzebe. See Dryden, John

Bacon, Sir Francis, 31n, 161, 173
Barabbas, 32
Barbauld, Anna Laetitia Aiken, 224-5
Barnes, Joshua: edition of Euripides, 162
Baxter, John, 168-9
bearing: Extracts relating to, 63 (§84), 65 (§90), 67 (§100), 70 (§114), 74 (§135), 75 (§141), 81 (§162), 82 (§170), 85 (§181), 88 (§200), 89 (§202), 125 (§335), 133-4 (§357); as theme in LCB, 18
Beauties of the English Stage, The, 113n

"Beggar, The." *See* Moss, Thomas
Bell, John: edition of the English Poets, 155
Bernard, John, 8, 178, 182
Bible: Genesis, 23; historicity of, 23-4n, 34; authors of, 24; Old Testament, 30; miracles in, 33-4; divine authority of, 37; canon, 38; Leviticus, 39; marriage and consanguinity in, 39-40; Deuteronomy, 40; authenticity of, 41; TJ recommends reading, 156; prime source for Ossian, 171
Bolingbroke, Viscount (Henry St. John): Extracts from *Philosophical Works*, 24-38 (§§4-34), 40-55 (§§36-58); on God, 4, 24-5, 28, 29, 30, 34, 36, 40, 41, 42-3, 44, 45, 50; *Philosophical Works*, 5, 89n, 155; entries in LCB, 8, 213-14, 215; and TJ, 11, 155-7; and the Bible, 23n, 164; dedicatee of Pope's *Essay on Man*, 89n; handwriting of entries from, 196-8, 205; referred to, 163, 209
Boyd, Julian P., 184
Brock, David, 209
Brothers, The. See Young, Edward
Brown, Charles Brockden, 11
Buchanan, George, 8, 12, 157, 214; Extracts from *Jephtha, or The Vow*, 135-7 (§§367-72)
Buckingham, Duke of (John Sheffield), 13, 157, 158, 181; Extracts from epitaph, 63 (§83); from *The Tragedy of Julius Caesar, Altered*, 115-6 (§§297-8); from *The Death of Marcus Brutus*, 116 (§§299-300)
Burke, Martha Jefferson Trist: quoted, 6, 191; ownership of LCB, 15; inscriptions by, 218, 226
Burwell, Nathaniel, 185-6
Burwell, Rebecca: TJ's courtship of, 16, 185, 205
Butler, Samuel: Extracts from *Hudibras*, 92-3 (§§214-7); *Hudibras* referred to, 14; in TJ's libraries, 159; entries in LCB, 215
Byrd, William, 159n